THE
JEWISH
PARTY
BOOK

THE JEWISH PARTY BOOK

A Contemporary Guide to Customs, Crafts, and Foods
by Mae Shafter Rockland

SCHOCKEN BOOKS • NEW YORK

First Schocken paperback edition 1987
10 9 8 7 6 5 4 3 2   87 88 89 90
Copyright © 1978 by Schocken Books Inc.

Library of Congress Cataloging-in-Publication Data
Rockland, Mae Shafter
  The Jewish Party Book
    1. Jews—Rites and ceremonies.   2. Entertaining
3. Jewish crafts   4. Cookery, Jewish   I. Title
BM700.R53   392   78–54387

Design by Hermann Strohbach
Manufactured in the United States of America
ISBN 0–8052–0829–1

For
Jeffrey's
Eighteenth
Birthday

CONTENTS

PREFACE

There is a Yiddish folk song in dialogue form, popularized a number of years ago by Theodore Bikel, in which a student asks his rabbi, "Tell me, *rebenyu* what will happen when the Messiah comes?"

"When the Messiah comes," answers the rabbi slowly and intensely, "we will have a little banquet."

Continuing in question-and-answer form, they proceed to outline the epitome of the Jewish party, deciding what is to be eaten and drunk and the form of entertainment. The opening speech, *hokhmah* [words of wisdom], will be offered by King Solomon; Miriam, the prophetess, will dance; King David will play; and a substantial address will be given by Moses. And in response to the always pressing party-giver's question—"What will we eat at the *sudenyu?*"—the rabbi replies, "The behemoth and leviathan," those legendary monsters of the land and sea, which embody all evil and which in the Messianic Age will battle one another to the death, their flesh feasted upon by the righteous. This succulent dish will be washed down with plenty of *Yayin Hamshumor,* that very strong wine which has been preserved in its own grapes since the days of Creation and guarded and saved for this special banquet meal.

This book will not offer recipes for anything quite as esoteric as a Monster Stew, but, recognizing that "folkways are the social practices by which a people externalizes the reality of its collective being,"* within its pages you will find hospitality-related customs, foods, and crafts that are rooted in the folk experience. Folkloric beliefs and activities have flourished throughout the ages alongside the officially sanctioned religious practices; they serve to make the celebrated events more accessible to ordinary people—you and me.

Among the commandments enumerated in the Talmud (Shabbat 127a) "which yield immediate fruit and continue to yield fruit in

*Mordecai M. Kaplan, *Judaism as a Civilization* (New York: Schocken Books, 1967), p. 432.

time to come," on an equal plane with honoring parents, studying, attending the dead, visiting the sick, helping the needy, and making peace between people is the *mitzvah* of providing hospitality. As a child at the Sabbath dinner table, I never tired of hearing my mother describe how her father in Poland would bring a different guest home with him almost every Friday night from synagogue. These were usually travelers (itinerant craftsmen, salesmen, beggars, or saints) who would go to the synagogue on Friday evening hoping for just such an offer of a Sabbath dinner and a place to stay. After the meal my grandfather would take one of the heavy wooden doors from its hinges, rest it on four chairs, and make up a bed. What fascinated me, of course, was trying to imagine taking the doors off in our Bronx apartment. It seemed truly like a fairy tale, and yet what has remained with me as something I want to emulate and transmit each time I have a guest is that willingness to truly open myself and my home, to make the person feel as though he is in his own home, only better, a bit more pampered.

Volumes of important Jewish scholarship are produced every year, along with a vast amount of Sunday-school material. Yet today's American Jews, probably one of the most affluent Jewish communities ever to exist, often do not quite know what the holidays (with the exception of Passover) are about, and many of our celebrations have grown—or deteriorated—into extravaganzas which are only incidentally linked to the event they are meant to celebrate. This preamble is not intended to lead the reader to despair, for after all we have only been in this country in any great numbers for less than a century. And in that time a lot has happened. While the American Jewish community took root and got on its economic and cultural feet, European Jewry was all but wiped out and the State of Israel came into being. With European Jewish life no longer there, except to feed our imagination, and Israel beset with very real military and economic problems, the responsibility for cultural and religious growth is very much our own. And slowly, we are beginning to develop a true Jewish-American life style. Some of the things we do in what I consider this transitional time are awkward and unsure, but I feel confident that with time American Jewry will produce yet another Golden Age in Diaspora history. This book is a self-conscious attempt to bridge the gap between our nostalgic longings and our responsibilities to future generations.

As I began *The Jewish Party Book* and throughout its growth and development, I asked almost everyone I met what would be useful in a volume such as this. The answers varied widely. Those people with minimal Jewish education asked for as much in-depth source material as possible. Both Jews and non-Jews were honest with themselves as well as with me when they admitted the unlikelihood of their digging into any primary sources. They wanted their Jewish education in a popular format. Then there were those friends steeped in Judaic knowledge, whose Jewish education is infinitely more thorough than my own. They know exactly how to find the sources, but were hoping I could provide them with ideas to add contemporary styling and enjoyment to traditional practices. They wanted creative interpretations of the materials.

In the hope of being helpful to as many people as possible, this book is something of a potpourri. Each section, therefore, is a blend of historical material and projects—culinary or craft—growing out of that background. Some sections pay more attention to food; others to decorations, invitations, or the creation of objects related to the particular celebration being discussed. There are activities for different age and interest groups, and a variety of inspirational and instructional projects are proposed. Not every section goes into equal detail in each area. The reader is encouraged to combine techniques from one section with thematic material from another. Indeed, it is my hope that this book will enrich American Jewish life not only through the material presented in these pages, but by encouraging you in your creation of an environment that expresses and fulfills your needs as a Jew in America today. I have tried to be simultaneously evocative of all those celebrations tucked away in a corner of our nostalgic minds (which perhaps never happened that way in the first place) and provocative in the sense of offering suggestions for bringing tradition up to date.

In that this is a volume about hospitality and it has always been within the Jewish tradition to open the door and feed the stranger, "for we were strangers in Egypt," I'd like the book to serve as an invitation to the Gentiles among whom we live to become familiar with our customs. The text and illustrations reflect and depict contemporary American ways of celebrating Jewish events, and will therefore, I hope, be of interest to the non-Jew who wants to learn something about the lives of his Jewish neighbors, and to the future historian as a document of the times.

Tishri 5739 / October 1978   Mae Rockland

ACKNOWLEDGMENTS

It would take another book to fully describe and credit the contributions made to this book by many friends and colleagues, ranging from crafts, cooking, and bartending to finding the perfect quotation, photography, religious and historical insight, and cleaning up after the events. I hope they will all recognize themselves somewhere in these pages and that we will continue to enjoy many *simhahs* together in the years to come. Thank you:

Arena (Carol Atlas), Leo Arons, Rabbi Albert S. Axelrad, Tova Be'eri, Cindy Pearlman Benjamin, Martin and Joan Benjamin-Farren, Jay Craig, Dashara (Loni Heisman), Judy Feierstein, Roz Freund, Sarah Fuhro, Beverly Glassman, Rabbi Melvin J. Glatt, Bob and Linda Shafter Goodman, Martha Gray, Debra Hirshman Green, Nancy Hersh, Ilse Johnson, Jane Kahn, Everette and Cherie Koller-Fox, E. Jan Kounitz, Lillian Lapidus, Robert Leverant, Susan Male, Leslie Mitchell, David Moss, Telemachos Ch. Mouschovias, Kayla Niles, Cecelia Rosenblum, Tom Savonick, Helen Schlauffer, Ruth Schulman, Jeffrey Segelman, Tamara Selig, Bernie Shanfield, Betty Smith, Lisa and Roz Staras, Barbara Tropp, Helen Tupa, Shirley Watson, and Hal Wolpert.

The photographic work has been credited with each image, but I want especially to thank Bill Aron, Kenneth M. Bernstein, and Jim McDonald for their patience, artistry, and humor.

Even as I write these words of appreciation, I am deeply grateful to my editor, Beverly Colman, who lets nothing pass her desk without the benefit of her meticulous attention to detail; her insights and provocative comments throughout the crafting of this book have been invaluable—and she's fun to work with.

Food is the indispensable element of every party, and in order to know how to cook one must know how to eat. First you have something you think delicious, then you begin to figure out what went into it and how you can duplicate it and even improve upon it. For that very basic appreciation of food I must (all jokes aside) thank my mother, Bella Dunsky Shafter, who always serves generous portions of love with every morsel to be eaten.

My children, David, Jeffrey, and Keren, provided inspiration and criticism, love and labor, all of which made an incalculable contribution to these pages.

Most of all I am deeply indebted to Myron Tupa, not only for his expert aesthetic and technical advice, as well as assistance with many of the projects in this book, but for his unfailing moral and spiritual support throughout its writing and production.

In everyone there is something precious, found in no one else; so honor each person for what is hidden within—for what they alone have, and none of their fellows.

—Hasidic saying

BEFORE WE BEGIN—A FEW GENERALIZATIONS

ATMOSPHERE

The question of what makes a party *Jewish* is obviously the first thing to be considered as we begin this book about making a "Jewish party." While the concept of hospitality is an ingrained positive value in Jewish life, the notion of making a party for its own sake is not. Traditionally one makes a *seudah* [feast] in honor of a particular event or holiday, and family and guests join together to celebrate the occasion. Other occurrences, such as the completion of the study of a particular book of the Bible, also provide the opportunity for a little social refreshment. Jews, like anyone else, enjoy friends dropping by and the spontaneous party that results. The celebrations discussed here, however, are those that are based on traditional observance. The basic outlines of the ceremonies connected with the particular events will be described, along with suggestions for the attendant festivities, because they give the party its very reason for being. Some readers may think there's too much "religion" in these pages; others may find there is not enough. It is my intention to point out the religious background and the nature of the events celebrated, but to leave the degree of formal observance to the reader.

Every party we give is an opportunity to share our heritage with friends and family and to transmit our values to future generations. The manner in which we interpret and celebrate Jewish occasions reflects these values as much as the prayers we say. Literature, anecdotes, and films combine with our own experiences to provide stereotyped versions of many Jewish celebrations. In some people's minds, the idea of a a Jewish party instantly invokes the image of Mt. Sinai carved out of chopped liver. It is not my intention to undermine the catering business. Nor do I contend that all of our parties should be casual affairs where we sit on the floor with paper plates. But, along with the rabbis who in many other times and countries instituted sumptuary laws, I feel that too often we sacrifice good taste as well as the sanctity of the occasion to sheer ostentation. My hope is that by presenting some options in the way celebrations can be personalized, readers will find ways to make Jewish parties that are richer, more memorable, and more sheer fun than a conventional party.

As you begin to plan your parties, some introspection is perhaps in order, both as to your own religious sensitivities and those of your guests. When I made the Sukkot party described here, most of the people I invited had never been near a *sukkah* and had no idea what the holiday was about. Therefore, the invitation I made had on it a great deal of background information as to the nature of the holiday and the meaning of its observance. The *hanukkat habayit* invitation, on the other hand, was sent to people to whom the ceremony involved was already familiar, and therefore uses Hebrew without explanation. With the invitation itself you begin to define the kind of party you will have.

HELP

There are as many different kinds of parties as there are people to give them. Only give the kind of party that you can do comfortably. If you have your heart set on staging a huge event but are terrified of it, hold off until you feel you have the expertise to handle large amounts of food and people. Decide how simple or elaborate your party will be, according to your temperament, the size of your house, and your purse. If you are relaxed and having a good time, everyone else will too. This all seems very obvious, but it needs saying, because I have been to entirely too many parties that were stilted and unnatural and seemed to provide no pleasure for the giver. No matter how large or small the event you are planning, make sure that you have enough help (of the kind that is genuinely helpful), so that you don't find yourself in the kitchen throughout the festivities. Party help is available in many guises. For those who want it, there are catering establishments that take over every last detail of the event once you have chosen the day and menu.

If the party you are planning is too big or too elaborate to handle yourself, even with the help of friends, you can hire help without going the total "catered affair" route. List the factors that make a big party go smoothly, then decide what part you and your family will do and how many people must be hired for the day or evening.

1. The food must be prepared and the buffet table set up, or the food served to seated guests.

2. Someone has to tend the bar or fill the punch bowl or look after the keg of beer.

3. Someone should greet the guests and tell them where to put their coats (or make an attractive sign).

4. There should be someone emptying ashtrays and collecting glasses, napkins, and plates during the party.

5. The cleanup.

Many cities have agencies that provide professional party help. These tend to be expensive because the agency gets a commission, but the people are trained. Experienced help can often be found through your favorite (or any good) local restaurant. Also, if your local synagogue has a social committee, ask them. College fraternities and sororities as well as college and high-school placement services often can supply you with students who regularly work as party helpers. Explain everything you expect to be done to the helpers beforehand. With professionals this can be done an hour before guests arrive, but with inexperienced student help it's a good idea to have a calm run-through the day before, at your house or wherever the party is to be. It's worth the extra effort to write down important instructions (what time the casserole goes into the oven, ingredients for the punch, etc.). When you know that your helpers are attending to things without your immediate supervision, you can enjoy your own party.

MUSIC

Jewish music, whether it is meant to provide entertainment or a background for conversation, is an excellent way of giving a party a Jewish atmosphere. Most cities have at least one group that is familiar with the standard *freylakh* music or with Israeli music. Many musicians are willing to learn your favorites from records or cassettes. Or you might simply want to use your own records or tape collection, or make a composite tape of your favorites arranged to provide variety. Music can add to everyone's enjoyment, or it can destroy the feeling of community you want to create; the style and volume are both very important in determining the effect it will have. Whether you have live or recorded music will depend on the size of the party and its location, as well as the cost and availability of musicians. In some situations a single instrument can offer just the right note (sic). Usually parties are not the time to begin teaching songs, but if you have a friend (or family member—or yourself) who, with or without an instrument, feels comfortable leading people in song or humming along, this can be very pleasant, so long as there is a voluntary, uncoerced quality about it. Heavy "performances" usually sit poorly when guests would rather move around, socialize, eat, and drink, so be careful whom you ask to do what and for how long. It helps to be specific.

I have made my own collection of cassettes of different musical backgrounds for different parties. For example, for the Purim Masquerade, to emphasize the Oriental Palace motif, I made a cassette with selections from a variety of Greek, Turkish, Sephardic, and flamenco records. At my parents' anniversary party I had a cassette of different Yiddish melodies, folk songs, familiar Second Avenue show tunes, and popular Israeli songs. I wanted music people are familiar with, which will, if played softly in the background, provide a feeling of familiarity and warmth. I prefer a cassette to a pile of records, both for its variety of performers and moods, and because it can run longer without interruption or attention.

FOOD

The Jewish preoccupation with food is proverbial. There is a tradition that every holiday should be celebrated "half and half"—half for God and half for people. The people's half usually means food. With rare exceptions, Jewish life in the Diaspora has been one of poverty, and one is always concerned about what one doesn't have. Much of our classic favorite dishes owe their existence to the ingenuity of generations of cooks producing soul-satisfying meals with the cheapest possible ingredients. Some of the recipes given here are for foods we readily identify as traditionally Jewish, since for the most part they are of East European origin, which is where most American Jews trace their ancestry. Others are traditional among Jews in other parts of the world. Still others are foods that, though part of the general American cuisine, seemed borrowable to me and could be given a Jewish flavor, or they lent themselves well to a particular celebration. I have not provided sample menus, because in all of my cookbook reading I rarely find them useful. So, instead, the customs surrounding the traditional foods are described and some of my favorite recipes are offered, in the hope that you will combine them with your own favorites, and those culled from the growing number of Jewish cookbooks, to make unique and memorable festive meals and parties.

CRAFTS

Part of the joy and simultaneously the responsibility of creating objects for religious use is that, because of their very function, they are destined to take on an aura of significance and to outlive us. Quantities of outmoded and half-worn domestic articles of every description are given to rummage sales and flea markets, but we hold indefinitely (if we are fortunate to have them) on to the last threads of our grandmother's *matzah* cover or our grandfather's battered *kiddush* cup, no matter what shape it's in. Craft projects are included in this party book because the objects we use are very much a part of our lives and celebrations. Beautiful handmade things can enhance a party as much as delicious food and fine music.

Crafts are universal. At one time or another, most peoples have exploited the different basic ways of making things. For different cultural reasons at different periods in their history, different groups became more or less identified with a particular craft. Since ancient times the Jews have particularly been known for calligraphy and textiles. For the past four or five centuries, paper-cutting has flourished as a popular form of folk expression. At various times, depending upon local guilds and customs, Jews have been active in the metalcrafts. While many of us would like to have lovely ceremonial objects of precious metals, the craft projects described in this book emphasize materials that are most easily accessible to the home craftsperson: fabric and paper and, to a lesser extent, wood and clay. Those readers with skills or facilities to work in the more difficult media should feel free to borrow and adapt any of the ideas and designs given here for their own projects, for they are meant to serve as inspiration and departure points. It is my hope that readers will be excited by the Judaic source material and, using their own skills and inventiveness, go on to make things that will further enrich their lives and add to the growing body of Jewish-American folk art.

PART ONE
THE PEOPLE

1 (photo: Bill Aron)

We are born, we die—and somewhere between those two events we reach puberty and most of us marry and have children, adding another link to the chain. From the beginning of time, human beings have marked these major events in the life cycle with special ceremonies and feasts. In every culture these times of transition—birth, puberty, marriage, death, and, to a lesser but still significant degree, the anniversaries of these occasions and other changes such as moving into a new home—are fraught with intense emotion, a combination of exhilaration and fear. At such times the individual feels most alone and most vulnerable. The rituals, celebrations, and gatherings that are the folkways of a group serve to mitigate this aloneness and to tie the individual and the family to the community. It is our own loss when we deny ourselves the strength and joy such ceremonies are designed to provide, substituting the "efficiency" and expediency of modern institutions for the warmth of our cultural heritage.

The only fact I retain from a college Sociology course is that all peoples have essentially the same problems to solve and the same events to celebrate; it is the particular solutions they find to the universal experiences and the manner in which they mark the changes in the life cycle and the seasons that differentiate one group from another.

The Jews developed a system of beliefs based on ethical monotheism, in which a single ethical supreme being is responsible for all the natural phenomena. At critical moments, it is to this one God that Jews turn for aid, comfort, and support. Judaism, however, is as much an orthopraxy as an orthodoxy: one's conduct is as important as one's philosophy. Thus, every event in Jewish life is sanctified in one way or another. Many of the popular customs of the people, however, are only connected to the central theme of Judaism by great stretches of the imagination, for they come from prehistoric times or were picked up from surrounding cultures. Despite rabbinic sanctions against many of these practices, the ordinary folk have refused to give them up, because they seem to produce the desired results and they are fun. So over the centuries rites which have superstitious or magical roots have been incorporated into what we now accept as the "traditional way." It is this combination of religious philosophy and folkloric customs that serves as a vehicle for transmitting our values from generation to generation.

3

We are proud to announce
the birth of our daughter
Alana Loren Rockland
on July 19, 1985 at 8:34 pm, 6 lb. 10 oz.
Please join us for Alana's
naming ceremony & celebration
at noon Sunday, August 25th

(photo: Mae Rockland)

BABIES

Yiddish proverbs tell us that "the *nakhes* [pleasures] we get from children are far more precious than gold," "each child brings his own blessing into the world," and, "if the world is ever redeemed, it will be through the virtues of children." Those of us with some experience at being parents may also find truth in the proverbs that say, "little children, little troubles; big children, big troubles," and "little children won't let you sleep; big children won't let you live." But even so, most parents will agree that, although "your child may be a robber, yet you dance at his wedding."* The intense Jewish commitment to having and teaching children is indeed proverbial. Children are thought of as the inheritors of the past, the transmitters of sacred values, and the creators of the future. A baby is part of the Jewish people from infancy, and the anticipation and arrival of a new child is traditionally surrounded by many customs and ceremonies.

It cannot be denied that, while girls have not been entirely neglected, boys have usually received a bigger welcome into the world. With the growth of Jewish feminism, this is beginning to change. There are valid reasons for these changes and for the attempts to minimize sexism in ritual put forth by supporters of egalitarian Judaism. Further, it seems to me that with the annihilation of almost half of the Jewish population of the world in World War II, along with the fact that we as a people are having fewer babies than we used to, *every* newborn should be accorded a full, vibrant welcome into the Jewish community. Whether you choose to celebrate the arrival of a baby in a traditional or contemporary way, I suggest that you discuss the possibilities with your rabbi well in advance of the big day and also explore both the old and newer literature for source material to help make your celebration unique.**

Leo Rosten's Treasury of Jewish Quotations (New York: McGraw-Hill, 1972).

**For historic background, see Hayyim Schauss, *The Lifetime of A Jew* (New York: Union of American Hebrew Congregations, 1960). For innovative as well as traditional ideas, see Sharon and Michael Strassfeld, *The Second Jewish Catalogue* (Philadelphia: The Jewish Publication Society, 1976).

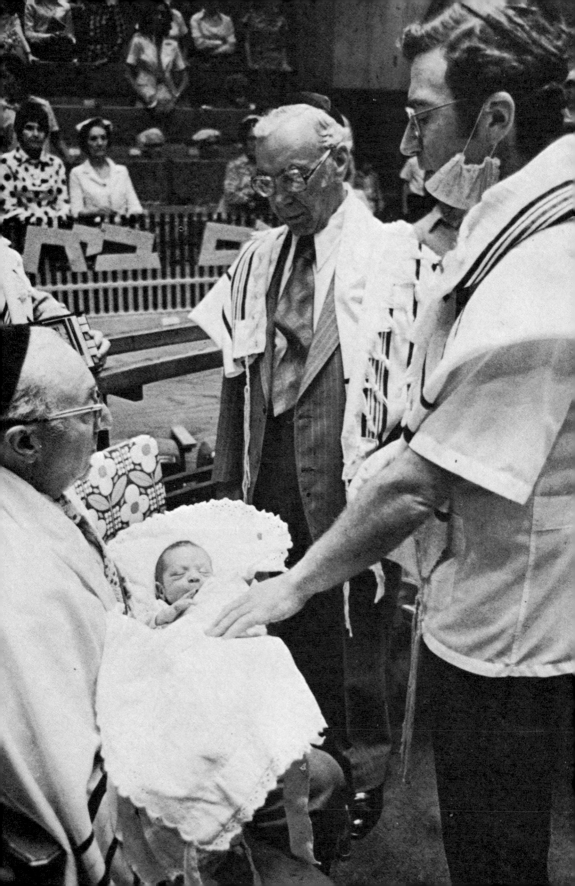

While one is always enjoined to look after the needs of orphans, and custom says that people who "rear orphans in their home are regarded as having given birth to them" and "whoever teaches the son of a friend Torah is deemed to be his father," adoption as we know it has no standing in *halakhah* [religious law]. In modern Israel, a form of adoption has been developed that legally protects the rights of the child in regard to maintenance and inheritance, while skirting the religious difficulties. The current generation of young parents who, for whatever reasons, adopt babies—often going through great difficulties to find a baby in this age of contraception and abortion—are not at all shy of the fact that their baby is a chosen one. It is therefore very appropriate that the ceremonies and festivities surrounding birth be expanded to include adopted children as well.

Customarily, every Jewish child has a Hebrew as well as a civil (English) name. This practice began in the Middle Ages. Ashkenazim name babies only for deceased relatives, and there are strong sensibilities against using the name of a living person or of someone who died young. Among Sephardim the reverse is true, and babies are named to honor a living relative, frequently the father or grandfather. In ancient times a baby was named as soon as it was born. Today the tradition is generally observed of naming girls in the synagogue when the father is called to the Torah, either in the week after the birth or about a month later, when the mother can also be present. Among Sephardim, baby girls are named only at home, when family and friends and sometimes the rabbi are invited to a big meal. Boys are named as part of the *brit milah* [covenant of circumcision] ceremony, which, unless the baby is sickly, invariably takes place on the eighth day after birth. This can be held either at home or at the synagogue. The ceremony is followed by a *kiddush* of wine and cakes. *Branfn* [whiskey] and *lekakh* [honey cake] are traditional among Ashkenazim, while some Sephardim serve a preserve made of poppy seeds and honey along with strong coffee. Some families turn the event into a full-fledged feast complete with Sabbath and holiday dishes. There is a strong tradition in favor of making a *brit* an occasion of great festivity. Despite the fact that as far back as biblical times the real origins of circumcision have been obscured by legendary tales, Jews have tenaciously held

3 *Brit milah* in a synagogue. The infant is being held by his godfather while the *mohel* says the blessing before beginning (photo: Bill Aron)

to this form of covenant and have circumcised baby boys even at times when the penalty for doing so was death.

Some people think that, as long as the baby is circumcised, he has been welcomed into the religious convenant between the Jews and God. This is not so. In order for the circumcision *(milah)* to be a covenant of circumcision *(brit milah)*, it must be performed on the eighth day after birth, or as soon after as the child's health permits, and the customary prayers and blessings said. While it may seem more efficient to have the operation done by the obstetrician or pediatrician the day before the mother and child leave the hospital, there is nothing then that is Jewish about the procedure, which has become almost standard for American baby boys.

Because we suffered for it, the rite grew in importance. It is said that the observance of circumcision, along with that of the Sabbath, has been instrumental in preserving the Jews as a people. Over the centuries festivities and customs formed an island in an ocean of hostility; in our time they can provide a similar resting place from the pressures and tensions of contemporary life.

The popular misconception that equates the word *brit (bris* in the Yiddish form) with circumcision sees it as only for boys. *Brit* means "covenant," and because the concept of an eternal binding agreement between God and humanity is so central to Judaism, I am delighted that in recent years many creative people have designed *brit* ceremonies for girls. I like the idea very much of knowing that, whether the infant is male or female, a *brit* can be planned in advance for the eighth day after birth; a *mohel* [a person to do the circumcision] is tentatively lined up in case it's a boy, but otherwise the same preparations can be made. Some people prefer to wait a month or so to have a ceremony for a girl, either because by then life has settled down to a more normal pace, or because they would rather have the girl's ceremony totally different than that for a boy. My own feeling is that the week after birth is so extraordinary and emotions are so high with the very newness of the infant, by putting it off to a later date, when most people will already have seen the baby, the special feelings of immediacy are lost. Also, since the eighth day of life has been special for the *brit* ceremony for thousands of years, it seems fitting to me to use it to bring girls as well as boys into the covenant.

Baking and freezing an assortment of cakes and other delicacies can be a pleasant way to pass the last weeks of pregnancy, knowing that—whether it's a boy or a girl—there will be a festive reunion of family and friends. There is a warmth and intimacy about a baby's

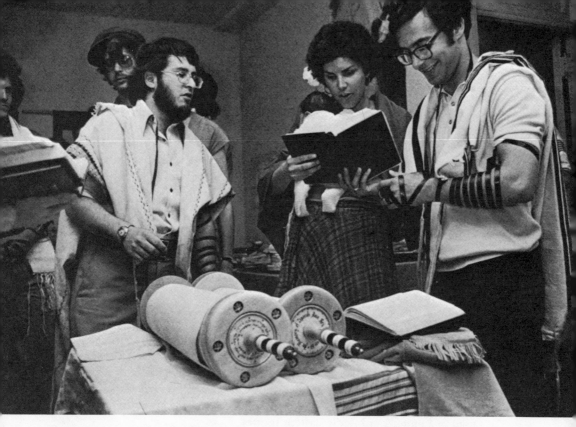

4 Baby girl's naming ceremony at home. The men are wearing *tefillin* on their arms and foreheads (photo: Bill Aron)

naming, whether it takes place at home or in the synagogue, which fortunately precludes overly elaborate food. Buy some things and ask friends to help, especially if this is your first baby and you are planning a *pidyon haben* also.

Originally all firstborn sons (unless their birth was preceded by a girl or a miscarriage) in each family were to be consecrated to the service of God. The reason for this priesthood of the firstborn was said to be that the Hebrew firstborns were not killed along with the Egyptian firstborns during the night of the Exodus. Their function was later taken over by the tribe of Levi. The custom grew up of "redeeming" the firstborn of a Jew who is neither a Kohan nor a Levite by paying five silver shekels to a Kohan during a short ceremony on the thirty-first day after birth; if this falls on a Sabbath, the *pidyon haben* is postponed one day. The tradition is based on Exodus 13:2: "Consecrate to Me every firstborn; . . . the first issue of every womb among the Israelites is Mine." While some people choose to ignore this ceremony, seeing it as archaic, others feel that it should be expanded to include girl babies. If you plan to have a redemption ceremony, consider adding readings of your own selec-

9

tion to it. Cakes, cookies, and pastries baked and frozen even before the birth will come in handy, since it is customary to have wine, tea, and cake for the participants

There are enough recipes for cakes that freeze well in other sections of this book. Here I'd like to mention a simple traditional snack that appears at many fetes associated with fertility. *Nahit* [chick-peas] are a special favorite at another little-known gathering variously called a שלום זכר *shalom zakhar* [peace for the male], or among the Sephardim *midrash* [study]. It is held the Friday night after the birth, when the father, his friends, and male relatives stay up all night studying Torah and visiting. Their study is usually fortified with tea, cakes, and typically peppery chick-peas.

NAHIT

Cover dried chick-peas, which can be bought in health-food stores and many supermarkets, with cold water and soak for 12 hours. Drain, rinse with cold water, and cover with cold salted water. Simmer covered for 40 minutes, or until tender but not soft. Drain and sprinkle with salt and pepper. Serve warm or cold. Any that aren't gobbled up like peanuts can be added to salads or soups; they are also used in a number of Middle Eastern recipes.

Another traditional get-together which is seldom observed these days is that of Watch Night. This is similar to the *shalom zakhar*, but takes place the night before the circumcision because, since that night is the last chance for malevolent spirits to affect the baby before he is made safe by the covenant, it is "necessary" to have an all-night vigil to protect him. Originally, a table laden with food was set out for a protecting deity. Later this borrowed custom was reinterpreted as a welcoming feast for Elijah, the prophet/angel who is the protector of newborns. Today when the night of watching is observed, it is seen more as a *mitzvah* feast in prelude to the joyousness of the *brit*, with the food being consumed by the guests, rather than as a vigil to counteract demons.

ANNOUNCEMENTS AND AMULETS

The joyousness surrounding the arrival of a new child into the family provides sustenance for the spirit, so the simplest fare is both satisfying and allows family and friends to concentrate on the baby rather than the food. Sharing the news is both exciting and exhausting. The telephone is certainly a useful device for telling closest family and friends about the baby, but written announcements not

5 (illustration: courtesy David Moss)

only allow you to inform more people for less money, they provide an opportunity for creatively commemorating the event. Packages of printed cards are available, but my preference is to make a personal and unique statement. One of the nicest announcements I've received was sent by Rita and Theo Bikel to announce the birth of their first child. The cover had a soft gold-and-sepia-hued color photograph of Theo holding the infant. Inside the message said: "Another reason to work for peace." What makes the card especially meaningful is that, along with the lovely double portrait on it, the father is wearing a *yarmulka*, immediately identifying the people and card as Jewish. (If you're handy with a camera and going to visit friends with a new baby, why not snap some photographs? A gift of these pictures, taken just when the parents don't have time to do it—would really be appreciated.)

If photography is not your forte and you are intent on keeping the cost of reproducing the cards down, consider a simple personal drawing or paper-cut (see pp. 218–223 for instructions) as a graphic to be printed by a commercial printer. In this instance, unless the work is done well in advance and you just fill in the baby's name, date of birth, and whatever other information you consider pertinent, I suggest having the cards printed rather than doing them yourself because of the time and energy they cost. Hebrew quotations can also add to the personal feeling you want to convey.

For example, you might use the blessing written on traditional Torah binders described later in this chapter, or the phrase ברוך הבא ["Blessed be he that cometh"], which the assembled people stand up and say when the baby is brought into the room for a *brit milah.* (If one is having a covenant ceremony for a girl, the phrase can be written in the feminine form: ברוכה הבאה.) Another possibility is to use the child's Hebrew name as the departure point for a design. The painting in Fig. 5 was done for my daughter, Keren Chaya Faigle, by the calligrapher David Moss. The artist used the block letters of her name as a background for a unicorn and a bird, because Chaya is Yiddish for a wild beast and Faigle for a bird.

Folklore supplies us with a rich source of ideas and motifs for announcements and other projects surrounding the arrival of a new baby. It is rarely acknowledged that Jewish superstition and magic are as ancient and deeply rooted as rabbinically sanctioned Judaism. Dream interpretation, divination, demons, and angels are all mentioned in the Bible. The word "magic" is derisive; when we call it "mysticism" it becomes acceptable. After the expulsion of the Jews from Spain in 1492, mysticism flourished and grew in the Sephardic Jewish world, adding new interpretations to the old ingrained body of folkways and beliefs. In his book *The Lifetime of A Jew,* Hayyim Schauss points out that "people seldom recognize the inconsistencies of their beliefs and religious practices," and "the striking use of amulets and the preponderance of superstitions associated with the life cycle suggest that the greater the danger, the more precious the moment. Thus magic and superstition serve to enhance and affirm life's value." Changes of status—birth, puberty, marriage, and death—are times of both the greatest sanctity and the greatest vulnerability. At such crucial moments the line between religion and superstition begins to blur; magic is somewhere between religion and medicine. The underlying element is a faith in the power of good coupled with the belief that the use of an appropriate "prescription" will avert danger.

Amulets and charms of various sorts have been used to ward off evil spirits ever since people decided they were to be feared. At the birth of a child the greatest danger comes from Lilith, Adam's first wife, and her cohorts. In recent years Jewish feminists have rallied to the support of Lilith, who was created along with Adam as his peer. When she demanded the equality she was entitled to, and Adam insisted on keeping her in a subservient position, she pronounced a magic incantation and removed herself from the Garden of Eden. Three angels, Sanvei, Sansenvei, and Semangelof, were sent to bring her back. She refused to return and Eve was then created, as we know from a rib in his side, to be Adam's wife. According to patriarchal interpretations of the legends, Lilith then became the enemy of pregnant women and infants; she consorted with demons and produced hordes of demonic children of her own, who also prey upon the children of Eve. A few years ago in Mea Shearim, the Orthodox quarter of Jerusalem, I bought a printed broadside which is commonly used to hang on the walls of the rooms of new mothers and infants. The key phrase is directed against Lilith, and Sanvei, Sansenvei, and Semangelof are depicted in the middle. Whether or not you are a political feminist and find yourself siding with Lilith, it is very nice to have three protective angels hovering about a new baby. They also provide a charming decorative motif for announcements, wall decorations, or embroideries for the baby's room. The three angels are traditionally represented in a curious bird-headed form, which is possibly a survival of similar charms used during the Graeco-Roman period.

6 Paper-cut and India-ink design of the three angels to use as an amulet or birth announcement

The *hamsa* [five-fingered hand] is another popular form for an amulet which is indigenous to North Africa and has been in use since at least 1000 B.C.E. It is still used by Moroccan and Tunisian Jews to ward off the evil eye. We see it often now as a popular motif in Israeli jewelry. It has been the Moroccan custom to draw a hand on the wall of the labor room. Among the Jews of Bukhara (which was once a part of the Persian Kingdom and is now a province of the Uzbek Soviet Socialist Republic), when a son was born the midwife would bring into the room where the family was awaiting the birth a silver bowl containing a wax candle in the shape of a *hamsa* set in a circle of plain candles. Everyone present would light a candle and place a silver coin in the bowl; then the midwife would light the central candle. In some centuries it was the custom to say "*Bal hamsa*" ["With five"] to a beautiful child, because the expression protects against the evil eye.

The ceramic *hamsa* mirror frame in Fig. 7 was made as a gift for a friend's new baby. The mirror in the center is an ordinary round one in a plastic frame with a tiny handle which I bought in the local five-and-ten-cent store. The size of the available mirror determined the size the clay surround would be. I drew a paper pattern and traced it onto a ¼"-thick slab of clay. I cut out the clay with a sharp knife, and a ceramist friend fired it in her kiln. The inexpensive mirror was then glued on the back with epoxy and lined with felt. The original plastic handle of the mirror, now on the back, is a loop and so serves as a hook to hang the mirror on the wall. Find the

7 Ceramic mirror frame, 6" x 7", with a 2¼" round opening for the mirror (photo: Jim McDonald)

mirror before beginning the ceramic work. This project would also be nice to make in wood.

In the first centuries of the Common Era, the birth of a baby was commemorated by planting a tree in the garden: a cypress for a boy and a pine for a girl. Wood from the trees was then used as part of the *hupah* [wedding canopy]. This custom, adopted from the Romans, was based on the belief that the life of a person was related to the growth of a tree. Even stripped of its magical quality, the custom itself is very appealing, whether one plants a tree at home, at the synagogue, or in Israel by sending money to the Jewish National Fund's reforestation program.

Besides their use for announcements and decorative objects, some of the folkloric symbols I've been discussing might be incorporated into a tiny *yarmulka* and other special clothes for the *brit*, or decorate the borders of a naming certificate,* a receiving blanket, or a quilt.

THE WIMPEL

Whether the baby is a boy or a girl, making something special is a wonderful way to anticipate its arrival and to welcome it. Some people are uncomfortable with the idea of preparing baby things before the birth, preferring to wait until they are certain of a live baby. Like other deeply rooted fears, this is not one that can be argued with; I personally choose, if the pregnancy is proceeding normally and there is no medical reason to assume otherwise, to plan and make things in expectation of a healthy baby.

A delightful custom originated among the Jews of Germany and spread to parts of France and Italy and eventually to descendants of those congregations in this country as well. The swaddling clothes used at a baby boy's *brit* were embroidered or painted with his name, birth date, and wishes for a future of Torah, marriage, and good deeds and made into a wrapper for the Torah scroll. (A binder, which goes once around the Torah and clasps in front, or a wrapper, which is wound around several times and then self-tied,

---

*The Union of American Hebrew Congregations uses a printed form for naming ceremonies which, along with biblical quotations, says: "In conformity with Jewish tradition (space for baby's name) child of (parents' names) was named and blessed in the sanctuary of the Lord (name of congregation) and given the Hebrew name of: _____. May it become a name honored in the household of Israel." There are also spaces for the parents' and witnesses' signatures and the Hebrew and civil dates. An individually designed certificate would make a lovely gift for a friend's or relative's baby—or do one for your own.

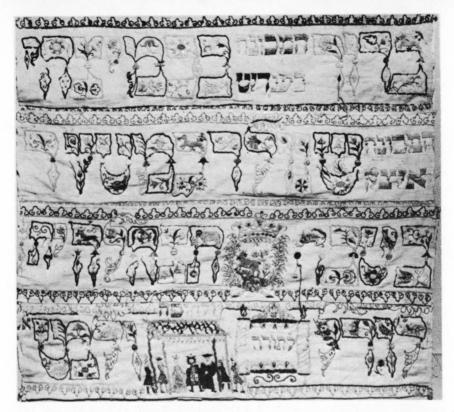

8 *Wimpel* Torah wrapper from Germany, 1735 (photo: courtesy Photographic Archive of the Jewish Theological Seminary of America, New York; Frank J. Darmstaedter, Curator)

is used to keep the heavy parchment of the Torah scroll from unwinding and possibly breaking; the mantle goes over this.) The personalized wrapper, called a *wimpel* (which is German for banner) would be used to wrap the Torah on the first day the child was brought to the synagogue, usually a year after his birth. It would be left on until the next time one was given and then stored until it was used again at the boy's Bar Mitzvah. Practices varied from congregation to congregation—some storing them in the synagogue, some with the family, and using them with varying frequency depending probably on how many others they had.

This is a lovely custom to pick up and reinterpret in a contemporary American idiom. Because they were traditionally made only for boys doesn't mean that we should ignore the possibility of making *wimpels* for girl babies too. Also, since we no longer "swaddle" our babies as though they were little mummies, and it seems artificial to me to make the traditional *wimpel* from cloth that has never touched a baby, I decided to rethink the project from the beginning. What I came up with was the notion of making a patchwork crib quilt, and embroidering the traditional blessing (see p. 20) in

16

the blocks, which could then be taken apart and reassembled into the more or less standard size (which is usually about 8" wide and 9'–12' long) to make it into a *wimpel* later. Once having come up with the idea and initial sketches, I called friends who were expecting their first child and asked them if they would like such a thing as a baby gift. They were delighted, and the expectant mother, Cindy Pearlman Benjamin—a very gifted calligrapher—collaborated with me by designing the lettering. A number of friends are helping with the embroidery. At this writing, both baby and quilt are still in progress. When the baby is born, the blocks allocated for the name and date of birth will be completed and then the quilt assembled. Two of the finished blocks can be seen in Figs. 12 and 13. Figure 9 shows all the pieces of the quilt top assembled on top of the polyester filling and the lining fabric. After the squares are all embroidered and seamed together with the spacing pieces, it will be finished by bringing the extra border of backing gingham around to the top and using that as a self-binding. Because the quilt will eventually be disassembled to make it into a *wimpel*, we will not quilt the layers together but will instead tie knots through all the small floral-printed squares.

9 The *wimpel*/quilt in progress (photo: Kenneth M. Bernstein)

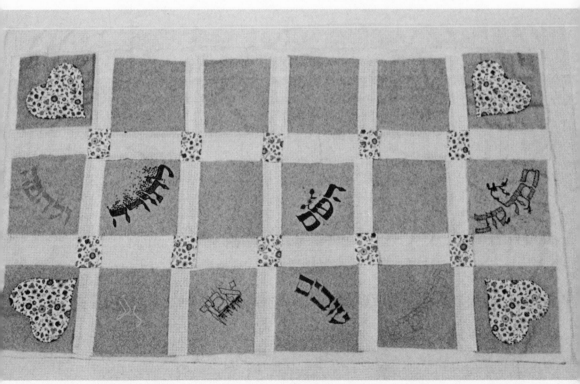

When the quilt is made into a *wimpel*, the parents may keep the four corners and make them into a pillow for the baby's room. If you want to make one like ours, directions are given below. You might use the blessing in English or write something original. Remember if you use the Hebrew that you have to adjust for male or female endings. I picked a gold-color permanent-press cotton fabric for the squares, yellow-and-white gingham for the lining and spacing strips, and a floral print with the same yellows, as well as orange, pink, brown, and green, for the hearts and corner squares. The designs are being embroidered in the colors of the print. Depending upon what it was made of and what condition it is in now, it might be nice to use the mother's wedding dress as the basic material or the lining fabric for the quilt. In fact, any way you can devise to make your *wimpel*/quilt unique makes it all the more precious.

Our finished quilt will be 32" x 54½". To make one like it, you will need (½" seam allowances are included):

eighteen 9" squares of permanent-press cotton fabric (Eighteen was a deliberate choice because the numerical value of the Hebrew word for life [חי] is eighteen.)
fifteen gingham strips, 1½"x 9", for the horizontal spacers
twelve gingham strips, 3" x 9", for the vertical spacers
ten 2" x 3" rectangles of printed fabric for the corner spacers
four 8" squares of the floral print to cut into heart shapes
four 3" floral-print squares for the corners of the border
a 33" x 55" piece of polyester quilt batting
38" x 60" gingham for the lining and borders (This allows 2" all around to fold over as the border, plus 1" to turn under as the seam allowance. If your fabric is wide enough, you might want to make the lining larger still, to allow for the possibility of its shifting and for the fact that the quilt will pucker when you knot it.)

Since the *wimpels* were originally made only for boys, the traditional blessing is in the masculine form; the child's name is given along with that of his father, and the mother's name isn't mentioned at all. The *wimpel*/quilt we are making for the Benjamin baby will have just the child's name, but we are allowing two squares (Nos. 3 and 4) to have a lot of room to embellish it. The diagram indicates which squares can be done in advance and which—because they are dependent on the gender of the child—will have to wait. Cindy has her drawings ready to go, so if the baby is a boy the

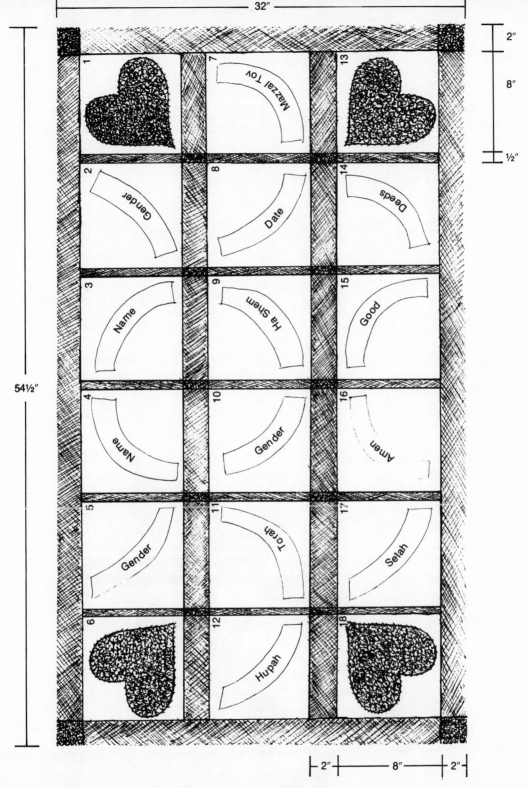

10 Diagram of the quilt, with measurements

quilt can be quickly finished by friends in the week before the *brit*. If the baby is a girl we will have more time, because the parents plan to wait until the weather is warmer and have an outdoor picnic for the baby-naming. If you decide to do the blessing in English, you can have almost all of it done before the birth.

The masculine form of the blessing reads:

הקטן *(name)* נולד במזל טוב יום *(date)*

השם יגדלהו לתורה ולחפה ולמעשים טובים אמן סלה.

The feminine form:

הקטנה *(name)* נולדה במזל טוב יום *(date)*

והשם יגדליה לתורה ולחפה ולמעשים טובים אמן סלה.

The English translation is: "The little one *(baby's name)* of *(parents' names)* was born with *mazzal* on *(date)*. May God bless him/her to grow up to the study of Torah, to the marriage canopy, and to good deeds. Amen. Selah."

11 Hebrew letters for AMEN

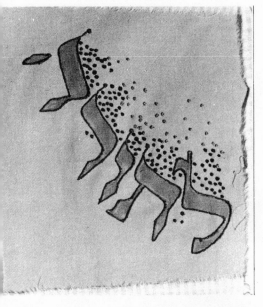

Quilt block that says TORAH. The letters were colored in with permanent felt-tip markers, then embroidered with outline stitch and French knots (photo: Kenneth M. Bernstein)

13 Quilt block that says HA SHEM ["The Name," a substitute for "God"]. The letters and a bit of floral embellishment have been colored with permanent felt-tip markers and embroidered with a combination of outline and running stitches, French knots, and detached chain stitches (photo: Kenneth M. Bernstein)

The Hebrew word *Amen* is shown actual size in Fig. 11. You can use this as a pattern if you wish. By studying the photographs and the diagram, you can see the way the letters were gently curved to form an overall pattern of arches. Traditional *wimpels* (Fig. 8) were often embellished by delightful pictures, either painted or embroidered, inspired by the blessing. As you can see, the possibilities are endless. Our *wimpel*/quilt is being made with a mixture of embroidery and permanent felt-tip markers. You might want to do some appliqué or even batik or dye-painting. Why not borrow from another American tradition and turn the quilt finishing into a party, too, in the manner of an old-fashioned quilting bee!

14 (photo: Mae Rockland)

BAR/BAT MITZVAH

My father was born in a now-vanished village in the Ukraine. When he was just a few years old, his father went to America in the hope, common to so many immigrants, of building a better life for his family. By the time my grandfather had saved enough money for his family's boat passage, his wife and two eldest sons had died, leaving the maternal grandmother and three boys: my father, then almost fourteen, and his ten-year-old and sixteen-year-old brothers. With their passage money the old *Bobeh* and the three boys made their way to Warsaw and from there embarked for America.

In the steerage section of the boat a *minyan* [quorum of ten] met several times a day for services. On Monday, Thursday, and the Sabbath, the Torah was taken out and read from. At one such service my father was called to the Torah. When he told the assembled group that, despite the fact that he had passed his thirteenth birthday many months ago, because neither of his parents was there and because of the hardships of the journey he had never had that honor before, the service spontaneously became a celebration and ended with a *seudat mitzvah* [meal celebrating a commandment]. Somehow from among their meager store of food an extra bit of wine and cake and perhaps a precious orange were found and transformed into a Bar Mitzvah feast.

My father came from an environment in which a boy began to read the Bible at five. By the age of ten, he was studying the oral laws and traditions. At thirteen, as part of a society in which study and prayer were as routine as eating and sleeping, he became "bound to the commandments," a Bar Mitzvah. This was thus a rite of passage into which he had grown organically. On the day on which this coming-of-age was celebrated (usually the Sabbath immediately after his birthday), he was called up to witness the reading of the Torah and allowed to wear *tefillin** for the first time. In some communities a *tallit* [prayer shawl] was also worn for the first time on this occasion; in others, wearing a *tallit* was reserved for married men. Depending on the abilities and talents of the child, he chanted the prayers before the congregation and read part or all of that day's biblical portion from the scroll of the Torah. Boys who couldn't read the handwritten unvowelled scroll witnessed the reading and recited as many of the prayers as they could. If the family could afford it, the boy had new clothes for the occasion. Most families had a Bar Mitzvah feast at home as the third meal of the Sabbath, during which the boy usually gave a short prepared speech.

This manner of preparation and celebration, which to us seems so deeply rooted, has in fact been the custom only since the late Middle Ages. Before that time, children were allowed to perform whatever religious *mitzvot* they were able to. Thus, at whatever age a child could responsibly look after *tefillin* and read from the Torah, he was allowed and encouraged to. In biblical and talmudic times and during the early Middle Ages, a young man reached majority at twenty, when he was considered responsible for his own financial and military obligations. The only change in his status as he passed from childhood through adolescence was that at thirteen his father was no longer responsible for his religious conduct or education and pronounced a benediction—which is still customary today—to that effect. Since nothing very ceremonially significant had taken place, there was no celebration or feast.

Today, despite the fact that Bar Mitzvah as we know it is of recent origin, it is one of the most widely observed of Jewish rites. Some people say that marking the age of thirteen the way we do is a throwback to a much more primitive time when a boy was initiated into the tribe at the onset of adolescence, and that possibly circumcision of all the boys of the same age was performed at that time. Others feel that in contemporary life dependency on parents is so protracted—lasting for many into the twenties—that a ceremony at thirteen marking "religious maturity" is meaningless. My own feeling is that the very reasons so often advanced by those who would

---

*Phylactories, two small leather boxes each containing four portions of the Pentateuch handwritten on parchment (Exodus 13:1–10, 11–16; Deuteronomy 6:4–9, 11:13–21). They are strapped to the forehead and left arm with leather thongs wrapped in a prescribed manner during the recital of morning prayers. Since they are not worn on the Sabbath, if the Bar Mitzvah ceremony takes place then, they will not be worn until the next day.

like to eliminate Bar Mitzvah or to postpone it to a later date in fact argue in favor of retaining and strengthening a custom that has proved its popularity and staying power over the last centuries and, unlike other celebrations, has also survived the trip to America.

A child of thirteen is indeed going through a remarkable set of changes. These are not only physical: the intelligence which at an earlier age was curious about everything takes on a more specific focus, and the world outside the family becomes increasingly alluring. While it is sad that for many children Jewish education ends with the Bar Mitzvah feast, it must be admitted that, if one eliminated the Bar Mitzvah ceremony, those very children would have nothing rather than little. Further, if the Bar Mitzvah program that the child, parents, and teachers espouse is truly meaningful, then even if the child "quits" immediately after, he is often left with a residue which will prompt him to seek further Jewish education and involvement later on. Therefore, for its emotional, familial, and educational values, I feel that Bar Mitzvah is a valuable institution—one that I hope will grow in profundity as more and more people take it seriously and divest it of some of the unfortunate trappings with which it has become encumbered.

A girl is traditionally considered to have reached religious majority at the age of twelve years and one day, but, despite her earlier maturity, it is only in recent years, with the growth of Jewish egalitarianism, that Bat Mitzvah as a religious ceremony has begun to take root. Occasionally in the past a family dinner was held to honor the girl's twelfth birthday, and the parents would recite the traditional blessing freeing them from responsibility for her religious conduct. Increasingly, Conservative and Reform congregations have embraced the idea of giving girls the same privileges and responsibilities at Bat Mitzvah (though usually preferring to postpone it until the girl is thirteen) as the boy receives at his Bar Mitzvah. Among Jewish feminists there is a divergence of philosophy, with some insisting on total equality and neutrality not only of the roles of leaders and participants in the service but in the language of prayer as well. Others feel that there should be equality but that the redefinition of women's roles does not mean that henceforth they should be treated exactly as men; rather, new and equally compelling ceremonies should be invented for women.

Fortunately, we do not have to solve these problems here; there is room enough in Jewish life for every variety of religious expression. The important point to be made is that a child at the age of twelve or thirteen is automatically bound by the commandments, whether or not the maturing process is formalized with a ceremony. The commandments themselves do not differentiate between men and women. Therefore, the Bar/Bat Mitzvah ceremony, if one elects to have it, should exercise the strengths and commitments of the child, regardless of sex, within the framework of whatever type of ceremony is most comfortable for the family.

Since both of my sons are blessed with fine voices and wanted to make their Bar Mitzvah day truly their own, they took over as much of the service as the rabbi would allow. To keep the regular Sabbath-morning service from turning into an egotistical display only for the benefit of visiting relatives, our rabbi wisely limited and spaced the parts of the service he turned over to them. Thus, they did a part of the preliminary service and chanted the entire Torah portion for the day, as well as the Haftorah reading; then, feeling really exultant, they went on to lead the Musaf (additional) service. My daughter is now beginning to prepare for her Bat Mitzvah and alternately wants to do either exactly what her brothers did or something that is special and different for herself. She still has several years to go and is fortunately involved in a fine program which will allow her this flexibility. It would be very painful if her enthusiasm and energy were dampened by trying to get her to accept conventional modes. Just as I want her to have everything she can attain through her own talents and efforts in her secular life, so do I feel that as a Jew she should be treated as as fully a member of the Jewish people as her brothers.

There are two aspects involved in planning a Bar/Bat Mitzvah. One is the religious service or ceremony itself; the other is the festive meal that traditionally follows it. Unfortunately, we all know some families for whom the social aspects of the event are of such overriding importance that they care little or nothing for the service and simply want their child "Bar/Bat Mitzvah-ed" so they can get on with the party. On a certain level these people are not entirely misguided in that they are often prompted by a genuine desire to forge a link with what they understand as Jewish tradition. In reality, they are cheating not only their child but themselves. While the follow-up festivities may be fun, genuine involvement in the spiritual preparation and education of the young person as Bar/Bat Mitzvah is approached is at least as enjoyable. The problem sometimes is that a family feels itself bound to a particular synagogue format which they find restrictive or do not really understand. If this is the case, the family should talk to the rabbi and the religious-school teachers, where appropriate, and enhance their own background or find ways of adding to the service readings meaningful to them. It is also possible to have a Bar/Bat Mitzvah service entirely of one's own design. A rabbi is not necessary, just a *minyan* and a Torah to read from. Scrolls can be borrowed from many synagogues and college Hillel Foundations. (One customarily makes a suitable donation when borrowing the Torah scroll.)

Many of us, however, are not emotionally or educationally prepared to take on the creation of an entire service on our own. Fortunately, there is an increasing number of congregations throughout the country that are rethinking their Bar/Bat Mitzvah programs and coming up with some creative approaches. Instead of, or along with, the traditional course of study, students are required to prepare a project of special significance to them. These projects vary with the interests and abilities of the child, but the idea is for the young person to share with the congregation some aspect of himself that reflects his Jewish values. A girl interested in ballet might dance like the prophetess Miriam; someone interested in archaeology might make a model of Masada and use it in the course of the services to explain the meaning of that resistance for Jews today. If this type of approach interests you and there is nothing like it in your area, start it yourself.

At the traditional service the parents usually present the child with a *tallit*. Most often this is purchased complete with the *tzitzit* [ritual fringes]. A *tallit* can be bought without the ritual fringes, which can be tied by the child with the help of the parents, or even with the parents just watching. Or the *tallit* can be made completely at home, again by either the child, the parents, or both together. Since women are also wearing *tallitot* with more and more frequency, Fig. 15 shows one possible form for a female *tallit* to take. At the egalitarian traditional service on the Brandeis University campus, one can see *tallitot* in every variety of fabric, color, and form. The only requirement for a *tallit* is that it have four corners for the *tzitzit*. I've seen *tallitot* made of denim and of lace; some in the shape of ponchos, others with hoods. Since many women who wear a *tallit* also would like to cover their heads but don't feel happy with a *yarmulka*, the hooded *tallit* is a comfortable solution. The *tallit* in the photograph was made from a handwoven shawl, slightly shaped with a seam in the back to form the hood. All that is required for a *tallit* is a rectangle of fabric that the wearer will be comfortable with. Sizes can vary as much as with any garment. Sew patches of strong attractive material on the back of the corners to reinforce them before cutting holes through which to thread the

15 (photo: Jim McDonald) 16 Batik velvet *tallit* bag (photo: Jim McDonald)

tzitzit. These holes should also be reinforced with decorative stitches (see Fig. 16). The neckband or borders can be embellished as desired with embroidery, fabric paint, or any means one finds attractive. My own preference is for white or off-white woven wool or synthetic fabric with some form of stripe near each end.

The most important part of the *tallit* is the *tzitzit.* We read in Numbers 15:37–39 that "The Lord spoke to Moses, saying: 'Speak to the children of Israel and instruct them to make fringes on the corners of their garments throughout their generations. . . . Look at [them] and remember all the commandments of the Lord, and observe them.'" You can make your own *tzitzit* from lengths of yarn or buy a package of *tzitzit* strands at most Hebrew bookstores. Whether you make or buy them, it is a good idea to practice with a bit of scrap fabric before beginning on your *tallit.*

You will need sixteen strands—twelve short ones and four long ones. Separate these into four groups, so that for each corner you have one long and three short strands. Even up three short strands and one long one at one end and push them through the hole you have prepared. Fold the strands in half, evening up seven of the ends and leaving the longest strand, called the *shammash*, free for winding. Take four strands in each hand and pull them toward the side of the *tallit* and tie them into a double knot near the edge of the fabric. Now wind the *shammash* thread in a spiral around the other seven threads, making sure to end where you began, so you have exactly seven turns. Use all the threads to make another double knot. Spiral the *shammash* thread around eight times. Tie a double knot. Next make eleven spirals and a double knot. Spiral the *shammash* around thirteen times and make a final double knot. Before you begin, study the knots on a completed *tallit* to see the finished effect.

A *tallit* needs a *tallit* bag. These can be purchased, but it is much more rewarding to make one, for yourself or for a member of your family. Figure 16 shows the batiked velvet shoulder bag I made for my daughter's *tallit*.* I used an off-white velvet to begin with, then wrote her name and drew the bird, flower, and border with *permanent* felt-tip marking pens. Her name is Keren Chaya Faigle. I wrote only Keren Chaya and used the bird—*faigle* in Yiddish—to fill out the design. Then, with hot wax melted in the top of a double boiler, I painted over the marking-pen designs. The fabric was then dyed, using a cold-water batik dye from the hobby shop (a dye that needs simmering will remove the wax). Enough extra fabric was dyed to use for the strap and sides. The back has an allover design like the border. When the dyeing process has been completed, allow the fabric to dry and iron out the excess wax between sheets of newspaper. It takes a lot of ironing.

When the child is well under way with his studies and the type of service has been decided upon, attention turns to the *seudat mitzvah*—the feast celebrating the fulfillment of a religious commandment. Rabbinic justification has been found for this feast by interpreting Genesis 21:8, "Abraham made a great feast on the day Isaac was weaned," as weaning not from his mother's milk but from the "evil inclination"—i.e., attaining religious majority. When the child is well prepared and committed to the ideas inherent in the concept of Bar/Bat Mitzvah, and the family too is in-

---

*There are directions for patchwork, embroidered, and needlepoint *tallit* bags in my book *The Work of Our Hands* (New York: Schocken Books, 1973).

volved in the learning and growth process, there is indeed a great deal to celebrate.

I have been to some Bar Mitzvah celebrations that had the feeling and flavor of a Roman orgy in a New Orleans bordello as staged by Ed Sullivan. I'm not sure why, in this liberated age, these extravaganzas seem to be put on principally in connection with a Bar Mitzvah and only rarely for a girl's Bat Mitzvah; but I won't take issue with it, since this is a case where the women are better served. I admit to a certain perverse pleasure in going to these affairs and sitting at a table (at a safe distance from the band) with eight or ten of my peers and making snide remarks about the *glatt* kosher "mock shrimp cocktail." (How can anyone who is *glatt* kosher know what a shrimp cocktail tastes like in order to fake it? Why would they want to?) I find amusement in the struggles of Aunt Anna in her décolleté tight pink satin—first to keep her bosom covered in the synagogue, now to make sure that it is shown to advantage—and the décor ("We had a choice of yellow and white, but that reminded us of eggs; blue and white, but that seemed so *obvious;* and red and black, which they use for businessmen's conventions and since today he is a man . . ."). Sometimes if I am in a benevolent mood, or if someone else is making the nasty cracks, I will wax sentimental about the poverty of the *shtetl* and comment that these same *shtetl* Jews now have money and are acting out a fantasy of elegance by dancing at noon under the glistening chandeliers of Murray's Chez Français.

The end of my tolerance came at one such affair during the ritualistic lighting of the birthday cake. A new *minhag* [custom] had been invented. In what seemed to be a parody of *aliyot* to the Torah, people were "called up" to light birthday candles. A Master of Ceremonies was in charge, and he invited the honored guests, one by one, to come up to the bandstand and light a candle. This time, after calling upon the maternal grandfather, followed by the maternal grandmother (both of whom haltingly and shyly did what was expected of them), he called for the paternal grandfather and no one, in this audience of two hundred, made a move for the dais. He called again, making bathroom jokes, and along with the snickers was a growing silence. Then a whisper filled the room: "He's dead, tell him that he's dead." The emcee carried on with great aplomb, euphemistically explaining to the world at large that "Our beloved grandpa is no longer with us," and, having thus paid his respects to the dead and been reassured that the rest of the family was still alive and well, went on with the show.

I have no intention of wreaking havoc with the catering business; nor do I maintain that the event itself should not be the focal point of a wonderful family and community celebration. Just the opposite is true. Caterers perform many genuinely useful services. I just wish that the prevailing mode among them was not so blatantly gross. The responsibility is *with us;* if we do not request that type of ostentation which makes the Jewish community the object of ridicule in film and literature, it will fade away. This is not a new problem; from time to time in the past the rabbis have issued sumptuary laws aimed at reducing the lavishness of Bar Mitzvah and wedding feasts. For example, the leaders of the Jewish community in Cracow, Poland, were so aroused by this issue in 1595 that they placed a tax on such celebrations in order to keep them from becoming extravaganzas. They feared, as we do, that the significance of attaining religious majority would be dwarfed by an overly sumptuous party.

Closer to our own time and place are the following excerpts from the "Resolutions on Moderation in Serving *kiddush* at Bar and Bat Mitzvahs," which were drawn up at the annual membership meeting of Temple Beth El in Troy, New York, in 1927:

> Members henceforth [are] to limit their Bar Mitzvah celebration on Temple premises following Sabbath services to a modest repast, which . . . will rather be in the traditional spirit of a *seudah shel mitzvah*, a meal appropriate to a religious moment.
> Resolved, that the entire congregation be limited in the serving following a Bar or Bat Mitzvah, to a *kiddush*, not a meal.

MENU GUIDE

> a. Wine, liquor (grape juice or soda for children)
> b. Cake, cookies, candies, nuts
> c. Chopped herring or pickled herring or gefilte fish (with accompanying bread, crackers, or *kikhl*)
> d. Coffee, tea, or punch
>   (Note: no sandwiches, hors d'oeuvres; no meat or hot dishes.) The above menu is meant as a maximum; no family need feel obliged to serve items c. and d. if they prefer not to.

> Resolved, that the Board empower the president to inform all Bar and Bat Mitzvah parents that our kitchen will not be available to any members who do not agree to abide by the rules.

The options then open to us, if we agree with the idea of simplicity but want to celebrate the event joyously, are those of genuine

17

hospitality and warmth. Just as with the service, the family should think through its own need and find ways of personalizing the *simhah* [joyous celebration]. Those families who have decided to mark the attaining of religious majority outside the synagogue will also have their *simhah* at home or some other location. The Bar/Bat Mitzvah has served some families as the opportunity to have an extended family retreat and reunion. These have been held at summer camps and hotels, providing sleeping space where needed and the chance for lots of visiting. Other families have marked the event by a trip to Israel, and some have made arrangements to have the Bar Mitzvah at the Western Wall. Since most of us will not undertake anything like this (aside from other considerations, even the "simplest" retreat or trip is expensive), I can probably be most helpful by describing the festivities surrounding the Bar/Bat Mitzvah ceremonies of my own children and those of friends.

As I described earlier, my sons' Bar Mitzvah ceremonies took the form of active participation in a traditional Sabbath-morning service. This service always ends with a *kiddush*, the sanctification of wine and then the sharing of *hallah* and perhaps some cookies. Our feeling was that, since our children's commitment was being recognized by the community, we wanted to provide the food for the *kiddush* and to invite the congregation as well as our own family to celebrate with us. Several other Bar/Bat Mitzvah candidates' mothers all joined together and helped one another. As each Bar/Bat Mitzvah date approached, we baked and filled our freezers with cakes and breads for the *kiddush*. To allow the host family the most freedom to relax and visit with well-wishers during the *kiddush*, friends poured the wine, looked after refilling the platters, and so on. Two college students were hired to serve punch to the children and to wash the glasses, and a local woman to clean the social hall afterward.

The grandparents had come Friday afternoon and shared a Sabbath dinner with us before we all went to Friday-night services. Our family is large and many had come from quite a distance, some leaving their homes at dawn to arrive in time for the Sabbath-morning service. We wanted to enable the family to rest and visit before undertaking their long trips home, and we were particularly concerned for the comfort of the elderly great aunts and uncles, with whom we are blessed with a fair number. If my house had been large and comfortable enough, I would have invited everyone back home for some warm food and the chance to lie down. But the town I lived in had a small private women's club in an elegant, sprawling old house. It rented its facilities—which included a huge

18 Bar Mitzvah posters

dining room, parlors, and several upstairs rooms with places to rest—to families like ours which wanted an intimate and informal atmosphere for family gatherings such as Bar/Bat Mitzvah lunches and weddings.

Recently I had a call from a friend in Pine Bluff, Arkansas, to tell me about the plans for her son's Bar Mitzvah this fall. It will be the first Bar Mitzvah in Pine Bluff in eighteen years. The Jewish community is tiny; there are sixteen children in the religious school. Everyone in town is looking forward to the event enormously, Gentiles as much as Jews. The family will put an announcement in the town newspaper, saying that no invitations will be sent in town and all friends of the family are cordially invited to the Sabbath-morning services. Their family is also large and quite spread out geographically. Carolyn Greenberg described an old Southern custom which would be wonderful to transplant. She says that the local friends play host to the visiting friends and family, seeing to it that they never have to buy a meal. Different friends take turns having lunches and dinners for all the out-of-town visitors. That way, by the end of the weekend old and new family and friends all know one another. The food itself can be absolutely basic—sliced salami and potato chips—but the warmth and the fact of being looked after in a strange town are the essential ingredients in the shared meals.

Now that we've moved to a larger house, I hope to be able to have my daughter's Bat Mitzvah *seudah* at home. It is too far in the future to be planning a menu. We might have a buffet of all cold foods or, most likely, since it will be in mid-February, I'll do a lot of cooking beforehand and have it heating while we are still in synagogue. In any case, every freezer in the neighborhood may be called into service. Extra tables and chairs can be borrowed or rented, as can tableware of almost every description. Most liquor stores are very accommodating about delivering an estimated oversupply of wine and then picking up the unopened bottles. Many of them have punch bowls and glasses which they will lend at no charge or for a small breakage deposit.

One way to give the guests a meaningful souvenir of the occasion is to make the invitation a work of art. The Bar Mitzvah announcements in Fig. 18 and the Bat Mitzvah announcement on the T-shirt (Fig. 14) were made as posters. The ones in Fig. 18 are 12" x 18" and were sent in large manilla envelopes. Robin's was 18" x 24" and was sent in a mailing tube. I designed them all and had the first two printed by offset; I screen-printed the edition of Robin's. Since I was hand-printing them, I printed the T-shirt in Fig. 14 as well, so that for weeks before her Bat Mitzvah Robin could tell the world what she was doing. All these announcements, as well as others like them, take their imagery from the Torah portion for that particular Sabbath. Robin's Torah portion, for example, was Exodus 6:2–9:35. In it seven of the ten plagues are described—not a particularly cheerful source of pretty pictures for a Bat Mitzvah announcement. The passages tell us that God will act with a strong hand to get us out of Egypt, and with a benevolent hand we will be guided. I therefore usd the downward-directed hand wrapped in a serpent to portray pestilence, hail, and blood; the hand with the heart-shaped fingernails depicts gentleness. I like using the Torah portion itself as the basis for the invitation design because it tells people immediately what is important about the event.

An announcement was made for my oldest son's Bar Mitzvah by a friend. She said that all she needed from me was a good snapshot of David, and she would do the rest. So one afternoon David posed with a *tallit*, prayer book, and *kiddush* cup, and I shot a roll of film. I sent the best snapshot to my friend, who had the image developed onto a screen and then hand-printed his invitation. That was her Bar Mitzvah gift to David. Whether you look for design motifs in the liturgy or decide to use a photograph, a personal drawing, or a quotation, if you invest it with a unique quality it is sure to be treasured.

I know that in some communities it is the common practice to decorate the *bimah* [platform] with masses of floral arrangements. I've never been partial to this custom. If flowers or plants are called for, I prefer to use live seasonal plants. Afterward, these can be planted in the home or synagogue garden and provide a lasting reminder of the day. The bush of white roses we planted after David's Bar Mitzvah seven years ago is really lovely now.

Our synagogue did not have really nice tablecloths to cover the *kiddush* tables. Rather than renting them from a linen-supply house, I bought yards of inexpensive, brightly colored cotton fabric and made the cloths. Later, I gave them to the synagogue.

As presents for my son's tutors and the friends who helped with the baking, I made *mizrahim* and ceramic *mezuzot*.

The Bar/Bat Mitzvah will undoubtedly receive many gifts and, after everything has returned to normal, will sit down to write thank-you letters. Since music was one of David's main interests, he made a linoleum-cut print which he called "The Group." We had it reproduced by photo-offset on foldover 6" x 8" cards, which then

19 "The Group,"
lino cut by
David Rockland

became his personalized way of expressing appreciation to all the
people who had joined him on his special day.

In the century and a half since Reform Judaism in Germany instituted the confirmation ceremony, it has undergone many changes.
Initially, considering the child at thirteen as too young to be
thought of as a religious adult, it was seen as a replacement for the
Bar Mitzvah and held after the fourteenth birthday, usually when
the child was about sixteen. There was no specific day for the ceremony, which borrowed its name and some of its forms from the
Lutheran Church; it was held on a special Sabbath such as that
which falls during Hanukkah or Passover. Finally Shavuot, the Festival of the Giving of the Torah, which was the day when a Jewish
child in the Middle Ages traditionally began studying, was selected
as the day for confirmation ceremonies. This group ceremony originally took place in the religious school; it later moved to the
synagogue. Like the Bar Mitzvah, it was initially only for boys, but
now girls participate in it fully.

Resistance to confirmation has faded and it has been accepted by
Conservative and most Orthodox Jews in addition to Bar Mitzvah
rather than as a replacement for it. Confirmation programs have
won acceptance because of the earnestness of the students who par-

ticipate in them, proving that, when the need is felt, Jewish life can expand and create new forms or fill borrowed ones with treasured values.

20 Poster invitation to a confirmation service, designed and sent to the entire congregation by the confirmands

21 (photo: Robert Leverant)

WEDDINGS

King Solomon had a daughter who was beautiful, bright, and charming. He doted upon her exceedingly. When she reached marriageable age, he determined that she would wed the finest, wealthiest prince or king in the world. He sent messengers everywhere to announce that he was searching for such a groom, and the princes and kings came from near and far. But the princess, who was as modest as she was sweet and beautiful, did not like any of them, and they were sent away.

Solomon was uncertain what to do next, so he consulted the readings of the stars to see what the future held for his daughter. He was not at all pleased with what he found out. The stars foretold that in a certain season of the year, under the influence of the prevailing stars and planets, the princess would fall in love with a poor youth and would marry him, and that this was God's will. The king was aghast and determined that his daughter would not marry without his permission; he would test God. He had a castle and fortress built on a small uninhabited island several miles out to sea. As the season foretold by the stars approached, he outfitted the castle with everything he could think of for his daughter's pleasure and diversion, stocked it well with food and brought her there. To attend her every whim and to guard that no one should approach the castle, he installed seventy elders. The princess lived quite contentedly in her retirement. When she became restless or felt confined, she went to the roof of the castle and walked around, and this soothed her. Every day a boat was sent from the mainland by the king to ask after the well-being of the princess, and every day the news was the same.

There lived in the town of Acre a poor young scribe, who, full of energy and enthusiasm, set out to see a bit of the world before returning to the honorable profession of his father and grandfather. After many adventures, he found himself one evening in a barren and dismal area; it was raining, he was cold and hungry, and with night rapidly approaching he looked about for some way to comfort himself. There was nothing. Then he saw the partially devoured carcass of an ox lying nearby. He praised God for having provided him with shelter, and crawled inside the animal and went to sleep. During the night an eagle came, picked up the carcass, and flew with it out to sea. He put it down on the roof of the princess' castle and picked away the remaining flesh from the skeleton. In the morning when the princess came up to the roof for her daily exercise, she found the youth, took pity on him, and brought him down to her chambers, where he bathed and she provided him with clean clothes and warm food. He remained in her quarters and, since the seventy elders only came when they were summoned, no one knew of his presence.

The young scribe and the king's daughter became fast friends, and, as the stars predicted, she fell in love with him. One day she asked him, "Do you love me? Would you take me to be your wife?" "I do love you," he replied, "but you are the daughter of the king and I am a lowly scribe; how can I marry you?" "We will declare our love before God, and the angels Michael and Gabriel will be our witnesses," she said. And so he drew blood from his arm and with it wrote a marriage document, with God's angels as witnesses.

The seventy elders who had spent their days and nights in constant vigilance of course knew nothing of this marriage. So when the season foretold by the stars drew to a close and King Solomon came to the island, they reported to him that all was well and as he wished. The king called for his daughter, and she appeared, bringing her new husband. The king was initially furious and then amazed as he heard the story of the youth's arrival at the castle and the writing of the marriage document. As he listened, he realized that not even Solomon the Wise could outsmart God. He saw what a fine young man had been chosen to be his son-in-law and announced that everyone would go back to Jerusalem for seven days of feasting to celebrate the marriage of the princess to the scribe.

Most of us were raised with tales such as this, where marriages are made in heaven. But such notions of romantic love leave us totally unprepared for the complex realities of marriage in mid-twentieth-century America. Much of what is written about weddings assumes that the bride and groom are young and innocent, still under the protection of their parents, and certain to live happily ever after. By perpetuating an overly romantic, simplistic view of marriage, a disservice is done not only to those people whose situation is far from that depicted in fairy tales but even to the idealized young couple marrying for the first time. Everyone cannot be fit into the same storybook wedding picture.

Consider the wedding I attended last May. The bride was thirty-seven, the groom forty; between them they had six children. This was their third wedding, the second to each other. The Jewish bride had been married for fourteen years; after her divorce, she met and fell in love with a divorced Unitarian. They lived together for a year and finally were married with a civil service, essentially for the sake of the children. The home they created was very Jewish, and the groom felt himself more and more attracted to Judaism and began to study seriously. Several years later he converted and had a *brit*, and since he had not been circumcised as an infant (as so many American boys are nowadays), he entered the hospital for surgery. The traditional *Aufruf*, when a groom is honored by being called to the Torah at a service shortly before his wedding, was simultaneously his Bar Mitzvah. A few weeks after his *brit*, he was standing under the wedding canopy, feeling, he said, very self-indulgent. He'd converted entirely for his own sake (his wife, in fact, had discouraged him); being Jewish was something he wanted totally for himself. And, on top of that, to have the opportunity, after four years of happy marriage, to declare one's love and commitment once again to his wife/bride within a supportive community in a time-honored ceremony was one of life's most beautiful experiences. Their six children held the *hupah* poles for one of the loveliest weddings I've ever seen.

Or what of the elderly couple living together unmarried because they are dependent on Social Security and cannot afford to get married. They approach a rabbi and ask to have their union sanctified with a religious wedding, which is not reported to the civil authorities. Some rabbis, for reasons of conscience, will perform such weddings; others, also for reasons of conscience, won't. Such couples should know that within Jewish tradition they really don't need a rabbi to get married.

According to the Talmud, there are three ways of being legally married (cohabitation, contract, or gift of value to the woman), none of which requires a rabbi. All three require the presence of two adult male witnesses who are not related to the bride or groom or to one another and are in good standing within the Jewish community. Before the two witnesses the groom declares that he takes the woman to be his wife, according to the law of Moses and Israel, by cohabitation. The couple then retires to another room while the witnesses remain outside. Understandably, this form of marriage is not particularly in favor.

The second and third forms are, however, definite possibilities

41

and can be combined to make a moving, personal, and traditional ceremony. In the presence of the two witnesses (and of course anyone else the couple cares to have attend), the groom gives the bride a document or an article of easily determined value, such as a ring or a coin, with the following declaration, and she accepts it. As the groom places the ring on the bride's right forefinger (because that is the finger generally used for pointing and the ring can be shown to the witnesses; later it is usually put on the left ring finger), he says:

הרי את מקדשת לי בטבעת זו כדת משה וישראל.

Hare at mekudeshet li betaba'at zo kedat Moshe v'Yisrael. ["Behold, you are consecrated unto me with this ring as my wife, according to the law of Moses and Israel."] (It should be mentioned at this point that there have been cases of children playing at weddings and then needing a religious divorce, because the little boy, with a dimestore ring or a coin, acquired a "wife.") This basic transaction can take place under a *hupah*, wine can be drunk, additional readings add-

22 Appliqué-and-embroidery *hupah*: "Let the heavens rejoice and the earth be glad" (photo: Mae Rockland)

ed, the traditional glass shattered—in fact, anything the couple desire to make them feel they are indeed married.

The essential ingredients of a Jewish wedding are the same around the world, but over the centuries various Jewish communities have picked up local customs. Thus in America some Jews hold to customs brought with them by their immigrant forebears, while other American Jewish weddings look very similar to those we've seen in the mass media and come to accept as the Standard Wedding. The customs surrounding the Jewish wedding are so rich with symbolism and warmth that couples looking for ways to personalize their wedding day would do well to turn toward tradition for inspiration.

Orthodox, Conservative, and some Reform wedding ceremonies take place under a *hupah* [wedding canopy]. The *hupah* is essentially a rectangular piece of cloth large enough for the bride, groom, and rabbi (and sometimes other members of the wedding party) to stand under. The four corners are attached to four poles which can be held by friends or inserted into permanent supports. The idea of using a *hupah* goes back to the tent of the bridegroom in which the marriage was consummated, but for us today it signifies the new home about to be started. A *tallit* is often used as a *hupah*, and it has become the custom in Israel for a soldier's wedding to have his buddies support a *tallit* using four rifles as poles. Sephardic Jews often use both a *tallit*, draping one over the couple, and a large fabric canopy which can accommodate the rabbi and family members as well.

A handmade *hupah* which could be hung in the new home after the wedding would surely become a cherished family heirloom. It is a time-consuming project, but a very gratifying one, especially if relatives and friends help. Many techniques are possible, from weaving to batik and screen-printing. The one shown in Fig. 22 was made by appliquéing bright-colored cotton and velvet fabric to a purple wool background. It was made for the Elmont Jewish Center in New York; between weddings it hangs on the wall of the synagogue entrance. One could also make a *tallit* and use that as the *hupah*. If your synagogue has one which is serviceable but unattractive and you don't have the time or inclination to make a new one, perhaps with a bit of ingenuity you could spruce up the existing one—that would be a service to the community as well. I have been to weddings where the *hupah* was made of fresh flowers. No doubt this is some florists' idea of elegance. I find it totally objectionable. If there is that much money around to be spent on the poor cut corpses of fresh flowers (these *hupahs* usually cost hundreds of dollars), the money should be given to charity. On the other hand, I can imagine a few sprigs of fresh flowers or greens from your own garden or that of a friend tacked onto a cloth *hupah* as being very attractive and unostentatious.

The *hupah* can be set up or carried anywhere; the preferred places are a home or a synagogue, either inside or outdoors. Restaurants, country clubs, and other commercial establishments tend to be devoid of human warmth and certainly lack even the remotest aura of sanctity, so that even though they can be of assistance for the social part of the wedding day, my preference is to keep away from them. It is easier to arrange for food and help to be brought in than it is to prepackage and export religious atmosphere. If your home isn't big enough or you are not affiliated with a synagogue, consult your local rabbi anyway. In college towns there are usually Hillel chapels which—especially when the students are on vacation—can often be used.

The ceremony under the *hupah* is the culmination of a series of preliminary events. In earlier times the bride and groom were formally engaged a year before the wedding, and a legal betrothal document—called *tenaim,* specifying the obligations and material objects that each partner brought to the marriage, as well as setting the wedding date and place—was drawn up and signed by both parties as well as two witnesses. Because the betrothal is legally binding and can only be nullified by divorce, and in troubled times, with the couple essentially married but living apart, problems could and did arise, by the Middle Ages it became customary to sign the *tenaim* immediately before the wedding. In searching for ways of equalizing the marriage ceremony today, many couples are turning to the ancient custom of *tenaim* and finding in it a flexibility which suits contemporary lives. Unlike the *ketubah* [marriage contract], which will be discussed shortly, the *tenaim's* form can be accommodated to express the needs of the individuals, and both the bride and groom sign them, whereas only the witnesses sign the *ketubah.* By writing *tenaim,* the couple has the opportunity to think through and express what it is they expect of the marriage and what they will bring to it. The document can reflect profound emotional commitment while even listing, if desired, who does the dishes and who takes out the garbage. The couple described earlier drew up *tenaim* and had the document gorgeously lettered and illuminated by a gifted scribe. They felt that the language of the *ketubah* did not really express their stage in life or their relationship. They have an ordinary printed traditional *ketubah* because it is the required legal document which records where and when their marriage took place and validates it, but the *tenaim* is the document that means the most to them. In it the bride and the groom promise to "guard, nurture, and educate the children of the bride and groom" in the manner that is customary according to the ways of the Jews. The careful choice of language allows them to express concern for the six children by their previous marriages.

Brandeis Hillel Rabbi Al Axelrad recommends the writing of *tenaim* for all couples. He sees this as a way to make the couple really aware that they are entering a new stage in their lives, one that broadens the scope of their feelings and ideas. He suggests having a small ceremony at home, perhaps the week before the wedding, or after Havdalah on a Saturday night close to the wedding, when the symbolism of Havdalah—the separation of Sabbath from the rest of the week—can also be interpreted as the separation from one stage of life and entry into another. Unlike the wedding, which, especially if it's a first one, will have lots of people and tumult, this could be a simple ceremony in which both people read their agreement, sign it, and share wine and a little food with a few friends or close family. Whether the document is written in Hebrew or English or both, it can also be beautifully drawn and illuminated by a calligrapher. When a Jew marries a Gentile, they cannot have a *ketubah* which recognizes their marriage according to the law of Moses and Israel, since in fact their marriage is *not* according to that law. But they can draw up *tenaim*.

Among Orthodox and Conservative Jews, the groom is honored by being called up to the reading of the Torah, a custom which is called an *Aufruf* (*ufruf* in Yiddish). The *Aufruf* can take place at any service when the Torah is read most frequently it takes place on the Sabbath morning before the wedding. As the groom chants the same blessings he first recited at his Bar Mitzvah, he is showered with sweets. (The traditional fertility omens—raisins and nuts— have in many places given way to cellophane-wrapped candies, symbolic of a happy sweet life, because they are easier to clean up.) It is customary for the groom's family to provide a simple *kiddush* for the congregation and invited guests on this occasion. Some rabbis call the bride to the *bimah* and bless the couple. It is traditional for a bride to present her future husband with a new *tallit* to wear for his *Aufruf* and from then on. Making a *tallit* and/or a *tallit* bag adds even more to the significance of the gift. Often on the day of the *Aufruf* the bride's family will present the groom with a *kiddush* cup, and the groom's family will give the bride candlesticks, which can be used for the first time at the wedding.

The Jewish wedding ceremony is a religious service incorporating a legal contract and is designed to start the couple's life together upon a foundation of care, understanding, and sanctity. Before the procession to the *hupah* takes place, the *tenaim*, if they have not been signed before, are signed and the groom is asked if he is ready to take on the responsibilities outlined in the *ketubah*. He signifies his willingness by accepting a handkerchief or other object offered him by the rabbi. The two witnesses to this sign the *ketubah*.

It is said that the practice of having a procession to the *hupah* originated with God Himself when He "brought" Eve to Adam. It is also felt that the bride and groom are a queen and king on their wedding day and should therefore have an escort. Traditionally the groom's parents bring him to the *hupah*, holding him by either arm, and then the bride's parents escort her there. At some Jewish weddings this lovely custom has given way to the American practice of the bride's father or other male relative accompanying her down the aisle toward the waiting groom, to "give her away." To me, the old-fashioned custom is really more suitable for contemporary couples, in that it treats them both equally while signifying that two families as well as two individuals are joined at a wedding. Who accompanies the bride and groom is not a matter of fixed religious law. Custom has hallowed the parental role for this *mitzvah* of attending to the couple, but there are many circumstances when the parents cannot or should not fulfill this role. If the parents of either the bride or groom are dead, divorced, or separated, substitute escorts are chosen; sometimes the other parents will then also forgo their traditional role in order not to cause the couple any discomfort. If either or both the bride and the groom have lived away from home for a long while, or have been married before, it usually seems inappropriate (unless they are very young and the first marriage was of brief duration) for the parents to escort them to the *hupah* as though they were really bringing their child from the parental home to the next stage in life.

While children of the first marriage should be included in the festivities of a second marriage, to turn them into the escorts is putting a large burden of emotional responsibility on them. If they are psychologically prepared for the role, they might help hold the *hupah*, or read something, act as a flower girl or ringbearer or whatever is meaningful to the family, depending on the elaborateness of the wedding and the age of the children. The role of escorting the

23 Reproduction of an antique wedding ring (photo: courtesy The Jewish Museum Shop, The Jewish Museum, New York)

couple might be given to siblings of the bride and groom or to friends, or they might choose to walk unescorted (even together) to the *hupah* or to "just appear" there with no fanfare. At a first wedding, the parents of the couple receive a lot of attention, with flowers for the mothers, et cetera. Where there are children, their feelings and needs should be looked after and their participation planned well in advance of the day itself, which may be difficult for them. I've been to some weddings of friends where the children were really happy and having a marvelous time, because they weren't treated as excess baggage or leftovers from another life. If anyone is to have flowers, it should be the children instead of—or as well as—the couple's parents. Some children, even if they like the parent's new mate, want nothing to do at all with the wedding because it raises too many painful emotions for them. Their wishes too should be respected, and they shouldn't be expected to perform when they'd rather run away from the reality of life's changes. Most psychologists feel that children are better off attending the wedding, even if it takes a bit of encouraging to get them there; a loving family member, friend, or familiar babysitter should be with them throughout.

The rest of the entourage—maid or matron of honor, best man, bridesmaids—will depend on the elaborateness of the wedding. Even at the simplest wedding it is usual to have at least one female and one male attendant, generally sisters or brothers or the closest friends of the bride and groom. Sometimes all of the family members walk to the *hupah* to await the bride and groom and then surround them during the ceremony.*

*For a full discussion of the formal Jewish-American wedding with many attendants, I refer you to Lilly S. Routtenberg and Ruth R. Seldin, *The Jewish Wedding Book* (New York: Schocken Books, 1968).

47

The ceremony begins with an invocation incorporating verses from Psalm 118, starting with "Blessed may you be who come in the name of the Lord."

The blessing over wine is recited and then the betrothal benediction. The groom and the bride drink the cup of wine.

The groom then puts a ring on the right index finger of the bride and recites the phrase that solemnizes their marriage: "Behold, you are consecrated to me with this ring as my wife, according to the law of Moses and Israel." The ring must be the property of the groom and must be solid metal (usually gold), with no stones. Wedding rings are not mentioned in the Talmud but they were probably used in Roman Palestine; they became a regular part of the ceremony in the seventh or eighth century. In the Middle Ages, engagement rings were worn by men rather than women. In Germany, a gold ring was given to the groom by his father-in-law at the betrothal; the bride received hers on the morning of the wedding. A Jewish Museum reproduction of a type of ring that appeared around the sixteenth century is shown in Fig. 23. These rings, often enormous, had little houses on them, which were sometimes very stylized and at others very realistically modeled. They usually had the inscription *mazzal tov* on them. There is some speculation as to what these rings were actually used for. Despite their explicit symbolism, they are never mentioned in either writing or pictures of the time, and, since Halakhah clearly says that the marriage ring must be the property of the groom, it is unlikely they were used at the ceremony itself. It is most commonly believed that they were owned by the community and lent to the new bride for the week following the marriage, when because of their size they were worn on a chain or ribbon as a necklace and good-luck charm. Others feel that they may have been designed to hold small bouquets of flowers. Whatever their original use, they have made a small but precious and interesting contribution to the world of Jewish ceremonial art. Adaptations of this style are available from the Jewish Museum Gift Shop in New York and on special commission from a growing number of gifted Jewish metalsmiths who are committed to the design and creation of contemporary Jewish wedding bands as well.* Reform and Conservative and even many Orthodox ceremonies may include the presentation of a ring to the groom as well as to the bride. Additions to the traditional ceremony are very popular and appealing at this point.

*For names and descriptions of their work, see my book *The Jewish Yellow Pages* (New York: Schocken Books, 1976), pp. 31–40.

After the ring has been given and accepted, the *ketubah* is read and given to the bride. In the first century of the Common Era, when the *ketubah* first came into use, it was a progressive document, for it provided a woman with legal protection by outlining her husband's responsibilities to provide for her well-being while married and in the event of his death or of divorce. Today, many couples feel that the traditional *ketubah* does not reflect their concept of themselves or their marriage, which they see as uniting two persons of equal status. They would like to have a marriage contract that outlines the shared life they anticipate. Most Conservative and virtually all Orthodox rabbis, however, won't use anything but the traditional document. One rabbi, when asked why the *ketubah* stipulates that the husband is obliged to provide for his wife but does not obligate the woman to provide for her mate, responded that the last time a woman (Eve) tried to feed her husband it caused enough trouble for all time. The more usual response is simply that anything but the standard document will not be acceptable in Jewish law.* Some couples have "solved" this by having two *ketubot*, the traditional one (usually a printed form), which is the only valid one according to Halakhah, and then another equalized, personal version. Quite a few couples use only the modernized one, feeling that since they will be legally married according to Jewish law by virtue of the ring ceremony, they can improve upon the form of the *ketubah*.

Rabbi Al Axelrad greatly encourages the writing of creative *ketubot*. He is as concerned with the relationship of the couples he marries as with the fine points of Halakhah. He would like to see a groundswell of revised *ketubot*, which, over time, will produce the desired changes in religious law. Rabbi Daniel Leifer has written a thoughtful essay "On Writing New *Ketubot*,"** which gives several examples of contemporary marriage contracts, as well as the rationale for writing one's own. It is recommended reading for any couple considering this course. Whatever you decide to do about your *ketubah*, you should discuss it fully with the officiating rabbi.

---

*Quite a few farsighted Conservative rabbis use a *ketubah* that has a clause stating that if there is a civil divorce, either party (not only the husband) can appeal to the Conservative rabbinical court for a religious divorce. This clause was instituted to protect women whose husbands withheld religious divorce, preventing them from being remarried by an Orthodox or Conservative rabbi, as a form of financial extortion.

**This essay can be found in *The Jewish Woman: New Perspectives*, edited by Elizabeth Koltun (New York: Schocken Books, 1976).

24 *Ketubah* of Mr. and Mrs. S. Rosedale, by David Moss (photo: David Moss)

In certain instances, even a traditional *ketubah* will be objectionable to some rabbis. Among Reform Jews a marriage certificate is given to the couple, but it is usually not read at the ceremony.

While the text of a traditional *ketubah* is never meant to vary, the border decorations have over the centuries been remarkable in their variety as well as beauty. Illuminated *ketubot* have been produced all over the world, the style of ornament varying from country to country. A particular high point was reached in seventeenth- and eighteenth-century Italy, where intricate paper-cut embellishments were used, as well as colors and gold leaf. The cost of preparing these became so great that the rabbis limited the amount that could be spent on making one. Because of the so-called advances of industrialization, generations of couples have had machine-printed *ketubot* of little aesthetic interest. Today, in the wake of the general rebirth of interest in handicrafts, the calligrapher's art is once again finding an appreciative market. Therefore, whether you use a traditional or a revised text or simply a certificate commemorating the occasion, you might want to commission a scribe or artist/calligrapher to make a document you will enjoy hanging in your new home. The prices vary, but they are not inexpensive. Nevertheless, parents, siblings, or grandparents might really be happy to help pay for something of such lasting value and beauty.

Unlike a Torah, *tefillin* scroll, *mezuzah*, or bill of divorce, which must be written by a male scribe, anyone can do a *ketubah*. Women calligraphers all over the country are producing outstanding works of art as they enter a field of endeavor traditionally dominated by men. You might even want to try your hand at doing your own. Although I had never made a *ketubah* before, and have a genuine horror of the prospect of doing large amounts of lettering, when my sister was married she and her husband asked me to letter and illustrate theirs, I consulted with both the rabbi who performed the ceremony and my congregational rabbi all along the way, and produced the *ketubah*. Since I knew they would want it framed, before beginning I searched in antique and junk shops until I found an oval frame with a domed glass. I then cut the parchment my sister bought from a scribe on New York's Lower East Side to fit the frame. The scribe, by the way, was absolutely delighted that a "modern" young woman would want a hand-drawn *ketubah* and that it would be her sister who would do it. The contemporary *ketubah* in Fig. 24 was done by David Moss, a California artist. Calligraphers and scribes can be found in my book *The Jewish Yellow Pages*.

After the *ketubah* has been read, another glass of wine is poured and the Seven Benedictions *(Sheva Berakhot)* are recited over it. Usually the rabbi recites or sings these blessings, but in some locales the different blessings are recited or chanted by friends or family members. Sometimes the assembled group joins in for part of the seventh benediction, singing along with the rabbi, "Soon may there be heard in the cities of Judah, and in the streets of Jerusalem, the voice of joy and gladness, the voice of the bridegroom and the voice of the bride." The bride and groom then drink from the second glass of wine.

With the ceremony complete, tradition now calls for the groom to break a glass by stepping on it. This custom, though it has no halakhic standing, is so deeply ingrained in the popular imagination that even Jews having a civil ceremony often want to keep the rite. There are many interpretations for the breaking of the glass. The one most frequently offered is that it is a symbol for our mourning for the destruction of the Temple. Indeed, at many Sephardic weddings, "If I forget thee, O Jerusalem, let my right hand forget its cunning. Let my tongue cleave to the roof of my mouth, if I remember thee not; if I set not Jerusalem above my chiefest joy," is recited as the groom crushes the glass. Others are quick to point out that the custom is a really ancient one and exists simply to frighten away evil spirits with noise. It is likely that the former is an interpretation of the latter to make it more Jewish, less heathen. I prefer some of the more contemporary interpretations of the custom, which tell us that, as the shattering of the glass is irreversible, so should the marriage last into eternity. Or that this momentary violence and sadness should be the only bit the couple will have. At this high point everyone usually shouts "*Mazzal tov*," and the bride and groom kiss. At some weddings the ceremony is now over. At others, the rabbi will pronounce the priestly benediction:

> May the Lord bless you and keep you,
> May the Lord show you favor and be gracious to you,
> May the Lord raise His face to you and grant you peace.
> Amen.

The ceremony described above is, with some variations, the basic traditional one. Depending on your sensibilities and those of your rabbi, it is possible to add readings of biblical verses or poetry or to incorporate original statements by the bride and groom.

Before joining the guests where they are surrounded by good wishes, joy, music, and dancing, many couples follow the old custom of *yihud:* retiring to a private room to be alone with one another for a few minutes. While this is no longer the time when the marriage is consummated, it is still a very practical custom, giving the couple a chance to take a breather and, if they have fasted before the ceremony, to break their fast together, or at any rate to share a little wine and cheese. Then, when they return to their guests, they are very much more a couple for having had the few minutes alone.

King Solomon had seven days of feasting for his daughter's marriage, and in many places this custom of a weeklong celebration, which it is said began when Jacob made such a feast for his mar-

The invite you
to share in our
simcha, the
marriage of our children

Elka
and
Joseph

Sunday, the twentieth
of August
nineteen hundred
and seventy-two

יוסף

אלקה

at two o'clock
in the garden
of the
Princeton Jewish
Center
435 Nassau Street
Princeton, New Jersey

Dr. and Mrs.
Max Gershon Frankel
Dr. and Mrs.
Julian Jurand

Let me be a seal upon thy heart. שׂימני כחותם על-לבך

25 Paper-cut wedding invitation

riage to Leah, continues. Most of us, however, are content with a
wedding reception and meal following the ceremony. In some circles it is fashionable for the wedding meal to have as much food
(and to cost as much) as if it were meant to provide sustenance for a
week. My preferences are much simpler. There is an increasing
number of small catering establishments—sometimes only one or
two people working out of their own home kitchens—who can
provide simple but delicious meals without a lot of the unnecessary
extras. Often they will also be happy to include food made by
friends or family and can help with the arrangements for serving.
One of the nicest, friendliest wedding feasts I attended was served
buffet-style and featured the favorite foods of bride and groom,
made by their mothers. There was a casserole of macaroni, beef,
and tomatoes and stuffed cabbage made by loving hands. And so
that the mothers would not have to make vast quantities and be
exausted by the effort, the menu was filled out with purchased roast
turkey and salads brought by friends. A huge *hallah* graced the
central table. Admittedly this was a huge table, and at right angles
to it going off into an adjoining room was another overlong table.
Friends set up many small bridge tables in the garden, with one

53

Inside the invitation image:

 וארשתיך לי לעולם וארשתיך לי
בצדק ובמשפט ובחסד וברחמים

Please share with us
in celebrating the marriage of
our children

JUDY and DAVID
Sunday, the ninth of July, 1978
The simcha will be held at
Temple Israel
Natick, Massachusetts

Chuppah at one o'clock
Luncheon to follow

Milton & Lenore   Joshua & Edith
Feierstein   Epstein

HOSEA 2:21   And I will betroth you unto me forever...
in righteousness and in justice,
in lovingkindness and in compassion...

26

long head table at the far end, and had platters of food served, family style, at each table by college students.

Unless the wedding is really tiny, you will probably want printed invitations rather than handwritten notes or phone calls. Perhaps it is in reaction to the many years I spent in diplomatic circles, but I tend to avoid the formal invitations described in etiquette books. The invitation is the first opportunity most of your friends and family will have to share in your *simhah*, and so it seems to me that it's more meaningful to have it warm and personal rather than "correct." I particularly like those that include a favorite verse or quotation of the bride and groom. The formal American wedding invitation is usually written in the name of the bride's parents, since they are the hosts. Typical Jewish wedding invitations, however, while they are usually sent by the bride's family, will be in the names of both sets of parents. Older or previously married couples will often want to issue the wedding invitation in their own names. Those shown here were designed using the technique of the paper-cut to define the basic shapes; I made the first; the other was made by Judy Feierstein for her wedding. Paper-cutting is an excellent means of design (instructions will be found on pp. 218–223). The invitations were printed on heavy colored card stock by photo-off-

54

set, a considerably less expensive process than that of engraving. Quotations for the invitation, to embellish the *ketubah*, or to have engraved on wedding rings can be culled from the wedding ceremony itself or from psalms or proverbs; Solomon's Song of Songs is particularly rich in romantic imagery.

The date you choose will possibly be influenced by custom as well as convenience. Weddings are not held on festivals, the Sabbath, or the intermediate days of Sukkot and Passover; they can be held on Hanukkah and Purim. During the seven weeks of counting the Omer between Passover and Shavuot in the spring, Orthodox and Conservative rabbis won't officiate at weddings, since it is said that the students of Rabbi Akiba were victims of a plague during this period and it has therefore become a time of semi-mourning. There are several days on which exceptions are made, including Lag Ba-Omer, when the plague is said to have miraculously lifted for a day. Most recently, Israeli Independence Day was approved by the Israeli Rabbinate for weddings during the sefirah period. For many people the time between the sowing and reaping of the spring harvest was considered an unlucky one for marriages, giving rise to the large number of June weddings. During the summer most Orthodox and Conservative rabbis will not perform marriages between the seventeenth of Tammuz and the ninth of Av, since these three weeks constitute a period of mourning for the destruction of the two Temples. Even though Reform Judaism doesn't recognize these two periods, many Reform rabbis will not perform weddings on the ninth of Av. The period between the new moon and the full moon while the moon is waxing is considered auspicious, and the latter half of the lunar month less so. It's considered unlucky to be married on a Monday; Tuesday and Wednesday, however, are lucky days—Tuesday because on the third day of creation the phrase "and God saw that it was good" occurs twice. Iraqi Jews preferred Wednesday, because the sun and moon were fashioned on that day. The Mishnah says that a widow should marry on Thursday so that her husband can devote three days to her—Thursday, Friday, and Saturday—before going back to work. These days Sunday seems to be the most popular, because of the convenience it affords the guests.

In Kurdistan and Iraq it was considered a bad omen if there were no musicians at a wedding, and among East European Jews there is a Yiddish expression that something is "as sad as a wedding without musicians." I'm sure we've all been to weddings where we'd happily accept a little bad luck for some peace and quiet. The

27 (photo: Pace Photography)

three-piece *shtetl* band was one thing, but today's amplified "groups" are often nerve-shattering. There are quite a few musicians in America familiar with Jewish wedding music, or who can learn melodies or pieces you want played from a cassette or record.

The music should enhance everyone's experience, not ruin the digestion. If the wedding is at home, a single instrument—guitar, clarinet, or flute—can provide just the right festive touch.

Like musicians, photographers are sometimes a mixed blessing. We would all like to have a record of the important day, but surely it isn't necessary to have the photographer stop the procession to the *hupah* to get a better shot, blind a nervous bride with flashbulbs, rearrange people who are happily dancing with and for their friends, and generally make a nuisance of himself. All couples have different ideas of what they want in the way of wedding pictures, so it is a good idea to carefully instruct the photographer you hire, even if it is a friend doing you a favor, and to tell him clearly beforehand what you would like: whether or not to photograph during the service, a few candid shots of friends and family, or formal portraits.

When we think of bridal clothes, what immediately comes to mind is what we've seen in magazines, movies, and on television: the long white gown and the groom in a tuxedo or basic blue suit. There are no religious requirements as to what the bride and groom may wear. In this country, based on European tradition, it is customary for the bride to wear white and to be veiled, and among Orthodox Jews for the groom to don a white garment, known as a *kittl*, over his regular clothes and to wear his *tallit*. The custom of a bridal veil, we are told, goes back to biblical times, when Abraham sent his servant Eliezer to find a bride for Isaac. When the servant had persuaded Rebecca to marry Abraham's son, he brought her to Canaan. As they approached the tents of Abraham and Isaac, and Isaac came out to meet her, "she took her veil and covered herself." Since then, it is said, Jewish women wear bridal veils as a sign of modesty, so that they will be seen only by their husband. In the fifteenth century in the Rhineland the veil was often a gift from the groom. In the seventeenth and eighteenth centuries, some communities forbade the wearing of gold on the veil, indicating that it must have been popular to the point of offense. In the nineteenth century golden veils were common among Tunisian brides. In some hasidic groups, brides have their face completely wrapped.

The groom's *kittl*, which looks very much like a bathrobe, is the same as that worn both on the somber Yom Kippur and the festive Passover, and is therefore seen as suitable for a wedding. The *kittl* shown in Fig. 27 has hand embroidery (blanket stitches) around the cuffs and edges, as well as a silk rope belt; these give it a more festive and personal look than the stark ones sold in religious book-shops. If the groom wants to wear one, it certainly seems a worth-while and challenging undertaking to make it as handsome and interesting as the wedding dress.

In the East, Jewish brides have often worn the most colorful and exotic wedding clothes.* Yemenite brides wear a gold-encrusted, helmetlike headdress. In Iraq, the bride's fingernails are painted with henna; she is ornamented from head to foot, with silver bells in her hair and a golden nose ring. In Salonika, Greek brides wore long white gowns embroidered with gold thread, a white scarf, and a veil hanging from a crown of artificial flowers. Gold and white was also popular for bridal gowns among Bukharan Jews. It seems that with so much interest these days in ethnic clothing and "peas-ant looks" of one sort or another, it would be nice to have a wed-ding dress that is in some way specifically Jewish, even if it means stretching the imagination a bit.

The dress shown in Fig. 28 was modeled after a Bukharan bridal gown in the Israel Museum in Jerusalem. The original gown is of cotton tulle, with the Jewish amuletic motifs embroidered in gold sequins. The contemporary version of the dress was made of antique-white cotton velvet and embroidered by machine, using sequins that are attached to a thread and sold by the running foot. An ordinary shift pattern with bell sleeves was used for the dress. (The sleeves of the original dress are so long that, with the arms down, the edge of the cuff is well below the knee. The original also has a much higher neckline, and more embroidery.) After the pieces were cut out, the dress was pinned for fit. Seam lines were drawn along the pin lines on the inside with a pencil. The pins were then removed so the sequins could be embroidered in place while each section of the dress was spread flat. Patterns for the de-signs were made on tracing paper and then pinned in place on the dress sections. The designs were traced onto the fabric with dressmaker's carbon paper and a tracing wheel. I used my own hand for the hand shape on the sleeves. The spacing and size of the design motifs were determined by the shape of the dress and the size of the bride. Hold the sequins in place by pinning across them. As you work, you may become confident enough to "draw" with the ribbon of sequins, and then you will only need a few pins. I

---

*For many magnificent illustrations of wedding clothes in different countries and epochs, see Alfred Rubens, *A History of Jewish Costume* (New York: Crown Publishers, 1967).

28 Bukharan bridal gown (photo: Bill Aron)

finished off all the ends with slightly larger individual sequins and tiny pearl beads. Larger individual sequins with pearl bead centers were sewn on the sleeves and as centers for the small circles on the skirt. The touch of hand-sewing was pleasant to do and adds a nice finishing touch. The neck was edged in a ready-made sequin braid. Strips of this braid sewn together make up the little cap, which holds the veil in place. The dress is special enough for a wedding dress but not so obviously bridal that after the wedding it is destined to remain in the back of the closet forever.

The wedding cake as we know it in America is not particularly Jewish, and yet it makes its appearance at many Jewish weddings. For my sister's wedding, instead of a many-tiered cake, I made a large flat one on the shape of a big flower (using three fan-shaped pans from Mexico). For the figurines on top, I made low-fired ceramic caricatures of the couple, with their names and date carved into the base. It didn't occur to me then, but the next figurines like this I do will have a *hupah* over them, using tiny flag dowels as the supports and a patch of fabric for the *hupah* itself.

In this chapter, I've put a great deal of stress on getting away from the basic features of the American wedding: department-store gowns, country-club food, the gentile band playing tunes from *Fiddler on the Roof*. My reasons are not only aesthetic. How many weddings have you been to where the cost was reckoned in the thousands of dollars and the bride and groom then moved into a home furnished with cheap things that won't last five years? Where the cost of the reception would have made the down-purchase payment on a home for the young couple? Where they were isolated at a head table, sometimes even raised on a dais, with the immediate families (with whom they had already spent most of their time during the preceding days and weeks) and far from the friends with whom they wanted to share the day? Where the number of friends the couple could invite had to be limited to accommodate the friends or business associates of the parents? I cannot overemphasize that the wedding belongs to the bride and groom, not to their parents. Making the kind of wedding *they* want will enhance not only the wedding but the marriage itself in years to come.

> When their time of marriage arrives, God, who knows each spirit and soul, joins them as at first, and proclaims their union. Thus when they are joined they become one body and one soul, right and left in unison, and in this way "there is nothing new under the sun."
>
> —From the Zohar

FAMILY REUNIONS

This story was narrated by Glueckel of Hameln (1646–1724) in one of her seven volumes of memoirs which she addressed to her twelve children after the death of her husband:

One very windy day, a bird set out to cross a wide sea with his three tiny nestlings. The only way to get them across the raging sea was to carry them, one by one, in his claws. When the bird had gotten halfway across with the first fledgling, the storm turned into a gale, and the parent said to the child, "See how I am struggling and risking my life on your behalf. When you are grown up and I am old, will you look after me as well?" "Oh yes," the baby bird answered, "just get me across and I will do anything you ask." On hearing this, the parent bird dropped the fledgling into the sea, saying, "That's what should happen to all liars like you." The bird then returned to the shore and began the trip again with his second child. Upon getting to the middle of the sea, he asked the second child the same question, received the same answer, and promptly allowed him to drown as well, saying, "You are a liar too!" He then returned to shore and set out once again with the third baby bird in his claws. When he reached the middle of the sea he asked the same question, and got this response: "Father, dear, while it is true that you are struggling mightily for me and I would be ungrateful not to try to repay you in kind when you are old, I can't promise to do so. But I know that when I have children of my own I will do as much for them as you have done for me." To this the parent replied, "Well said, my child. For the sake of my grandchildren I will carry you ashore."

The story vividly makes the point that while children will tire of doing as much for their parents as their parents have done for them, "We should put ourselves to great pains for our children, since they are the foundation of the world." This traditional Jewish view is right at home in today's youth-dominated society; on the other hand, the concept of honoring one's parents seems alternately archaic and guilt producing. The positive commandment to honor

61

29 (photo: Jim McDonald)

one's parents is not meant merely to produce obedient offspring; it helps us to recognize that parents personify something greater than themselves. They represent the continuity of the past and are the transmitters of human values.

Because of our busy contemporary lives, it often seems difficult to find time for different generations to come together to enjoy each other. When it comes to visiting with aunts and uncles, it is even harder. As a result, we often don't see family members for years, unless there is a wedding or a funeral.

When I was a child, one of my great-uncles would organize a family picnic every spring. We had to travel for what seemed endless hours by subway and bus from our tenement to the park, but the afternoon of roasting hotdogs and marshmallows, spent with warm and benevolent people who were so familiar while being almost strangers, was always worth the trip, and those days are indelibly etched in my memory. As I grew older I became too involved in my own teenage social life to attend all the family reunions. But these lovely people continued to remain interested in me, and later, when I returned home for a visit from school or my own home, my parents would invite the family and a few friends who had watched me grow up for an informal meal so we could catch up on the intervening years. Since leaving home at seventeen, the closest I've ever lived to my parents and the rest of the family is seventy-five miles, so these reunions are always precious.

Last year my sister and I decided that too much time had gone by since the last reunion and that, with our parents getting older, it was our turn to provide the opportunity for the family to get together. There was a new crop of cousins to meet, and we all love seeing who looks like whom. We also wanted to express the affection and gratitude we feel for our parents—and what better way than by imitating them! We knew how pleased they would be to have a little party, like the ones they used to make, made in their honor. We decided to use their wedding anniversary and the fact that our father and my sister's daughter both have birthdays in the same month as excuses for a family party.

30 Party invitation

31 (photo: Jim McDonald)

Since my sister and I live almost three hundred miles apart, we were at first a bit intimidated by the problems we thought we would have in preparing for forty people. We were tempted to invite everyone to join us at a restaurant. But since what we wanted was to recapture the warmth of the family gatherings we had experienced as children and to let our children meet with their cousins in the same way as we had, we decided to have the party at our parents' apartment. That way the children could retire to the bedroom and play games in the piles of coats, and everyone could visit informally instead of having to sit in one spot while being waited on.

The invitations were handwritten on cards which were printed inexpensively by offset on 8½" x 11" stock; these were folded in half to produce a 5½" x 8½" card with plenty of space for the message inside. For the design I chose a phrase from the prayer book—

"From generation to generation we shall proclaim Your greatness"—and added a few floral motifs and birds as symbols of domesticity. The original artwork I gave to the printer to be reproduced was a much larger screen print which I also printed on fabric to use as Passover cushions.

We asked my mother for the best kosher delicatessen near her house and ordered a presliced roast turkey, potato salad, cocktail franks, knishes, drinks, and bread to be delivered the morning of the buffet party, which was to begin at three in the afternoon. My sister, who lives in the same city as my parents, was to bring green salad and herring in wine sauce. Since I live a five-hour drive away, I brought the paper plates and cups and the cake and fruit for dessert. As most of the food was not homemade, I wanted to add a personal touch and decided to bake my own cake. I needed one that could be made several days earlier and would travel well; the gorgeously frosted whipped-cream cakes we so often associate with birthday and anniversary parties would not have survived the trip. Further, most older people really are not overly fond of these elaborate confections and, while the children are impressed by them, they usually take one taste of the too-sweet dessert and leave it on their plate. A friend suggested making either a giant strudel (or several placed together end to end) on a piece of 2" x 4" wood which could have the seventy-two candles for my father's birthday, plus the four for my niece's, strung out lengthwise. I liked the idea, but the thought of transporting the super-long strudel deterred me. Instead, I made a double recipe of Chocolate Applesauce Cake, which is simultaneously simple and rich enough to satisfy many different tastes.

CHOCOLATE APPLESAUCE CAKE

2	cups sifted flour	3	rounded tablespoons cocoa
1½	teaspoons baking soda	1½	cups granulated sugar
¾	teaspoon salt	2	eggs
1½	cups light or dark raisins	1½	cups applesauce, homemade or
½	cup soft shortening		canned
1	teaspoon cinnamon		

Sift the flour, baking soda, and salt together. Toss the raisins with 2 tablespoons of the flour mixture to coat them and prevent them from sinking to the bottom of the cake. Using an electric mixer at medium speed, cream the shortening, cinnamon, and cocoa together until light; slowly add the sugar, beating until fluffy. Add the eggs one at a time, blending well after each addition. At low speed, blend into this alternately the flour mixture and the applesause, beginning and ending with the flour mixture. Do not overbeat—mix just until smooth. Stir in the coated raisins. Pour into a well-greased 3-quart ring mold; a Bundt pan or angel-food pan may also be used. Bake in a preheated 350° oven for 55–60 minutes, until a cake tester inserted into the center of the batter comes out clean. Cool in the pan on a rack for 10 minutes; turn the cake out of the pan and continue cooling on the rack.

When the cake is completely cool, wrap it in aluminum foil and store it for at least 24 hours before serving. The flavors are so strong that a day or two is necessary to mellow and blend them. This cake freezes well, so I usually double the recipe and make two, putting one in the freezer for future use. The cake is delicious served unfrosted or with a scoop of ice cream. To dress it up a bit for my parents' party, I made a paper stencil the size of the top of the cake with the words שלום ואהבה ["peace and love"] cut out. Then, using confectioners' sugar in my flour sifter, I filled in the letters with sugar. The paper was carefully lifted away, leaving the sugar only in the places where the letters had been cut out. A Hebrew *alef-bet* for stencil letters appears in Fig. 103. On occasions when I don't use letters, I've used an ordinary lace paper doily as the stencil for an intricate powdered-sugar design.

One of the highlights of the afternoon was the presentation of a custom-printed T-shirt to Zaydeh [Grandfather] by his two youngest granddaughters. With the T-shirt craze sweeping America and everyone wearing personalized shirts of one sort or another, the children came up with the idea of making a special one for Zaydeh. He immediately put it on, and we all enjoyed seeing him model the shirt emblazoned with the slogan "Zaydeh Power." My great-uncle Layzer had created one of his coveted cut-paper cards for my parents' anniversary. Uncle Layzer started doing paper-cuts as a child in Poland and now makes special ones, using scraps of patterned wallpaper, for everyone's special events.

The most satisfying result of the party for me was that one of my cousins issued an invitation on the spot for another reunion to take place in a few months at her house. If you need an excuse to find out how nice your own family is, hinge it on any holiday, birthday, or anniversary, or perhaps, as we did, just to honor *your* parents.

32 Uncle Layzer's paper-cut

33 Putting up the *mezuzah* (photo: Bill Aron)

HOUSEWARMINGS

Moving into a new home—whether it's the first one away from that of one's parents, a temporary "pad," a dream house, a vacation home, or a smaller place after the children are grown—is a demanding and exciting experience. Whether one moves around the corner or across the country or ocean, there is sure to be a mess at both ends. As one packs and then unpacks, many decisions have to be made about what to take physically and spiritually to the new home. When finally one is settled (or almost, since it seems some of us never finish unpacking and hanging the last picture), how marvelous it is to feel that one has survived the move with one's values (as well as the china) intact and to invite friends and family for a housewarming to dedicate the new home to the same beliefs and ideals you have always cherished and brought with you.

According to the rules of war set forth in Deuteronomy 20:5, if a man has built a new house and not dedicated it he is exempt from service and can return to his house, "lest he die in the battle, and another man dedicate it." This passage suggests the likelihood that homes were ritually dedicated in biblical times. The custom apparently lapsed, and until recently very little attention has been paid by Western Jews to *hanukkat habayit* [dedication of the home].

Among the Sephardim a *hanukkat habayit* service developed. In Iraq, the Babylonia of ancient days, a housewarming was a very significant event. The new home was dedicated before the furniture was installed. Local officials and religious leaders were invited, as well as family and friends. The mistress of the house greeted them at the entrance by sprinkling them with water and kernels of wheat, a wish for prosperity and luck. After the *mezuzot* were put up and selections from the Mishnah read, a festive meal was served; only then were the furnishings finally brought in. As additional protection against evil spirits, some people put deer antlers and a horseshoe above the door. Until recently, Ashkenazim simply affixed the *mezuzah* and said the blessing. In the nineteenth century the British rabbinate compiled prayers for the occasion, including Psalms 30 and 15 and those verses of Psalm 119 that acrostically compose the word *berakhah* ["blessing"], as well as other prayers of dedication.

A housewarming party modeled after the Iraqi one described above is, it seems to me, as appropriate for our mobile society, where we may set up many homes in the course of a lifetime, as it was for a more stable environment; for we really need the feelings of rootedness that traditions such as these can give us.

While working on this book I moved from New Jersey to Massachusetts, and even though I knew that I'd only be living in the apartment I was setting up until I could find a house, I invited all my new friends and neighbors, as well as some old friends who were able to make the trip from New Jersey, for a housewarming party when the *mezuzot* were put up. By the time you read this, I will be in my new house and preparing my next *hanukkat habayit*. Planning the parties—thinking of how nice the house will look and of opening my home to friends—helps to inspire me when I get tired of all those cartons to be packed and unpacked.

We left our *mezuzot* affixed to our old house in New Jersey, since Jews were going to be living in it. This meant we needed all new ones for our apartment. In reality this custom of leaving *mezuzot* applies only to the handwritten scroll containing the two scriptural passages of Deuteronomy 6:4–9 and 11:13–21; that is, we could have taken the *mezuzah* containers and left the scrolls by putting them in other containers or even affixing them with tape. But we preferred leaving the *mezuzot* and containers intact and making new *mezuzot* for our new home. My daughter and I spent several marvelous afternoons making ceramic *mezuzot*. Visitors have liked them so much that eleven-year-old Keren is now in the *mezuzah*-making business. If you have a kiln available to you (ask at the local Y or at an elementary, high, or adult school), you might want to try making your own.

If you have the facilities, glazes could be used to embellish the surface, but ours are quite attractive made from a dark stoneware clay body. If thinking about "sculpting" clay inhibits you, treat the clay as though it were cookie dough. Roll out a 3"–6" "cookie," wrap it around a small tube of rolled newspaper, and use a fork or kitchen knife to pinch the edges closed. The wad of newspaper will help the *mezuzah* keep its shape while it is drying and then will burn out in the kiln. With a sharp knife, cut a hole in the back into which you can later put the parchment scroll. A window can also be cut in front to see the word שדי [Shaddai, Almighty], which is written on the outside of the parchment scroll. Anything that produces a pleasant design can be used to emboss the clay if you want to add texture to it. Be certain to make the holes for the screws or nails large enough; otherwise, once it's fired you could easily break the *mezuzah* when you try to hang it.

Mezuzah containers can also be made of just about any material, from precious metals and exotic woods to glass, fabric, and found objects such as shells. In ancient days a slightly different version of the inscription was written or carved directly on the doorpost; only later were the two biblical passages we are familiar with written on parchment and attached to the wall. (In Israel I saw a *mezuzah* placed in a space left empty for it by omitting a brick and then covered with glass.) To protect the parchment from the elements, some inventive soul enclosed it in a reed, from which we derive our present traditional form of a cylindrical *mezuzah* container.

I would love to encourage you to write your own *mezuzah* scroll, but in order for it to be considered kosher it must be written on parchment by a scribe. These hand-lettered parchment scrolls are available at Hebrew bookstores and synagogue gift shops. If you can't find them locally, your rabbi will be able to tell you where to order them by mail. They are not inexpensive (prices usually begin at around $5 to $7, depending on quality and size), but when you consider how many nations have inscribed their creeds on enormous monuments of stone whose messages have been obscured by time and how the tiny handwritten *mezuzah*, affixed anew at each Jewish home, has tenaciously survived, you know you are getting a bargain.

The *mezuzah* is affixed on the upper third of the right-hand side of the doorway as one enters the room. One is used for each room, except the bathroom, and for the entrances to the house. It is attached to the doorpost diagonally, with the top leaning toward the inside of the house and the bottom toward the outside. It's a good idea to predrill the holes in the doorpost for the nails or screws.

Before putting up *the mezuzah*, it's nice to say a few words of welcome to your guests and to explain its meaning. Many people have the mistaken notion that it is a good-luck charm or amulet. And indeed it has had a long history of treading the thin line between religion and superstition. At various times different magical formulae were also written on the parchment. The rabbis managed to eliminate them, the last remaining vestige being שדי [Shaddai], which is an acronym for "guardian of the doors of Israel," written on the reverse of the parchment. For me the *mezuzah* is a statement that this is a Jewish home—that as we enter and leave it or live in any of the rooms we are committed to the teachings and ideals of the Torah and are aware of the Divine Presence in our lives. Before putting up the *mezuzah*, the following blessing is said:

ברוך אתה יי אלהינו מלך העולם,
אשר קדשנו במצותיו,

וצונו לקבע מזוזה.

["Blessed are You, O Lord our God, King of the Universe, who has sanctified us with His commandments, commanding us to affix the *mezuzah*."]

ברוך אתה יי אלהינו מלך העולם
שהחיינו וקימנו

והגיענו לזמן הזה.

["Blessed are You, O Lord our God, King of the Universe, who has kept us alive and sustained us and permitted us to reach this moment."].

Depending on your mood and your guests, you might want to read some of the psalms referred to earlier or to sing appropriate songs. We made our *hanukkat habayit* during Hanukkah, as you can see from the invitation, so after the *mezuzot* were in place we lit the *hanukkiah* and sang some Hanukkah hymns.

The invitations for our *hanukkat habayit* were made by my daughter. She drew the design on translucent Mylar with opaque India ink. This drawing was then used as a photographic positive to develop the design on a screen photographically. She then screen-printed the invitations and proudly signed her name, mine, and our cat's. They were printed on sheets of paper 9" wide by 17" long, so they could be folded, sealed with decorative notary seals, and sent through the mail without envelopes.

Friends who were having a *hanukkat habayit* asked me to design an invitation that could be inexpensively reproduced by offset printing. They wanted to incorporate the idea of "my home is my castle." So I put crenellations on the letters, which were designed to fill a houselike shape. The front of the card was drawn on the bottom left quarter of a folded piece of typing paper. The time, place, and other information were lettered in the top right quarter. Thus, after the card was printed, it could be folded and would open as a Hebrew book does, from the right. Since they really liked the house motif, as a housewarming present I made them a ceramic mirror in the shape of a house with *shalom bayit*—a wish for domestic peace —applied in a lighter clay.

...e to our *Hanukat Habayit* and *Hanukkah Party* — *Saturday* ...ber 10, 1977   8:00 PM   192 Winchester St., Brookline Mass

...S.V.P.: (617) 931-0142   Keren & Mae Rockland
(& Terra)

34   35

If you are invited to a *hanukkat habayit*, you too might want to
give a gift with some symbolic meaning—it's a lot more thoughtful
than giving dish towels. A lovely old custom is to bring a gift of
bread, salt, and candles as a wish for plenty of food and joy (sym-
bolized by light). Since a *hanukkat habayit* differs from an ordinary
open house in that it intentionally commits the home to Jewish values, it makes sense to give a gift that also is related to Jewish life.

Consider, for example, making a *mizrah* (a decorative marker for
the eastern wall) either as a painted panel, an embroidery, or, as
shown here, as a paper-cut (see pp. 218–223 for paper-cutting directions). The *mizrah* is a uniquely Jewish wall ornament and is suitable for any room in the house. The word *mizrah* originally meant
"rising sun"; it now means "east." When the Temple stood, Jews
turned in prayer to face the Holy of Holies; elsewhere in the Holy
Land they faced the direction of the Temple and Jerusalem. In the
Diaspora the custom grew up of marking the wall that faced east,
the direction where the Temple once stood. Sometimes this was
done by leaving a spot on the wall unfinished, omitting some stone
or plaster. But this practice changed and it became more typical to
embellish the eastern wall rather than to deface it.

Mizrahim can be made by any technique, using just about any

73

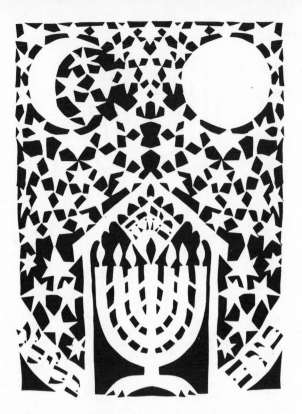

36 Paper-cut *mizrah*. The words on either side of the house say BY DAY and BY NIGHT; the center medallion in the house says MIZ-RAH

motifs you are comfortable with.* One friend of mine has an ongoing *mizrah*. On an eastern wall she has hung a very large piece of large-mesh needlepoint canvas. Near it she has a basket of wool and many needles and a rug hook. Everyone who comes is invited to add some stitches. She encourages all her guests to come up with their own motif for their little part; another possibility is to have some overall design or some motifs for people who feel inhibited about doing their own. She feels that the finished piece will be visually unified because she has selected the colors. This would make a fine project for a housewarming, to entertain the early guests while waiting for enough people to arrive to put up your *mezuzot*.

When there is a large crowd expected—with some of the guests arriving early and others late—I always like to have a lot of good things to nibble on for the early arrivals. There should also be plenty on hand for those who will stay on talking, dancing, and visiting into the night. I probably overprepare, but eating leftover party food the following week keeps reminding me of how nice it was to have a houseful of friends. I don't usually make a great variety of things—just *lots* of a few basic goodies. Then the foods brought by friends add a bit of variety. Since pineapple is an age-

The Work of Our Hands has patterns and directions for several *mizrahim*.

74

old symbol of hospitality, it seems particularly well suited for a housewarming.

Whenever I'm expecting a large crowd of people, I like to have all the cooking done well in advance; like many working women, I rely heavily on my freezer, cooking and baking when there is time and filling the freezer with foods that reheat simply. It seems that many parties I go to have almost the same food: cheeses and dips. While these are good and I also serve them, I often like to offer something a little more satisfying and less common along with the sangria that is my favorite party punch.

EMPANADAS (Turnovers)

These turnovers can be made whatever size you wish. They are delicious hot or cold, for a seated meal, a picnic, or a walk-around-with-a-glass-in-your-hand party. For a dairy variety, you can substitute tuna fish for the hamburger.

FILLING:		PASTRY:	
1	pound lean ground beef	½	cup non-dairy creamer
1	package dry onion-soup mix	2	teaspoons vinegar
½	teaspoon salt	2	cups sifted flour
4	tablespoons catsup	1	teaspoon salt
		2	teaspoons caraway seeds
		⅔	cup shortening

Lightly brown the meat and drain off any grease. Add the other filling ingredients and set aside while making the pastry.

Combine the non-dairy creamer and vinegar and allow them to curdle in a measuring cup. Sift the flour into a large mixing bowl and add the salt and caraway seeds. Cut in the shortening until particles the size of small peas are formed. Add the vinegar mixture all at once, stirring quickly with a fork to moisten the dough thoroughly.

Form the dough into two balls. Roll out one of the balls between two sheets of floured waxed paper into a 12" square. Cut into four 6" squares or nine 4" squares.

Place appropriate amounts of filling in the center of each square. Fold over to form a triangle. Press the edges together with a fork to seal; prick two or three times with the fork to allow steam to escape. Place the turnovers on an ungreased baking sheet. Repeat with the remaining dough. Bake in a 425° oven 10–15 minutes, until golden brown. These turnovers may be frozen or refrigerated before or after baking.

PART TWO

THE CALENDAR

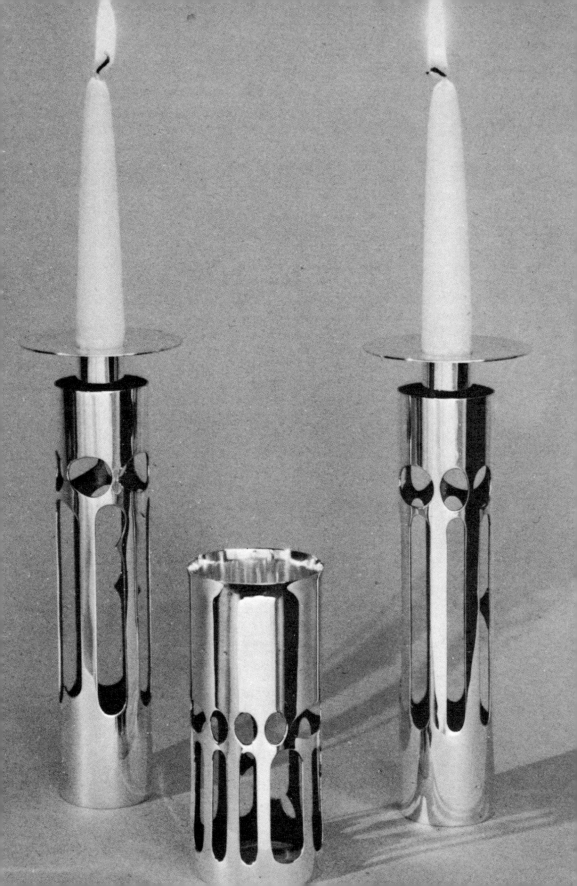

Teach us to number our days,
That we may get us a heart of wisdom.
—Psalm 90:12

The Hebrew calendar has long been known as the catechism of the Jewish people. In its orderly progress on through the seasons, it has served as a unifying force for Jews scattered all over the world for thousands of years. Observing the weekly Sabbath, the festivals, fasts, and holidays has traditionally provided a haven for Jews in many lands and epochs. Today this same observance can provide a refuge from the pressures of modern life while giving us the opportunity concretely to express our commitment to Judaism and our unity with the Jewish people. Secularists can enrich their lives by enjoying the seasonal and historical aspects of the holidays, while those with a religious point of view will identify the holidays with the action of God in nature and society.

Today science—our new religion—confirms through the use of sophisticated tests and machinery that which we have always known: despite our powers of reason, we are tied to celestial and seasonal changes. The cycle of holiday celebrations by which we mark these changes helps us arrange our lives in a coherent way. Further, enlarging the meaning of seasonal holidays to include real historical (or almost-true historical) events forces us to recognize that humanity is part of the world of nature.

To the extent that we desire it, Judaism can be an organizing factor in our lives. Because I have found pacing my year according to the Jewish calendar to be a tremendous source of strength and enjoyment, I'd like to share some of this with you. You might pick up this book only to find out something about Hanukkah, and then decide to try on Tu Bi-Shevat for size, and perhaps next year you'll have a ball on Purim. Whatever you do—have a good time!

37 Silver candlesticks and *kiddush* cup, by Moshe Zabari (photo: Eric Politzer)

THE HIGH HOLY DAYS

The series of fall holidays that begins with Rosh Hashanah on the first day of the Hebrew month of Tishri (corresponding roughly to September) and ends twenty-three days later on Simhat Torah provides many occasions for visiting with friends and family. The gatherings described in the following pages reflect the changing moods of this holiday period, which vary from intense seriousness and awe to lighthearted joy.

Rosh Hashanah

Rosh Hashanah, which literally means "the head of the year," marks the beginning of the Jewish calendar year (see Appendix for a comparative Hebrew/civil calendar); it is colloquially called the Birthday of the World, since in tradition the calendar originates with the Creation. Orthodox and Conservative Jews observe Rosh Hashanah for two days, while Reform congregations observe it for only one. The reason given for the two-day observance is that in ancient days the onset of the holiday was determined by the appearance of the new moon having been confirmed by witnesses before a high court. Since by the time the date was announced all over the Diaspora, inaccuracies arose, it became customary to obseve the holiday for two days. In our time, with worldwide instantaneous communication, this might seem anachronistic, but precisely because our lives are so speeded up I like the two-day observance. Often those people with whom we would like to share the holiday on one day are not available, and having two days gives us the potential for a richer, fuller celebration.

38 Dipping apple rounds in honey (photo: Jim McDonald)

Because the Hebrew and civil calendars do not coincide, it often seems that the Jewish holidays fall at the most inconvenient times. Just as the summer ends and parents with some sense of relief see their children off to school, the fall briskness fills one with a rush of energy to begin new projects; then along come the High Holy Days, on and off for three weeks, interrupting the demands of our busy lives. That is why every year the unifying effect of the Jewish calendar amazes me all over again. People who most of the year rarely think in terms of Jewish commitment go to synagogue or in some way—by visiting family or friends, perhaps—mark the beginning of the year.

A hasidic story tells of a king who decided to educate his only son by sending him to study in other countries so that he could be familiar with the languages and customs of the world. The king outfitted his son richly and gave him enough gold and attendants to enable him to live luxuriously wherever he went. After many years, with all his wealth spent, the prince found himself in a land where none knew of his father, the great king, and no one believed that he was of royal descent. In great misery and loneliness, he decided to return to his father's court, only to find that in the course of his wanderings he had forgotten his native language. When he tried by sign language to explain to the people of his country that he was the son of their king, they mocked him and beat him mercilessly. In desperation, he called and cried to his father. The king, hearing the wordless shouting outside his palace, recognized the voice of his child and ran to embrace him.

And so it is that each year, after immersing ourselves in the secular world, as the seasons begin to change, reminding us of our own mortality, we issue a wordless call—the sound of the *shofar*—and are once again embraced by our Father and our Jewishness.

GREETING CARDS

It is difficult to resist the pressures of the secular world in which we live for the most part of our days. Even if we live in a predominantly Jewish neighborhood and have only Jews as friends, it's hard to ignore the fact that most people in this country go into a greeting-card-sending madness around Christmas time. Many Jews do so as well, though they generally avoid sending cards that are blatantly Christian and simply join in the "holiday spirit" by sending "Season's Greetings" or secular (Common Era) New Year cards. But sending Hannukah cards has become increasingly popular. It

39 Screen-printed High Holy
Days greeting card

is, however, more traditionally Jewish to send greeting cards during the High Holy Days in the fall, marking the beginning of the New Year on the Jewish calendar. Since I can only endure one large all-purpose mailing a year, I prefer to send cards at Rosh Hashanah. They serve to catch up with friends I haven't seen in a long time. My non-Jewish friends usually reply with a Christmas card, and the time lapse allows for an exchange of thoughts rather than two greetings crossing in the mail. I like to do a simple design, leaving space either inside the card if it is a folded one, or incorporated into the design if it is a flat card, for additional messages. Since the fall holidays are so filled with visiting and shared meals, the cards sometimes serve as invitations as well.

This past holiday season my son Jeffrey suggested I make a Simhat Torah card rather than a more typical Rosh Hashanah card. He is particularly partial to Simhat Torah since he was born the day after that holiday and his Bar Mitzvah Torah portion was *Bereshit.* The suggestion pleased me, especially since I was planning an informal supper for the eve of Simhat Torah [Shemini Atzeret] and I could use them as invitations.

The cards were printed in an afternoon, using a simplified screen technique which is an excellent way to familiarize yourself with the rudiments of the screen process if you have never done it. I chose as my symbols the letters *lamed* and *bet*, a heart, and a bird. On Simhat Torah we read the last passages of Deuteronomy, ending with the word "Israel" (the final letter of which is a *lamed*), and the opening passages of Genesis (whose first word, "*Bereshit*," begins with a *bet*). These two letters spell the Hebrew word *leb* [heart]. The crowned bird was added as a symbol for peace and royalty, and also

83

to balance the design. A *menorah* form could have been used instead to fill the space.

The "screen" I used to print the cards was made by stretching a piece of silkscreen synthetic fabric (available from hobby shops and art-supply stores) on an embroidery hoop. I used an oval hoop, tracing the inner shape of it onto a piece of paper. That defined the space available for my design. Leaving about ½" all around, I played with the letters to form them into pleasant shapes and fill the space. Once the basic composition was decided, I covered the pencil sketch with visualizing layout paper (kitchen waxed paper can also be used; don't use ordinary tracing paper because it buckles and makes a mess of the design while printing) and retraced the design. I then used scissors and a hobby knife to cut the shapes out, being careful to keep the background paper intact. This was my stencil.

With the stencil thus cut and the screen assembled, all that remains is to get all your paper cut and folded to the size you want, your ink mixed, and a squeegee made to force the ink through the screen onto your cards. Standard screen equipment calls for a squeegee that consists of a hard rubber blade set into a wooden handle. For our simplified purpose, a stiff piece of cardboard or a rubber kitchen spatula will do as well. Screen-process ink is available at hobby and art-supply shops and is either oil- or water-based. The cleanup with water-based ink is easier, but since the oil-based ink is better with a paper stencil, I recommend it.

Place a piece of trial paper on a table covered with newspaper. Center your cut paper stencil over this. Lay your miniscreen, fabric side down, on top of the stencil, making sure it is in the exact position you want it to be. Use a spoon to put a drop of ink at the top of the screen inside the hoop. The ink should be the consistency of

40 Miniscreen printing sequence (photos: Kenneth M. Bernstein)
    [a] The equipment you need for the miniscreen process is laid out on a newspaper-covered table: paper folded in half to greeting-card size, tracing-paper stencil, embroidery hoop with silk stretched in it, and a piece of cardboard to use as a squeegee
    [b] Place the card stock on the work surface first; then stencil; and finally the hoop. Spoon a small amount of screen-process ink into the top of the hoop. Firmly "pull" the ink across the screen toward you
    [c] Carefully lift the hoop and admire the print

a

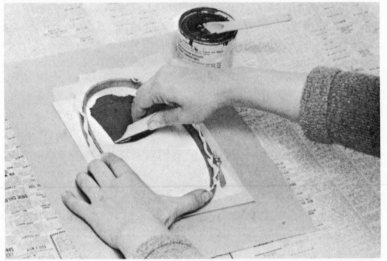

b

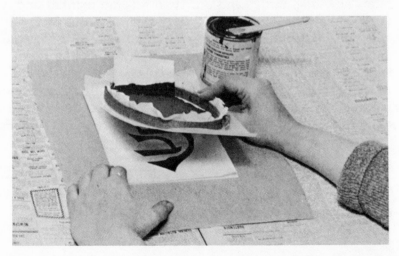

c

thick cream and drip from the spoon (yogurt or sour cream is too thick). If necessary, thin with thinner appropriate to the ink you have bought. Using the cardboard or rubber squeegee, gently but firmly pull the ink across the entire inner surface of the screen. This will force the ink through the mesh, causing the stencil to adhere to the screen in those places which have not been cut and depositing ink on your cards in the pattern of your design. Lift the screen carefully and admire your work. If you want any other white touches (let's say you forgot to put in the eye of the bird), just stick a snippet of paper onto the appropriate place on the bottom of the screen. Other minor adjustments can also be made with small pieces of masking tape. Continue printing. Since your hands will get dirty, it is helpful to have someone else act as a "printer's devil" and move the completed cards to another surface (or a clothesline) to dry and to place clean paper on the table for you.

When you have finished, pull off and discard the stencil and clean the screen thoroughly. The screen can be reused indefinitely if it is cleaned immediately. This miniscreen technique is also useful in the creation of patterned motifs on large areas (such as tablecloths) or as a simple way of adding a spot of a second color to a larger screen print.

TABLECLOTHS, HALLAH COVERS, AND SERVING DISHES

Since the destruction of the Temple, the home table has in many ways served as an altar. With everyone in a reflective and loving mood, it is especially nice to sit down to an intimate and beautiful dinner on Rosh Hashanah Eve. For me the way the table looks is as important as the way the food tastes. Because Rosh Hashanah signifies new beginnings and purity, the Torah mantles and Ark curtains in the synagogues will have been changed to fresh white. For those of you who like to keep that tradition, dressing the whole table in white can be very elegant and lovely. I find that a bit austere, however, and like to emphasize the festiveness and warmth inherent in the holiday season. While there are many beautiful tablecloths commercially available, I have never seen a Jewish one that I felt fulfilled the basic requirements of good design. So a few years ago I began making my own.*

*Directions for embroidered and appliquéd cloths are available in *The Work of Our Hands* and for a batik tablecloth in *The Hanukkah Book* (New York: Schocken Books, 1975).

When I was traveling in Israel I saw a tablecloth in the folk art museum in Tel Aviv that I really coveted. Imagine my absolute delight when my sister, knowing of my passion for beautiful Judaica, found a similar one in a New York shop specializing in Iranian imports and bought it for me. That cloth, which you can see in use at several of the parties later on in this book, was hand-printed on a heavy-weight cotton in Iran. It fits my table perfectly when the table has its extra leaves inserted. I decided to try my hand at making my own adaptation of this cloth to fit the closed table.

BATIK TABLECLOTH

Cold-water batik dyes are available in different qualities at most hobby shops. If you are familiar with the more difficult to use but more orilliantly colored procion dyes, go right ahead and use those. Measure your table and cut the cloth large enough to allow at least 6" all around for the overhang. My table is 42" square and has a very handsome pedestal, so I don't like to make the overhang too big; the finished cloth is therefore 55" square. Finish the edge by turning it under by machine. The design consists of the Hebrew blessing for bread repeated on each side of the tablecloth. I divided the phrase

ברוך אתה יי אלהינו מלך העולם המוציא לחם מן הארץ.

41 Batik tablecloth and *hallah* cover (photo: Jim McDonald)

["Blessed are You, O Lord our God, King of the Universe, who brings forth bread from the earth"] into five parts in order to fit them into lozenge-shaped forms. Using stencil paper from the hobby shop, I cut the letters out with a utility hobby knife. The letters are shown full size in Fig. 103. Adjust the spacing and size of the oval-shaped stencil or the letters themselves to fit your own tablecloth. (The design can also be embroidered rather than painted and batiked.) Lightly mark your tablecloth with pencil to indicate where the stencils are to go. Mine were placed so that when the cloth is on the table, the blessing goes around the edge of the table; you might prefer to use it as a border. Carefully place the stencils in their designated places and secure them with a bit of doublestick tape.

Mix a small amount of cold-water dye according to package directions (add the salt and fixer at this time). Use a stencil brush—or make a dauber by rolling a piece of felt *very* tightly into a cylinder about 1" in diameter; secure the felt with a tight girdle of masking tape. Saturate the brush or dauber and gently pat the dye onto the stencil. As you complete each oval, carefully lift the stencil away and with a fine nylon brush touch up any place that needs it.

When all of the letters have been painted, allow the fabric to dry overnight and then iron it lightly; this will heat-set the dye.

Then heat ordinary paraffin in a double boiler and paint over the lozenge shapes with a nylon brush. To make certain that the wax penetrates the fabric and protects the letters, it is essential that it be kept hot enough. It also helps to have the fabric stretched over a frame to prevent the hot wax from sticking the cloth to the surface you are working on. A wooden fruit box works well for this. Use a few push pins to hold the section of tablecloth you are working on taut, and as you complete the waxing of each area, unpin it and move the unwaxed fabric into place.

The border design—consisting of a thick–thin line—was done freehand using the Javanese batik tool called a *tjanting*. It, too, is available in most hobby shops and with a little practice is quite simple to use. It resembles a miniature kettle perched on the end of a wooden handle. The "pot" is dipped into the hot wax, which is then poured from the tiny spout onto the fabric. I use a small piece of cardboard to cover the spout as I lift the *tjanting* from the wax and bring it to the cloth; this avoids any unwanted wax splashes.

Once the ovals and the border had been waxed, I drew two straight lines on the fabric, using a darker-toned waterproof felt-tip marker. The fabric was then crumpled to break up the wax surface a

42 Screen-printed *hallah* cover
by students at Yadaim
(photo: Jim McDonald)

bit; this produces the characteristic veining we associate with batik. The entire tablecloth was then dyed according to the batik package directions.

While doing the tablecloth, I also played around with one of my favorite Jewish motifs, one very suitable for Rosh Hashanah: pomegranates (*rimmonim* in Hebrew), and made a round *hallah* cover. The fruit was drawn with different-colored permanent felt-tip markers, then waxed and dyed along with the tablecloth.

SCREEN-PRINTED HALLAH COVER

A group of students at Yadaim, the Jewish Craft Design Workshop sponsored by Brandeis Hillel, collaborated to produce dozens of screen-printed *hallah* covers (Fig. 42). We had been working for some time with paper-cuts when I confronted them with the problem of coming up with a fabric design that was thematically related to Rosh Hashanah and Sabbath and which would be attractive seen from any point at the table; it also had to be suitable for something other than a *hallah* cover, such as a cushion. The design we came up with is based on the theme of Creation. Since six people—each with a different style—were working on the project, we decided to break up the space geometrically and have different individuals make paper-cuts to fill the prescribed spaces. The center medallion represents the heavens; the four white spaces surrounding that have the Hebrew phrase, written in script letters

וירא ה' כי טוב

["And God saw that it was good"]; encircling this are birds and flowers; the earth is represented by the four corner designs of giraffes and trees. The border incorporates a wave-and-fish motif.

When everyone had done the individual paper-cuts, we assembled them and transferred the design photographically to a screen, then printed with textile inks onto an assortment of different washable fabrics. The edges were finished with simple self-fringing. We decided to put the design on the screen photographically because we wanted to print dozens of *hallah* covers in order to sell them and raise funds for the workshop. If you plan to do all your printing in one session, it is entirely possible to use the paper-cut itself as the stencil; see the description of a simplified printing process on pp. 83–86. To print something as large as a *hallah* cover, one obviously could not use the embroidery hoops described there; build your own frame or buy one from the hobby shop or screen-printing supply house, along with a rubber squeegee for printing. But use paper for the stencil. If you want a more durable stencil, you can use lacquer film or the light-sensitive photo emulsion we used. Both of these products are available at screen-supply stores. The photo emulsion is not as difficult to use as one might suspect. Workshop facilities at Brandeis are very limited, since the Yadaim project is in its developing stages, and we used ordinary inexpensive photo

43 Ceramic plate and bowl for apples and honey. They both have the traditional blessing recited before eating the apple and honey, the bowl in Hebrew: שנה טובה ומתוקה, and the plate in English: "A good and sweet year" (photo: Kenneth W. Bernstein)

floodlights as the light source, a sheet of plate glass and a block of styrofoam to hold the paper-cuts to the screen, and a bathtub in a dormitory for warm running water to wash out the unexposed emulsion. Indeed it would have been simpler to do this in an ordinary kitchen.

The ceramic serving dish and bowl shown in Fig. 43 were designed with the High Holy Days in mind but they can also be used throughout the year. A ceramist friend, Sarah Fuhro, threw the dishes, while I decorated them.

ROSH HASHANAH FOOD

Rosh Hashanah offers four opportunities for festive meals: dinner on the evenings before the first and second days and a midday *kiddush* and luncheon on the days themselves. Most of the traditional food customs associated with Rosh Hashanah reflect our desire for a happy and fulfilling New Year. We keep honey, symbolizing our hopes for a sweet year, on the table from Rosh Hashanah through Sukkot. We dip our *hallah* into it, and on the first night of Rosh Hashanah we eat apple (its roundness signifying our hope for a full and solid year) dipped in honey. On the second night it is customary to eat a new fruit, one that has not yet been eaten that season. As on the Sabbath, it is customary to eat fish, because of its age-old associations with fertility. Rosh Hashanah fish dishes tend to be sweet; the head of the fish is considered a special delicacy and is given to the head of the household—symbolizing, it is said, our wish to be leaders and not followers. Among Jews of Eastern Europe a popular dish that appears often through the holiday is *tsimmes* (the word also has another connotation: a hullaballoo of sorts). This can be made with or without meat but in most of its variations contains carrots in a sweet sauce, because in Yiddish they are called *mern*, meaning "to multiply." The hope is that our good deeds as well as our people will be multiplied in the coming year. Sweet-and-sour meat dishes are also typical. Traditional desserts for the holiday period include strudels filled with apples; *taiglach* (or *tayglakh*), a cookie–candy confection made by dropping balls of dough into hot honey; and of course honey cake.

GILDA ARONOVICK'S HONEY CAKE

This is a marvelously moist version of the traditional *lekakh* [honey cake]. If kept carefully wrapped, and even remoistened from time to time by brushing it with a bit of cognac, it will be delicious to serve throughout the holiday season, getting better as it ages.

6	eggs	¾	cup walnuts, chopped
¾	cup honey	3	ounces whole blanched almonds
2	cups sugar (1 granulated, 1 brown—or both granulated)	¾	cup dates, chopped
¾	cup salad oil	1	cup perked coffee, cooled and blended in an electric blender with 1 whole unpeeled seeded orange and 1 whole unpeeled cored apple
½	teaspoon vanilla		
5	cups flour		
2	teaspoons baking powder		
2	teaspoons baking soda		

Preheat oven to 350°. Grease and flour a 10″ tube pan.

Beat the eggs; add honey, sugars, and salad oil, blending thoroughly after each addition.

Sift together the flour, baking powder, and baking soda. In a paper bag shake the nuts and dates with 2 tablespoons of the flour mixture to coat them, so they won't all sink to the bottom of the cake.

Add the flour mixture alternately with the coffee mixture to the beaten eggs, again blending carefully after each addition. Add the vanilla, and stir in the dates and nuts. Pour into the prepared cake pan.

Bake at 350° for 45 minutes. Reduce the oven to 300° and continue to bake for another 30 minutes. (Since ovens vary, test for doneness carefully with a broom straw or cake tester.) Cool very slowly, leaving the cake in the pan on a cake rack for 25 minutes. Then carefully remove it from the pan and continue to cool it on the cake rack.

HALLAH

At all Sabbath and holiday meals (except Passover) it is customary to eat *hallah*, a golden egg bread, traditionally formed into braids. On Rosh Hashanah, and throughout the fall cycle of holidays, the bread is usually made in the shape of a round spiral. Some fanciful bakers will decorate the *hallah* further with dough birds or ladders, which help bring our prayers to heaven. The *hallah* can be made with or without the addition of raisins and dried fruits; some added sweetness—usually raisins—is traditional for Rosh Hashanah.

There is a biblical commandment that a portion of the dough be separated from the *hallah* before baking and given to the Temple priests. Since the Temple was destroyed n 70 C.E., this *mitzvah* is generally observed by taking a small olive-size piece of dough and

44 (photo: Kenneth M. Bernstein)

burning it in the oven, reinterpreting the ancient practice as a symbolic continuation of Temple offerings. (It has been pointed out, however, that even at the time of the Temple, when dough offerings were made, it was a common custom throughout the Middle East to throw a bit of dough into the fire to appease evil spirits.) Many Jews today burn the piece of dough as a conscious modern sacrifice, subtracting a bit from our immediate happiness to memorialize the destruction of the Temple and other holocausts. This is seen as a parallel to the breaking of the glass at the wedding ceremony and the removal of ten drops of wine at the Passover Seder.

While throwing a piece of the separated *hallah* into the oven, the following blessing is said:

ברוך אתה יי אלהינו מלך העולם אשר קדשנו במצותיו
וצונו להפריש חלה:

["Blessed are You, O Lord our God, King of the Universe, who has sanctified us with His commandments and commanded us to separate *hallah*."]

If you would like to try your hand at *hallah* sculpture but want to save time, try approaching your local baker and buying the dough from him. Some bakeries are willing to sell bread dough after the first rising. The price is usually half that of the finished product and is determined by weight. This allows you to do the "creative" part, skipping a lot of the time-consuming kitchen mess. It is a good shortcut to use when working with groups in a limited time.

Over the years I have collected more than a dozen *hallah* recipes. They are all similar, falling into three categories: *parve* (made with water and vegetable shortening), dairy (made with milk and butter), and fruited versions of either of these. *Hallah* can take quite a

93

variety of different forms, aside from the very lovely and familiar braid. The spices used to enhance the bread will vary too, depending on the country of origin. On the following pages you will find three of my favorite recipes.

Keep in mind as you work with the dough that yeast is a living thing. It needs to be kept comfortable. Extreme heat will kill it; cold will slow it down. So make certain that the liquids are lukewarm before coming into contact with the yeast. Test by putting a drop on the back of your wrist; it should feel comfortably warm, not hot. Kneading is the step that makes the dough change from a rough, sticky mass into a smooth, satiny, responsive, elastic ball. You can really feel it "come alive" under your fingers as the kneading progresses. Thorough kneading gives a better texture to the finished *hallah*. You can speed the rising process by adding more yeast (a packet or two). The bread will not taste of it as long as you haven't let it overrise. When setting the bread aside to rise, again remember the comfort of the growing yeast. It needs a warm place, free of drafts. An oven with a pilot light (as long as it never becomes hotter than 105°) will do nicely. If you have no pilot light, you can set the bowl of dough on a rack in the oven and place a roasting pan full of boiling water on the floor of the oven. The moisture helps too. For that reason, I always cover rising dough with a dampened cloth. To test for lightness when you think the bread has risen enough, press lightly with your finger near the bottom edge of the loaf. If the impression remains, the bread is ready to be baked.

SHAPING THE HALLAH

Shaping and decorating bread is very like sculpturing, with dough as your clay. While braiding is the most traditional way to shape *hallah*, you might want to try your hand at a few variations for the different holidays. If the basic three-strand braid is as much as you care to master, consider making the braids in graduated lengths and piling them on top of one another, brushing with water to make them stick.

The fish-shaped *hallah* (especially nice for Purim or any time in the month of Adar when the astrological sign is Pisces) was made by braiding four ropes of dough together. At the "head" the dough was simply pinched into a point; the tail was made by separating the four ropes at this end and pressing a fork into the dough. A snippet of extra dough forms the gill and raisins the eye; poppy seeds help suggest scales.

The tree (which also looks a bit like a sheaf of grain) for Tu Bi-Shevat or Sukkot was made with two four-strand braids piled on top of each other to form the trunk. At the top the strands were all separated into branches, the ends shaped into ovals and embossed with a fork to form leaves; additional leaves were made of scraps of reserved dough. The ladders were simply assembled from small ropes.

To make the dove, roll the dough into a 3" circle. Fold over the edges, forming a triangle, and seal with a bit of water. Turn the triangle over, sealed side down, on a well-greased baking sheet. Lift one point back against the center of the triangle and bend it into a head, pinching the tip to make the bill. With the edge of a fork, make creases for the wings, cutting through the dough at the last inch and pulling the wings away from the body. With the fork tines, press into the tail to make feathers. Use raisins, currants, or cloves for the eyes. As the bird rises it tends to droop its head, so you might prop it up with a bit of crumpled aluminum foil.

Small *hallah* rolls can be made with a one-strand braid. Shape a rope 3½ times as long as the finished loaf is to be. Bend the rope to form a loop, with one leg a little longer than the other. Pull the long end through the loop to make a simple knot. Twist the open half of the loop to form a figure 8 and carry the long end through from underneath.

Three-strand braids can be worked from either end—or, for a more even loaf, start by arranging the three strands to crisscross in the middle; braid from the crossover to each end.

To braid four strands, start with the strand on your right and weave it over and under the other three until it is the last strand. Repeat with the second strand, then the third, and so on until all

the dough has been used up and the loaf made. This is all done on a large greased baking sheet. I don't glaze the braids until they have risen again and are ready for the oven, because otherwise as the dough rises and expands, spots tend to be left unglazed. A 1" nylon paintbrush from the hardware store works well for brushing the beaten egg over the risen loaves. Depending on their size and your oven, the *hallah* will take between 30 minutes and 1 hour to bake. Test for doneness by tapping gently with your fingernail: if it sounds hollow, it is done. Remove the bread from the baking sheet and cool it on a wire rack to prevent condensation from ruining the crust.

Hallah can be served cold, of course, but I prefer to put it into the oven for a few minutes again before serving. If you have forgotten to separate a piece of the dough before baking, you can break it off and discard it before serving the loaf.

Traditionally, two *hallot* are served to symbolize the double portion of manna in the desert which was provided so no one had to labor and gather the manna on the Sabbath.

Several reasons are given for the custom of covering the *hallah* with a special cloth. We are told that it is sensitive and might have its feelings hurt when the *kiddush* for the wine is pronounced before the blessing for bread; that we cover the *hallah* to avoid confusing God, who has so many prayers coming at Him, when the wine is blessed; and that we cover it since the manna in the desert was covered with dew. Whatever the reason, it gives one the further opportunity of enhancing the holiday by making a special Rosh Hashanah *hallah* cover.

After the wine is blessed, the meal is begun by blessing the *hallot*:

ברוך אתה יי אלהינו, מלך העולם המוציא לחם מן הארץ:

96

["Blessed are You, O Lord our God, King of the Universe," who takes bread out of the earth."]

After the blessing and before eating, it is customary to salt the *hallah*. This is to partake of the mineral sustenance of the earth as well as the vegetable, and reminds us that "In the sweat of your face shall you eat bread" (Genesis 3:19). On Rosh Hashanah and throughout the fall holidays, the *hallah* is instead dipped in honey as a wish for a sweet New Year.

HASIDIC PARVE HALLAH

This recipe has seven ingredients, for the seven days of the week. Each measurement also has a symbolic meaning: one cup of sugar (there is one God only), two tablespoons of salt (for the tablets of the Law—or Moses and Aaron, in some versions), three cups of water (for the patriarchs, Abraham, Isaac, and Jacob), four packages of yeast (for the matriarchs, Sarah, Rebecca, Leah, and Rachel), seven eggs (six for the *hallah* itself and the seventh for glazing, just as the Sabbath embellishes the six days of Creation), ten tablespoons of oil (for the Ten Commandments), and twelve cups of flour (for the twelve tribes of Israel). The recipe is very generous and will make enough *hallah* for all the Sabbath meals of a family of four, plus a guest or two who likes to sit around and chat and nibble; but it can easily be divided in halves or fourths with a little simple math. It's a good recipe to use with a class of children, because it is less expensive than a milk-and-butter recipe, because it is *parve* and usable with either meat or dairy meals, and because of the symbolism of the measurements. Now the recipe:

1	cup sugar	4	packages (¼ ounce each) active dry yeast
2	tablespoons salt		
3	cups water	12	cups unbleached flour
10	tablespoons salad oil		cornmeal
7	eggs (reserve one for the glaze)		poppy seeds

Dissolve the sugar and salt in 1½ cups of very hot water. Cool to lukewarm. To help it cool, add the salad oil and 6 slightly beaten eggs. Sprinkle the yeast into 1½ cups of lukewarm water to begin the fermentation process. Sift the flour into a very large bowl and make a well in it. When all the liquids are lukewarm and the yeast has started to foam (this takes about 5 minutes), pour the liquids into the flour and stir with a wooden spoon. Turn the dough onto a well-floured surface and knead until smooth and elastic, adding a little more flour if necessary.

Rinse the bowl with warm water, dry it, and grease with vegetable shortening or salad oil. Place the dough in it, turning to make certain all surfaces are greased. Cover with a damp cloth and place in a warm spot to rise. Allow it to rise for about two hours, until doubled in bulk. Turn the dough onto a floured surface and punch it down. Divide it into the number of loaves you want to make (this recipe will make 4 big and impressive hallot, 8 medium-size ones, etc.) and place the dough you are not immediately using under a covered bowl to rest and keep from drying out. When your loaves are formed (see notes on braiding at the beginning of this section and read some of the other recipes for ideas), place them on well-greased baking sheets which have been lightly sprinkled with cornmeal. Cover with a damp cloth and set aside to rise again until doubled in bulk. The second rising usually takes less time. When doubled in bulk, brush with the reserved egg, which you can beat with a little water if you need to stretch it. Sprinkle with poppy seeds and bake in an oven preheated to 325° until golden brown (½–1 hour, depending on the size of the hallot).

SWISS HALLAH (makes 2 braids)

1	package active dry yeast	2	teaspoons salt
¼	cup lukewarm water	2	eggs, slightly beaten
1	cup milk		another egg for glazing
½	cup margarine	4½–5	cups flour
2	tablespoons sugar		

Sprinkle the yeast in the lukewarm water; allow to stand for 5 minutes to soften. Scald the milk and add the margarine, sugar, and salt. The margarine will melt and the sugar and salt dissolve, thereby cooling the milk. Add the beaten eggs. When this mixture has cooled to lukewarm, pour it into a large warm bowl and add the softened yeast. Gradually stir in the flour to form a stiff dough. Turn it out onto a floured surface and knead for about 7–10 minutes, or until smooth and elastic. Place the dough in a greased bowl, turning to grease all surfaces, and cover with a damp cloth. Let rise until doubled in bulk, about 2 hours.

Place the dough on a floured surface. Punch down and divide into eight balls. Cover them with an inverted bowl and let rest for 15 minutes. Shape the eight balls into 12″ strips. Place four strips on a well-greased baking pan. Pinch them together at one end. Braid by weaving the strip on the far right over and under the other three, until it is on the far left. Then weave the second strip through to the left side. Continue with the remaining strips and repeat the process until the dough is all used up and a braid has been formed. Pinch the ends together. Repeat with the other four dough strips. Cover the loaves and let them rise in a warm place until doubled in bulk, about 1 hour.

Glaze generously with a beaten egg, or yolk only. Bake the loaves in a preheated 375° oven until nicely brown (35–40 minutes).

DUTCH CURRANT CROWN HALLAH

Both because of its shape, symbolic of Torah crowns and the crown of merit, and because it is especially rich with fruit and eggs, this *hallah* is traditionally served in Holland with wine at the *kiddush* of such ritual festivities as circumcisions, Bar Mitzvahs, and weddings. Its symbolic shape makes it particularly suitable for Rosh Hashanah and Shavuot.

1	cup butter or margarine	½	cup currants or raisins
½	cup sugar	1	teaspoon powdered ginger
3	eggs	1	tablespoon orange marmalade
4	packages (¼ ounce each) active dry yeast	2	tablespoons candied lemon peel
		2	tablespoons candied orange peel
1⅓	cups scalded milk, cooled to lukewarm	3	heaping tablespoons candied cherries
6	cups flour	¼	cup chopped almonds
1	teaspoon salt	1	beaten egg for glaze

Sprinkle the yeast into the warm milk and let sit to dissolve. Cream the butter, sugar, and eggs together. Mix all the fruit, spices, and nuts with the flour and salt, coating thoroughly to prevent the fruit from sinking to the bottom of the bread. Add the flour mixture alternately with the dissolved yeast to the butter mixture. The dough will be sticky, but turn it out onto a well-floured surface and knead it well until it becomes smooth and elastic. Cover with a damp cloth and set it to rise in a warm place. It will take about 2 hours—maybe a bit longer because the fruits slow down the rising process.

When the dough has doubled in bulk, divide it into three long strands and braid them together. Join the ends together to form a crown. Place this circular loaf into a well-greased angel-food pan. Set to rise again for about 2 hours.

Brush the top with the beaten egg reserved for the glaze. Bake in a preheated oven at 375° for 35–45 minutes, until golden brown and done. Test for doneness by tapping lightly with your fingernail; if it sounds hollow, it is done. If desired,

frost with icing made by mixing 1 cup of confectioners' sugar with 1½–2 table-spoons of cream or milk; flavor with a drop or two of vanilla or almond extract.

TONGUE IN SWEET-AND-SOUR SAUCE

I always thought tongue was unbelievably difficult to prepare until my neighbor fixed it for me as a Sabbath dinner while this book was in preparation. My daughter—who, on seeing tongues in the delicatessen, had sworn she would never eat such a thing—adored it. Traditional recipes for the sauce are not much more complicated than this, but I get a kick out of these unexpected ingredients.

1	pickled tongue (3–4½ pounds)	⅔	cup ginger ale (regular, not dietetic)
½	cup catsup	¼	cup raisins or 6–8 halved prunes

Place the tongue in a large pot, cover it with water, and bring the water to a boil. Reduce the flame and continue to simmer, covered, until the tongue is very tender (3–4 hours). Turn off the flame and leave the tongue in the pot until the water is cool. Peel the tongue, removing excess fat, and return it immediately to the pot, permitting it to remain in the water until it is cold. This prevents the tongue from becoming hard and rubbery; it may be left overnight.

Make the sauce by combining the catsup, ginger ale, and raisins in a saucepan and simmering for 10 minutes. Add as many ¼" slices of the tongue as you need for a particular meal and simmer for another 10 minutes. If browning is desired, the tongue may then be baked uncovered at 325° for 10–15 minutes. Serve with rice or kasha (buckwheat groats).

Yom Kippur

Even non-Jews know that Yom Kippur, the Day of Atonement, is a fast day. Why then mention it in a book about parties? It is included here because describing the cycle of holidays from Rosh Hashanah to Simhat Torah without touching on the profundity of Yom Kippur seems frivolous. Also, there are in fact two special meals, often communal, associated with the holiday—one at either end of the fast. The ten days of reflection, penitence, and return begun with Rosh Hashanah come to an end with Yom Kippur, and according to the tradition our fate for the forthcoming year is sealed. The New Year really begins when we have, through a day of contemplation and prayer and denial of bodily pleasures, truly emptied the past year from our bodies and minds and begun anew.

There are no easy symbols identified with Yom Kippur—only the whiteness of the synagogue textiles and the *kittl*, a long robe worn by Orthodox men; the fast itself; and ultimately, of course, the sound of the *shofar*. The meal before the fast is usually eaten early to allow plenty of time to get to services. It is, of course, not the time for a big party, but it is pleasant—and keeps the amount of work per person to a minimum—to share it with a neighbor. Foods that are easy to digest and will not provoke thirst the following day are suggested. Round *hallah* dipped in honey usually begins the meal, and may be followed by chicken soup with *kreplakh* [small noodle envelopes filled with meat, equivalent to Chinese wonton or Italian ravioli], non-greasy food such as roast stuffed chicken, Cornish hen, or turkey, and green and yellow seasonal vegetables. For dessert one might serve baked pears or apples and simple cookies or loaf cake.

The men's club of the synagogue where I lived until recently has a very fine custom of having a Break the Fast meal for the entire congregation immediately after the holiday closes with the Havdalah ceremony. By the time the fast has ended, it is usually more than twenty-five hours since people have last eaten. The atmosphere is quiet but somehow permeated with a kind of shared peace and joy. The food then is really breakfast food: orange juice, coffee, tea, *hallah*, and honey and sponge cakes, as well as tiny gefilte-fish balls and herring. Having fish, especially herring, after the fast is understandably very traditional, because the mineral and salt content help the body return to normal after being dehydrated. In her marvelous *Israeli Cookbook* (New York: Crown, 1964), Molly Lyons Bar-David describes a dozen different international ways to prepare herring for post–Yom Kippur eating.

This past year I went to a communal Break the Fast in Cambridge, Massachusetts. Again the mood was both solemn and festive, becoming increasingly relaxed and joyful as the evening went on. Everyone who came brought food or drink to share. The hostess coordinated everything in advance by asking some to bring main dishes, others salads, breads, desserts, wine, etc. There was plenty of food, and it was all delicious, but the emphasis was on keeping it light. Most the guests were vegetarians, so I had another opportunity to expand my collection of menus of this type. There was a beautiful Mushroom Cheese Quiche and a salad with lots of interesting-looking grains. I have never yet made such a Break the Fast but I am planning to. When I do, I think I'll serve the Lemon Chicken Soup the Jews of Greece use to break the fast, because it is both refreshing and satisfying. Then I'll let my friends bring the salads and dessert to complete the meal, suggesting that they plan foods which can be prepared before the fast begins and served cold or reheated easily at my house.

SOUPA AVGOLEMONO (Greek Lemon Chicken Soup)

1	chicken (about 3 pounds)	3	tablespoons onion flakes
	oregano to taste	½	teaspoon salt
	salt to taste		black pepper to taste
	seasoned salt to taste	¾	cup rice
2–2½	quarts cold water	8	eggs
1	tablespoon celery seeds	½	cup lemon juice
1	tablespoon poultry seasoning		

Wash and dry the chicken; sprinkle, both inside and out, with oregano, salt, and seasoned salt. Bake in an oven preheated to 325° until it is browned on the outside (2–3 hours, depending on your chicken and your oven). To check it, turn a leg; if it pulls out, it is done.

Peel the skin off and bone the chicken. (Save the roasted meat to cut up and return to the soup before serving.) Put the bones, skin, giblets, and all the drippings from the baking pan into a deep pot. Add the cold water, cover, and simmer for at least 2 hours. (Cold water is used for making soup, since it draws the flavors out of the ingredients rather than sealing them in as hot water would.)

Strain the broth and discard the bones, skin, etc. Refrigerate the broth until the fat congeals and rises to the top, preferably overnight. Discard the fat from the top of the broth jelly—it will almost have solidified in the refrigerator.

Add the celery seeds, poultry seasoning, onion flakes, salt, pepper, and rice to the broth. Cook until the rice is done, about 20 minutes. Cool the soup, either by refrigerating it again or by filling the sink with cold water and placing the pot in the sink. When the water in the sink warms up, drain and replace with cold water.

Beat the eggs and lemon juice together until light and thoroughly blended. Pour the mixture slowly into the cold soup, stirring furiously. Heat slowly, stirring continuously until the soup thickens. Add the cut-up chicken meat you saved, and serve.

SUKKOT

In ancient days Sukkot was more important than Passover or Shavuot, the other two pilgrimage festivals, both in observance and in the popular imagination. Today it is hard to conceive of a time when Sukkot, the longest of the Jewish festivals, was also considered the greatest and most joyous.

The original name of the holiday was the Feast of the Ingathering. Coming as it did after the solemn New Year and the Day of Atonement, when all past sins and noxious influences have been cleansed, the Feast of the Ingathering celebrated both the successful outcome of the past year and the fresh beginning of the new one. It was celebrated variably whenever crops were ready for harvest. Later, as the calendar became based on astronomical reckonings, the Feast of the Ingathering was set to begin on the first full moon of the season—the fifteenth of the month of Tishri. It came to be characterized by enthusiastic partying, with lots of drinking, fireworks, and bonfires, customs universally typical of harvest revels. Along with actually bringing in the harvest, the main features of the holiday were the special ceremonies to bring on the winter rains and the custom of living in temporary huts called *sukkot*. These trellis-roofed booths gave the holiday its present popular name of Sukkot.

Later on, in order to give the holiday a historic as well as a seasonal meaning, the booths were interpreted to signify the temporary dwellings the Jews lived in during their forty years of wandering in the desert after the Exodus. This explanation doesn't stand up very well to pure rationalism, since it is obvious that a tent would be the typical shelter in the desert, rather than a hut made of difficult-to-find foliage. Nevertheless, the joyousness, hope, and confidence in the future signified by these booths, reminding us of epochs we as a people and as individuals have passed through to better times, make Sukkot a compelling holiday thematically and extend our simple happiness in the harvest.

45 *Sukkah* interior (photo: Edmund Jan Kounitz)

As a child, I only knew two Jewish families who owned their homes. Everyone else lived in apartments. One of the families was Socialist, like most of the neighborhood. The other was Orthodox, and every year they put up a *sukkah* in their tiny front yard. All the neighborhood children marveled at it, and our Socialist parents were at a loss to explain this anachronism. Later on, as an adult living in the "greater Diaspora" of suburbia, the only *sukkot* I seemed to see were those put up by congregations with decorations by the Youth Group. Then, during a summer trip, I visited the Israel Museum in Jerusalem and saw a nineteenth-century wooden *sukkah* from Southern Germany. This made me want to create one myself, which could be reassembled every year and would also someday be an heirloom.

When I returned to the States, I hired a carpenter and with his help designed the *sukkah* shown in these pages. Basically it consists of seven sheets of plywood forming an 8' square with a doorway 4' wide. The panels are joined at the corners by 2"x2" poles and 2"x2" lengths at the top edges of the panels. Three arches and one round window were cut in the walls, and vertical lattice stripping nailed to both the exterior and interior in order to suggest the wooden synagogues of Poland. 1½"x½" slats are used for the roof. I painted the exterior dark brown and the interior off-white, with the intention of carefully painting a mural of my town and Jerusalem on it, reminiscent of the interior painting I'd seen on the *sukkah* in the Israel Museum. But my original intention gave way to laziness, and I settled on some loops, lines, and flowers painted by my daughter. One of the panels was designated as the guest graffiti panel, and everyone who wants to can make a doodle or sign his name with a permanent felt-tipped marker.

This is not the simplest *sukkah* to put up: it takes two or more people several hours of work and concentration and is best done in daylight. Therefore, the closest we are ever able to get to the *mitzvah* of beginning the construction of a *sukkah* as soon as the Yom Kippur fast has ended is to carry out a few of the panels from the garage. Once it is erected, we decorate it with strings of cranberries and popcorn, and clusters of colored Indian corn, and pumpkins standing around.

The cranberries and popcorn can be strung by simply threading a yarn needle with kite-flying string and stringing the berries and corn like beads. Florists' wire can also be used, and then the lengths

46 *Sukkah* going up (photo: Mae Rockland)

47 Interior of the community *sukkah* of the Princeton Jewish Center before the foliage is put on the roof (photo: Mae Rockland)

of wired berries can be bent into circles or joined to make stars. Because this is time-consuming as well as fun, the children have often invited neighborhood or school friends home to help.

A number of years ago the Princeton, New Jersey, Jewish Center designed a new community *sukkah* which could be easily assembled and disassembled each year. It is simply constructed of 2"x4" uprights, with 1"x4" horizontal stretchers. Chicken wire covers the whole structure, to make it possible to tie decorations to the walls and attach foliage to the roof. For the solid parts of the walls, 4'x8' panels of outdoor-grade pressboard were used. Local artists were asked to paint Sukkot designs on these panels. For my panel I used the *ushpizin* motif and simply made a design of the seven patriarchal names, using letters with crenellated tops as a reminder of Jerusalem (Fig. 48). Each artist was asked to have a typical Israeli fruit, grain, or vegetable at the bottom of his design and I used one of my favorites—the pomegranate, both because of its beautiful form and because it is often used in Jewish art as symbolic of fertility not only of crops and human beings but of the Torah. You might consider using the design for embroidery or needlepoint.

108

As well as spending as much time and eating as many meals as possible in the *sukkah*, there is another ritual observance connected with Sukkot which also clearly reveals the agricultural origins of the holiday. That is the traditional ceremonial display of the *lulav* and *ethrog*, which represent the four species referred to in the biblical injunction on the manner of celebrating the Feast of the Ingathering. Leviticus 23:40 says that "On the first day you shall take the fruit of goodly trees [meaning the citrus tree bearing citron, *ethrog*], branches of palm trees [*lulav*], boughs of leafy trees [myrtle], and willows of the brook, and you shall rejoice before the Lord your God seven days." In the days of the Temple the four species were carried in procession once around the Temple grounds on the first six days of Sukkot and seven times on the last day.

Today, an almost identical procedure takes place in synagogues around the world. Even if one does not get to the synagogue, it is a *mitzvah* to hold the *lulav* [the palm branch tied together with the myrtle and willow branches] and *ethrog* and make the appropriate blessing.

Last Sukkot, as I was going about chores in my town, two young girls approached me. One was carrying a *lulav*, and the other a con-

48 *Ushpizin* panel, acrylic on weatherproof board, 4' x 8' (photo: Mae Rockland)

49 Jews from Persia used ornaments such as this antique cast-iron apple inlaid with silver to decorate their *sukkot*; they were often made in sets of different fruits and birds (photo: Jim McDonald)

tainer with an *ethrog* in it. When they caught my eye and I smiled, they immediately came up to me and asked if I had said the blessings for the *lulav* and *ethrog* yet today. I had not. They asked if I wanted to, and I did, and found it curiously inspiring and moving to cross a bridge thousands of years old there on the sunny New England street. I thanked the girls, they thanked me, and we all felt wonderful.

Lulavim and *ethrogim* are available through most synagogues and Jewish bookstores. Your local rabbi will be glad to help you learn the blessings and the manner of holding and displaying the four species. After the holiday, little can be done with the myrtle and willow, which dry out, but the palm is decorative to keep around and can be used at Passover instead of a feather to brush together the last of the *hametz*. My daughter came home from Hebrew school with a nice use for the *ethrog*. Cloves can be stuck into its thick skin, tightly patterning it; then dust it with cinnamon. When it dries (a week or two, depending on humidity), it can be used for the Havdalah spices at the end of the Sabbath or tucked into a drawer or linen closet instead of a sachet. It can also be made into preserves or jam.

ETHROG PRESERVES

You will need to add lemons, oranges, or limes to your *ethrog* to make enough and to enhance the flavor. The *ethrog* must be soaked and boiled to get rid of its bitter taste. The preserves can be used on

110

baked goods, or try adding them to tea or seltzer (carbonated water).

1	ethrog
6	lemons, limes, or oranges, or any combination
6	cups sugar

Soak the ethrog for four days, changing the water daily. Slice the ethrog very thin, leaving the skin on. Boil for 10 minutes. Change the water and boil it again. Repeat this at least seven or eight times. Taste the water to make certain it is not bitter.

Slice and seed the other citrus fruit. Simmer the sugar, fruit, and ethrog about 30 minutes, until everything is tender and the citrus peel looks transparent. Cool and refrigerate, or pour into scalded containers and seal with hot paraffin for long-term storage.

Over the centuries many magnificent *ethrog* containers have been made. The containers serve to protect the *ethrog*, keeping it from becoming blemished during the course of the holiday, and to enhance the *mitzvah* by having a beautiful ceremonial object. A simple *ethrog* container can be made of papier-mâché, using a

50 Making an *ethrog* box from a log

"Blessed are You, Lord our God, King of the Universe, who has sanctified us through His commandments and commanded us to sit in the sukkah."

בָּרוּךְ אַתָּה, יְיָ אֱלֹהֵינוּ, מֶלֶךְ הָעוֹלָם, אֲשֶׁר קִדְּשָׁנוּ בְּמִצְוֹתָיו, וְצִוָּנוּ לֵישֵׁב בַּסֻּכָּה:

Maximally, the commandment includes sleeping in it as well.

Ushpizin—Hospitality Sukkot is a tremendously universalistic holiday. In that it comes at the veritable end of time—at least the timeline of the year—it is symbolic and anticipatory of the messianic time. All the seventy nations are to participate in it as a foretaste or initiation of peace throughout the world.

In an analogy to harvesting, just as we gather our fruits together into the sukkah, so God gathers all His fruits together under His great sukkah—the Sukkat Shalom, the All-embracing Covering of Peace. An essential element of the holiday, then, is the extending of hospitality and taking in guests. In a symbolic form, we ask a different biblical person to visit our sukkah. There is an almost universal custom of inviting at least one person who has no sukkah of his/her own to join in the meals.

Brunch in our Sukkah Sunday, Oct. 10, noon until around four

sukkot

This is actually a composite of several holidays. It begins two weeks after Rosh ha-Shanah on the same day of the week and lasts nine days (eight in Israel). It falls on the 15th–22nd of Tishri.

As with many of the holidays, Sukkot has dual origins—being both a historical and agricultural festival. Historically, it represents the journey of Israel through the desert after the exodus from Egypt—during which time the people lived in booths of an obviously impermanent nature. Agriculturally, the holiday celebrates the final gathering of fruit and produce of the year. In this aspect it is referred to as Hag ha-Asif—the Holiday of the In-Gathering.

Unlike Pesah and Shavuot, the two other major festivals, Sukkot is referred to as Zeman Simhatenu—the Season of Our Joy. The singular nature of the festival is further emphasized in its being known simply as He-Hag—*The Holiday*. During this period (1) the verse הַזֹּרְעִים בְּדִמְעָה בְּרִנָּה יִקְצֹרוּ —"He who sows in tears reaps in joy"—is fulfilled; and (2) the High Holiday period of introspection and penitence is *finally* completed. As such, the essence of Sukkot is sheer joy. People go to extra great lengths to make the environment and ritual aspects of the festival beautiful and joyous (hiddur mitzvah). This joy, however, is somewhat dampened by our awareness that we are in the autumn of the year. The land has yielded its fruit; the days are shorter; winter (death) approaches. Ritually, as well, the joy is tempered at various points—we say Yizkor, we plead for life-giving rain. The holiday is thus in some ways a microcosm of the entire celebratory cycle which mixes and moves from joy to sorrow, fast to slow, high to low with little transition or insulation.

On Sukkot, the holiday of tabernacles (or booths), as on Passover and Shavuot, Jews from all over ancient Palestine converged upon their holy city, Jerusalem. The week-long celebration is, to this day, a harvest festival observed "after the ingathering from . . . threshing floor and . . . vat" (Deuteronomy 16:13). The agricultural origins of the festival are clear from the regulations for its observance—involving a sojourn in the sukkah (booth)

TABERNACLES: Tabernacle from S. Germany, 19th cent. Israel Museum, Jerusalem.

Sukkot at home
From Johann Christian Bodenschatz,
Kirchliche Verfassung der heutigen Juden

51 Sukkot brunch invitation

grapefruit, a large orange, or a small balloon as support for the papier-mâché in progress. A rustic container which is very appropriate to the holiday can be made from a small log. This project (Fig. 50) is not suitable for small children but young people with camping skills might try it.

During Sukkot, beside prayers of thanksgiving, there are also prayers for the winter rains. But after putting up a *sukkah* in your yard, you can't help hoping that the rains will wait until after the holiday so that you can have as many meals and guests there as possible.

My daughter usually invites her public-school class to have juice and cookies in our *sukkah* and we explain the holiday to the class, pointing out that the Pilgrims in Colonial America identified with the Jewish people and felt that their wanderings were like the Hebrew wanderings in the desert and that they had found their Zion in America. So they made a holiday which they based on the biblical Feast of the Ingathering. They called it Thanksgiving. The children are usually fascinated with this story, as well as with the custom of extending an invitation to the patriarchs to enter the *sukkah* on successive nights. Most of the children are familiar with biblical names from their own Sunday-school background, so they enjoy hearing that in the sixteenth century the kabbalist Isaac Luria established the custom of inviting the "exalted spiritual guests" Abra-

112

ham, Isaac, Jacob, Joseph, Moses, Aaron, and David to enter the *sukkah*.

Originally this custom of inviting the *ushpizin* (Aramaic for "guests")—one each on successive nights—was practiced only by the kabbalists, but the Aramaic formula of invitation became popular with other groups as well and even produced some interesting folk-art objects. On the back wall of my *sukkah* (see Fig. 45) hang two decorative *ushpizin* greetings. Both were bought in Mea Shearim, the very Orthodox section of Jerusalem. One is a lithographed *mizrah*, with the Aramaic greeting written in the margins and the names, with appropriate illustrations for each patriarch, arranged in medallions draped from festooned pillars and cornucopias. The effect is garishly baroque or, as we say in Yiddish, *ungepatchket*, but charming nevertheless because of the sincere naïveté of the superabundant ornamentation. The other *ushpizin* greeting is a small olive-wood box with a scroll inside which contains the invitation to the guest. Each day the scroll can be turned to allow the name of the patriarch for the day to become visible in the little window cut into the front of the box.

The story is told of a hasidic master who became so irritated with his disciples that he refused to see them, either for study or for help. He became in fact such a misanthrope that he would only see people when he went to the synagogue, which was rare, since he preferred even to pray alone. Sukkot found him alone in his *sukkah*, and when he recited the prayer inviting Abraham to join him, he indeed saw a vision of Father Abraham standing outside his *sukkah* door. When he asked Abraham why he would not enter, the patriarch replied that he would not go into a *sukkah* without guests and without joy.

An educational, stimulating, and fun *sukkah* party for children might center around acting out in an impromtu way what it might be like if indeed one or another (or all) of the patriarchs showed up. The teachers and children should obviously delve into background material about the identity and character of Abraham, Isaac, Jacob, Moses, Aaron, Joseph, and David. Then they might speculate on how, in the twentieth century, such a person would choose to travel, whom he might bring with him, what he would recognize about contemporary American Jews, and so on. This might be the evening entertainment for an overnight campout in the *sukkah*. After all, whether with just a few friends in the home *sukkah* or a classful in a community *sukkah*, an overnight can give children a

52 (photo: Edmund Jan Kounitz)

feeling of making a link with those generations that have gone before, even while they're simply having a good time.

BRUNCH IN THE SUKKAH

The *sukkah* is a lovely environment for an informal outdoor fall party. Brunch is particularly nice because it allows you to enjoy the warmest part of the day. Serving buffet-style makes it possible to have a lot of people in and around the *sukkah*.

Because I was aware that many of the people I was inviting to the party really knew little or nothing about Sukkot, I decided to make an invitation that would provide them with some background. I went to the library and Xeroxed various bits and pieces about Sukkot. This material was cut up and made into a collage, using black construction paper and felt-tip pens for emphasis. With a black ballpoint pen I drew over the Xeroxes of the old engravings, darkening the most important lines. I then made Xerox copies of the collage on legal-size paper and mailed them. That way, when my party guests came, they all had some idea of what we were doing in the funny little playhouse in my backyard.

I invited fifty people and expected about forty. I wanted to spend the day enjoying my friends rather than doing a lot of cooking, so the buffet I set up was quite simple. There were assorted seasonal fruit and nuts, a large wheel of cheese, herring in cream sauce, cream cheese with bits of lox mashed into it, *hallah*, bagels, and rye bread, honey cake, cranberry bread, and carrot cake. For drinks, I served sacramental wine, orange and tomato juice (with vodka or gin for those who wanted it), coffee, and tea.

Stuffed foods, such as stuffed grape or cabbage leaves, and strudel desserts are traditional favorites during Sukkot, signifying the abundance of the harvest season. Because pumpkins are so plentiful and beautiful during this time of year, I decided to serve a stuffed pumpkin as the *pièce de résistance*. Since the rest of the meal was dairy, and many of my friends are vegetarians, I concocted a vegetable–cheese filling in keeping with the harvest theme.

At another smaller *sukkah* party I filled three small pumpkins with three different mixtures. One was a smaller quantity of the recipe given below, omitting the cheese. The second was a meat–rice mixture I use to stuff cabbage leaves. The third was a Moroccan *couscous* recipe.*

The vegetable–cheese filling was prepared in the morning before my guests came, and the stuffed pumpkin put into the oven when the party began so that it would be ready to serve midway through, when just about everyone who would come was there and very few had already left. One of the best things about a stuffed pumpkin is that there is no pot or serving dish to clean afterward; you just throw away the shell.

There was much too much food to fit on the table inside the *sukkah*, so an additional table was set up under the swing set (with the swings removed—the garden is small) from which I had hung felt Simhat Torah flags.** I wanted background and folk-dancing music, so I simply moved my stereo speakers to the dining-room window, keeping the equipment inside and directing the sound outside. An

*See The Hanukkah Book, pp. 85–87.
**Directions for the flags are in The Work of Our Hands, pp. 25 ff.

outdoor party provides an excellent opportunity for children and adults to share festivities without some of the problems that arise in a more confined space.

STUFFED PUMPKIN

1	large (16″ diameter) well-formed pumpkin (make sure that with its handle it is not too tall for your oven; it should hold between 4 and 5 quarts when the seeds and fibers have been scooped out)	1	large green pepper, diced
		½	pound mushrooms, halved
		3	stalks celery, diced
		1½	pounds cottage cheese
		1½	cups uncooked rice
		4	eggs, beaten
6	tablespoons olive oil	½	cup parmesan cheese
4	medium-size zucchini	¼	teaspoon garlic powder
	bunch of broccoli	1	teaspoon fresh basil
1	cup minced onions	¼	teaspoon ground ginger
		½	teaspoon salt

Prepare the pumpkin by washing and drying the outside, cutting the top as though you were making a jack-o'-lantern, and scooping out the fibers and seeds. (The seeds can be salted and roasted for an extra treat.) Lightly rub the outside of the pumpkin with salad oil; this will keep the skin from drying out and produce a nice glazed effect.

Cut all the vegetables into large bite-size chunks, except the onions and green

53 (photo: Jim McDonald)

pepper, which are cut into smaller pieces. In a large skillet, heat the olive oil and lightly sauté the vegetables, just enough to tenderize them slightly. Cook the rice according to the package instructions.

In the pumpkin, combine the prepared rice and the partially cooked vegetables with all the remaining ingredients. Place on a large baking sheet and bake in a preheated 350° oven until the inner flesh of the pumpkin is tender. To test, open the pumpkin lid and pierce gently with a fork, being careful not to break the outer skin or your "casserole" will leak. Depending on the size of your pumpkin, it will take 1–2 hours. When serving, make sure to include pieces of the cooked pumpkin, which is a mildly flavored squash, along with the vegetable–cheese mixture.

If, in keeping with this Sukkot custom of stuffed foods, you would like to stuff something but the pumpkin seems too ambitious, consider stuffing a bread and using that as your bake-serve-and-eat casserole. Use a large round pumpernickel or rye bread. Cut off the top fourth to serve as a lid and carefully hollow out the center of the bread, leaving the walls and bottom about 1–1½" thick. The bread can be filled with any cold salad, even the old standbys of egg and tuna fish, and then heated in a 400° oven for 5 minutes to warm the outside and keep the salad cool. Or you might use a meat mixture, cooking the rice and browning the meat, and using an 8-ounce can of tomato sauce to moisten the mixture. Bake at 350° until the bread becomes darker and the meat mixture warm throughout, about 20 minutes.

CRANBERRY NUT BREAD

Throughout the period of the High Holy Days, people are always dropping by; this is particularly true during Sukkot, when neighbors—and people I don't even know who have heard about the *sukkah*—call and ask if they may see it. I always like to have something around which is appropriate to the holiday and yet simple enough that anyone who does come can have the experience of eating in the *sukkah*. The different varieties of fruit or vegetable quick breads, such as carrot, peanut, banana, or zucchini bread, serve the purpose admirably. They are easy to make; they keep and freeze well; and they are delicious at any time of day with cider, wine, coffee, tea, or milk. The recipe below is a favorite of mine. I like using cranberries at Sukkot, both for decorations and in foods, because of its association with the American holiday of Thanksgiving. The Pilgrims modeled Thanksgiving after Sukkot, and I return the compliment. Cranberries are native to the United States, and it is said that during that very hard first winter which killed so many of the early colonists, those young children who found wild cranberries and ate them (even though the adults thought they were poisonous) stayed healthier than the others and survived to celebrate the first Thanksgiving.

2	cups flour	¾	cup orange juice
1	cup sugar	1	tablespoon orange rind
1½	teaspoons baking powder	1	egg, beaten
½	teaspoon baking soda	½	cup nuts (walnuts, pecans,
1	teaspoon salt		filberts, or almonds), chopped
¼	cup margarine	2	cups fresh cranberries, chopped

Sift together the flour, sugar, baking powder, baking soda, and salt. Cut in the margarine until particles the size of small peas form. Add the remaining ingredients, blending well but not overmixing. Pour into a greased and floured 9"x5" loaf pan, spreading the batter higher in the corners and along the sides, since it has a tendency to become very high in the middle. (This recipe can also be doubled and baked in an angel-food pan.)

Bake in a preheated oven at 350° for 1 hour, or until a straw or cake tester poked into the bread comes out clean. Cool in the pan on a wire rack for 10 minutes, then turn the bread out onto the rack and continue cooling. As with most breads of this sort, it tastes better the second day.

GINGERBREAD SUKKAH

My daughter and I are dollhouse enthusiasts. It is our goal to make our dollhouses (there are three so far) Jewish homes on a scale of 1" to 1'. We have collected and are making Sabbath candlesticks, *hallot*, Seder plates, Hanukkah lamps, *mizrahim, mezuzot,* and indeed anything Jewish we can think of (see Fig. 62). Now in progress is a miniature *sukkah* modeled after my full-size one described earlier.

The world of miniatures now forms the second most popular collecting hobby in the United States. Perhaps it is this same fascination that partially accounts for the popularity of gingerbread houses. Sukkot, with its emphasis on joyousness, seems a perfect time to borrow a bit from the general folk culture and color it Jewish in the form of a gingerbread *sukkah*. If you'd rather not put in the baking time involved in making your own cookies, it is possible to fabricate an edible *sukkah* using store-bought cookies and graham crackers, and cementing them together with frosting. The *sukkah*

54 Gingerbread *sukkah* (photo: Bill Aron)

shown here was made using the same gingerbread and lemon–
honey doughs used for the stained-glass cookies on p. 150. This
dough is very easy to work with, and it keeps very well in the refrigerator before baking and unrefrigerated after baking. It is my
idea of the ideal indestructible old-fashioned cookie dough. When
baked it is very dense and hard; therefore the *sukkah* needs no
cardboard supports. The resultant cookie is ideal for dunking in
tea.

The most appealing characteristic of the typical gingerbread
house is a steeply sloped roof. Obviously for a *sukkah* this would
not be possible. I was at a loss for how to make the latticed roof of
the *sukkah*, which is its outstanding feature, when my daughter
suggested using pretzel rods. The length of the pretzel rods then
determined the other dimensions of the house. Gingerbread was
used for the walls with a bit of lemon–honey dough as decoration.
After the walls were cemented together with frosting and the pret-

zel rods laid in place, the "foliage"—candy spearmint leaves—was placed on top and secured with a little frosting.

Hanging from the inside of the pretzel roof are strings of broken popcorn, raisins, and gumdrops; chocolate pieces were used for ornaments at the base and seams. The house was assembled and finished on a large serving board, which was lightly frosted to hold the tinted coconut, raisins, and nuts that suggest a fall groundcover. We put a dollhouse table inside the *sukkah*, and some of the dollhouse family members came for a visit.

My family and friends enjoyed the *sukkah* very much, but no one wanted to eat it. Finally we brought it to a family luncheon at my daughter's Hebrew school, hoping that the children would finally demolish it. It was enthusiastically received, but instead of being eaten it was spontaneously auctioned off—with the $20 it fetched going toward the school's camp scholarship fund.

⅓	cup vegetable shortening	2	teaspoons baking soda
1	cup light brown sugar	1	teaspoon salt
1½	cups molasses	¾	teaspoon cinnamon
⅔	cup water	¼	teaspoon powdered ginger
6	cups flour		

Blend the shortening, sugar, molasses, and water together thoroughly. Add the remaining ingredients, mixing well. Turn out onto a lightly floured surface and knead for a few minutes. The dough can be used immediately, but it is easier to handle if it is wrapped tightly in plastic and refrigerated overnight. Allow it to sit at room temperature for 20 minutes before using.

Roll the dough out on a lightly floured surface until ⅜" thick. Cut it into one 7" square, two 7"x9" rectangles, and one 7"x4" rectangle. The square is the back, the two large rectangles sides, and the smaller rectangle is half the front, allowing for a 3"-wide doorway. The sukkah will be 7" high, 7" wide, and 9" deep.

Cut two arched windows into one of the sides, one arched and one round window into the other side, and an arched window into the front panel. Decorate with lemon–honey strips (recipe follows) cut from ¼"-thick dough.

Place the pieces on lightly greased cookie sheets. Allow space between the shapes, since the dough does spread. Bake in a preheated oven at 350° about 15 minutes, until the lemon–honey dough is golden brown. Cool on the cookie sheets on a wire rack. When completely cooled, assemble the sukkah, using your favorite frosting. Lay pretzels across the top, attaching them to the side panels with a little frosting. Ornament with candy spearmint leaves and anything else you can think of.

LEMON-HONEY DOUGH

⅓	cup vegetable shortening	1	teaspoon lemon flavoring
⅓	cup sugar	3½	cups sifted all-purpose flour
1	egg	1	teaspoon baking soda
⅔	cup honey	1	teaspoon salt

Blend the first five ingredients until light. Add the flour, baking soda, and salt, and mix thoroughly. Knead the dough lightly on a floured surface.

Bake at 350° about 10–15 minutes, depending on thickness. If the dough spreads more than you wish, add a bit more flour next time.

55 (photo: Bill Aron)

SIMHAT TORAH

Simhat Torah, which brings the three-week series of holidays begun majestically with Rosh Hashanah to a close, is a marvelous example of the way in which holidays change and grow to meet the needs of people. On Simhat Torah the last verses of the Torah (Deuteronomy) are read and the first portion of Genesis is begun. In talmudic times this holiday did not exist, and it was not until the Middle Ages that the Palestinian tradition of reading the Torah in three-year cycles was replaced by the Babylonian custom of an annual cycle. By the sixteenth century the Ashkenazic practices of taking the Torah scrolls from the Ark and making seven joyous circuits of the synagogue with them, of calling up young children in a group to a Torah reading under a communal *tallit* held by adults, and of calling up an unlimited number of congregants to the Torah were already entrenched in custom. The holiday developed over the centuries into an increasingly joyous one, with the children carrying flags—sometimes topped with apples and lit candles—much singing and dancing with the Torah, and even lots of drinking. In fact, a non-Jew visiting a synagogue for the first time on Simhat Torah would be a bit surprised at the general air of hilarity mixed with fervent religious intensity.

But until a very short time ago—a dozen years at the most—Simhat Torah was celebrated in America only by the very religious. When Eli Wiesel's book *The Jews of Silence*, which describes the situation of the three million Jews in the Soviet Union, was published in the mid-1960's, it coincided with a time of political activism and renewed Jewish identification on American college campuses. "He who has not witnessed the Rejoicing of the Law in Moscow has never in his life witnessed joy," writes Wiesel. "I am still waiting to see tens of thousands of Jews singing and dancing in Times Square or the Place de l'Etoile as they danced . . . in the heart of Moscow, on the night of Simhat Torah. They danced until midnight without rest, to let the city know that they are Jews." Simhat Torah has now become a time to show solidarity with the Jews of

56 Simhat Torah flag distributed by the Jewish Community Council. The back of
the flag says, in part: "This is the liberation flag of the Soviet Jews. The Russian
word is pronounced *svoboda* and means "freedom." The red *magen David* represents the Jews of the Soviet Union, recognized as a nationality by the Soviet
Union, their Soviet identity cards identifying them as Jews by nationality but
denying them the rights of nationality guaranteed by the Soviet constitu-
tion. . . . In the face of cruel oppression they have now raised their cry for
freedom!"

the Soviet Union, who, in defiance of the religious oppression in
their country, come to the synagogue on Simhat Torah Eve by the
thousands and dance and sing in the streets under the floodlights
set up by the Soviet authorities. American Jews haven't quite made
it in droves to Times Square, but the number of groups celebrating
Simhat Torah with dancing and by singing songs that have come to
us from the Jews of the Soviet Union grows steadily each year.

This past Simhat Torah, being new to the Boston area, I wanted
to go where there would be a lot of activity. I first thought of going
to Brandeis University in Waltham, where the students pour out of
the chapel and carry the Torah throughout the hilly campus. Then I
was told of a small synagogue in Cambridge, in a neighborhood no
longer Jewish. The median age of the congregation is about sixty,
and for the last few years it has invited all the university Hillel
groups in the area as well as the Somerville Havurah to participate
in its Simhat Torah service and celebration. That's where I wanted
to be. I invited a few friends over for an early holiday supper before
going to the Tremont Street synagogue. Although the menu was
simple (see recipes below), I wanted everything to be special, so I
prepared a meal around the motifs of roundness, fullness, and
sweetness emphasized throughout the fall holiday season.

When we got to the synagogue we were not disappointed. Even
though it was early, hundreds of people from all over the area were
there already. The congregation had provided ample quantities of

cakes and pastries, as well as wine, cognac, whiskey, and that favorite of Eastern Europeans, slivovitz (potent, clear plum brandy). A young man recently arrived from the Soviet Union spoke a few words, and, as the building filled to overflowing, the services began. The Torah processions were accompanied by enthusiastic singing and clapping; different songs burst out in different parts of the small synagogue and spread to nearby groups. After the second procession the crowd spilled out into the street, to find it already jammed with more people. It may not have been Times Square or Moscow, but it was wonderful.

When I invited my friends for Simhat Torah, I wrote notes on the silkscreened cards described on pp. 83–86 and asked them each to bring something. I told them that I wanted everything to be round, continuing the symbolic hope for a round, full, satisfying year. So one

57 Dancing with the Torah (photo: Bill Aron)

friend brought cherry tomatoes and beets for the salad, another a pair of round *hallot*, another large round cookies for dessert. I made a huge pot of hearty meat-based lentil soup with rounds of carrots and frankfurters floating in it. After lighting the holiday candles and blessing the wine, we began the meal with pieces of the round *hallah* dipped in honey. As on Rosh Hashanah, we nibbled on apple slices (core them and slice them crossways to keep them round) which we also dipped in honey. Besides the beets and cherry tomatoes, the salad also had chick-peas and sliced cucumbers tossed with lettuce. The soup, which we ate with more of the *hallah*, was so satisfying that we could barely handle the round cookies and the Melon Basket Fruit Salad, but we forced ourselves— reasoning that we would soon dance it off.

MELON BASKET FRUIT SALAD

The fall holidays are the perfect time to make this fruit salad, since you can enjoy the last of the summer melons mixed with the first pears and pomegranates of the fall season.

1	large honeydew melon	1	large pomegranate
1	cantaloupe	3	Bartlett (or other favorite) pears

With a pencil, lightly mark the outside of the honeydew with a sawtooth line around the circumference of the melon. Cut the melon along this line, with a sharp knife, into two "bowls." Remove the seeds and scoop the melon into balls, putting them into a large bowl. (Be careful not to cut through the melon skin, since the shell will be the serving dish.)

Make cantaloupe balls with the melon scoop (discarding the rind) and add them to the honeydew balls. Peel the pomegranate and add the tiny jewellike seeds to the melon. Add the pears, sliced crossways into rounds. Add 2 tablespoons of your favorite liqueur or brandy.

Gently mix the fruit and fill the two melon baskets with the mixture. This will serve 8–10 people.

As a table ornament for Simhat Torah, consider a platter of candied or caramel apples. Provide flags for your guests (children aren't the only ones who like flags), which you either make or buy from a Judaica shop or charitable organization. A number of suggestions for these flags appears in *The Work of Our Hands*, pp. 225–30.

HANUKKAH

I dread the Monday after Thanksgiving. It seems that no sooner has the turkey carcass been put into the soup kettle than our entire nation plunges into frenetic activity dictated by the shopping-days-until-Christmas countdown. Jewish Americans become quietly schizophrenic as we are pushed and pulled by the media, well-meaning friends and colleagues, as well as our own children, themselves in the throes of Santa-starvation. It would seem that, since Hanukkah usually falls within a week or two of Christmas, the cure for "seasonitis" (inflammation of the season) is readily at hand: play up Hanukkah. Indeed, recent years have been witness to diverse forms of magnification of what for centuries has been a minor holiday. During the late 1950's and early 1960's an aberration called the Hanukkah bush enjoyed a brief vogue. At that time a neighbor of mine built a six-foot-tall plywood driedel which was painted blue and white. This (to me pitiful albeit honest) attempt to counter the pressures of the outside world was annually set up in the entryway, decorated with flashing electric lights, and surrounded by heaped gifts. And the same commercial interests that have sentimentalized and distorted Christmas so that its profound spiritual and family qualities are all but lost in glitter and greed are ready to go to work on Hanukkah as well.

If we are to keep Hanukkah from becoming swallowed up in the general midwinter madness while it is coming out of the shadows and growing in importance, we must take care to preserve its meaning and integrity. The historical events that gave birth to Hanukkah are neither frivolous nor simplistic, and yet we persist in trivializing the holiday as though it were merely a way to get the children to stop lusting for a Christmas tree. On other holidays, notably Passover, recognizing the complexity of the messages we want to transmit to the next generation, we make special efforts to keep the children's attention. With Hanukkah we need to exert added effort to make it a holiday for adults as well as for children: when we as adults have internalized the meaning of the Maccabees' fight for

127

58 (photo: Bill Aron)

religious freedom and feel its relevance for us today, we can go on to enjoy the lighthearted aspects of the holiday with our children and friends, confident in the knowledge that that which we offer unambivalently and with enthusiasm will be received the same way.*

Hanukkah is the only Jewish holiday whose historic background can be fully authenticated. It commemorates the victory in 164 B.C.E. of a small band of Jewish guerrilla fighters led by the Maccabees—Mattathias and his five sons—over the Syrian-Greeks, or Seleucids, who had desecrated the Temple in Jerusalem and were violently enforcing decrees prohibiting the observance of Jewish

*I have devoted an entire book to this subject: *The Hanukkah Book* (New York: Schocken Books, 1975). In it you will find more detailed suggestions for celebrating the holiday.

128

laws and customs. The period of the Maccabean revolt must be seen in the context of the breakup of the Alexandrian Empire and the passing of world power from Greece to Rome; as first Greece, then Rome imposed its rule on the Middle East, the Jews too were trying to work out their own unique history. Unlike our time, when religion is seen as a personal matter, religion then was part of the total economic and political structure. With each new set of rulers, new sets of religious practices came into vogue and were more or less enforced to ensure conformity and monolithic support of the governments. Before Antiochus IV, the villain of the Hanukkah drama, came to power, the Jews paid taxes to his predecessor but were allowed complete religious and cultural freedom. While hellenization was not enforced, it went on nevertheless. Jews spoke Greek, took Greek names, and wore Greek clothes (this at a time when one's costume was a function of one's place and people rather than of fashion). Therefore, when Antiochus IV came to power and (not out of anti-Semitism as we understand that word today, but in order to insure political unity) erected statues of himself in all public places, including the Temple in Jerusalem, and banned Sabbath observance and circumcision, there were many Jews who had assimilated to the point where they did not feel themselves to be inconvenienced. A high priest from among the ranks of the ardent hellenizers was appointed. In a short time he introduced more Greek practices into Jewish life than had crept in in over a century. While Antiochus was off challenging Rome for the domination of Egypt, a group of religious Jews, called Hasidim* or Pietists—believing a false rumor that Antiochus had been killed in battle—staged a revolt against the high priest Menelaus and his adherents; they also destroyed statues of Antiochus and other visible symbols of his authority. Antiochus was not only alive, but he had been humiliated by Rome; when he returned to Jerusalem, he was in a state of frustrated wrath and in need of some sort of "victory." He therefore turned his army loose on the citizenry, using as his excuse the ill-timed revolt of the Hasidim. More than ten thousand people were killed, and more severe decrees issued. Death was the penalty for observing Jewish customs. Mothers found with newly circumcised babies were paraded through the streets with their baby hung from their neck, then thrown over the city walls along with other

---

*Today's Hasidism, though having the same name, do not originate with this earlier group but from the eighteenth-century Polish followers of the Baal Shem Tov (Israel Ben Eliezer, ca. 1700–1760).

participants in the circumcision ritual. The brutality of this suppression further divided the Jewish community. Some sought security, others martyrdom.

To be properly understood, the celebration of the first Hanukkah and the meaning of the holiday for us today should be viewed against this history of internal dissension in the face of external pressures. This is a situation with which contemporary Jews, who are concerned about the spiritual as well as physical survival of the people Israel—in the Diaspora as much as in the Holy Land—can well identify.

According to the First Book of Maccabees the spark that led to the chain of events commemorated at Hanukkah was ignited in the village of Modi'in, about halfway between Jaffa and Jerusalem. In line with his policy of enforced hellenization, Antiochus sent troops from village to village to ensure compliance with Greek religious ritual. When these mercenaries tried to stage a ceremony involving the slaughter of a pig on the altar in Modi'in and wanted Mattathias, the patriarch of the Hasmonean family, to officiate, Mattathias and his sons instead slew the Greek patrol, as well as a Jew who, trying to placate the troops, offered to go along with their demands. Knowing full well that his act of defiance would be harshly dealt with, Mattathias and his family immediately went into hiding in the surrounding hill country. There he was soon surrounded by many supporters drawn by his rallying cry, "Let everyone who is zealous for the Law and who would maintain the covenant come with me" (I Maccabees 2:27), and the nucleus of a guerrilla army ready to fight for religious freedom was formed.

Mattathias died during the first year of resistance, which was spent principally in enlisting the aid of the local populations and in training more volunteers.

> And his son Judah, who was called Maccabee, rose up in his stead.
> And all his brothers helped him.
> And all those who were adherents of his father.
> And gladly they fought Israel's battle.
>
> —I Maccabees 3:1–2

It took two more years and several major battles before the Maccabees finally forced Antiochus to end the persecution and were able to reclaim and rededicate the Temple. Thus, three years to the day on which the Temple was defiled, "it was dedicated afresh, with songs and harps and lutes, and with cymbals. . . . They decked the front of the Temple with crowns of gold and small shields. . . . Judah and his brothers and the whole congregation of Israel ordained that the days of the dedication of the altar should be kept in their season year by year for eight days, from the twenty-fifth of the month Kislev, with gladness and joy" (I Maccabees 4:54–60).

Celebrating the first Hanukkah did not mean that the war was over. The fighting went on for nearly twenty-five years, until political as well as religious freedom was attained, and Simon, the last surviving son of Mattathias, was named high priest by the Great Assembly. Simon established the Hasmonean dynasty and concluded a friendship treaty with Rome, little dreaming that his people would be driven from their land by this new world power, to live in exile for nearly two thousand years until, in our own time, the wandering nation Israel is home once again. It should come as no surprise, then, that since 1948, which saw the emergence of the modern political State of Israel, Hanukkah, combining the spirit of religious freedom with national autonomy, has come to be a holiday that engages the imagination of Jews.

When the Maccabees rededicated the Temple, "they brought the candlestick . . . and they lit the lamps that were upon the candlestick in order to give light in the Temple" (I Maccabees 4:49–50). The rekindled Temple lamp was not the nine-branched Hanukkah lamp with which we are familiar today; it was the ancient seven-branched *menorah*. The Maccabees and Hasidim hoped that by having a major eight-day (Sukkot-like) festival, they would offer the people something to compete with the pagan midwinter fire-lighting saturnalia. No mention is made of the miraculous cruse of oil which (we learned as children) kept the lamp alight for eight days when the supply was only sufficient for one. In the second century of the Common Era, when the authors of the Talmud sought to explain the fire-lighting that was attendant to Hanukkah with the legend of the cruse of oil, they were interpreting an ongoing practice in acceptable religious terms. The identification of lights with holiness has existed in Jewish ritual since earliest history. If the Jews of the Maccabean era were adapting local fire-lighting customs in the celebration of Hanukkah, they were doing it within an ancient (even then) tradition of using sacramental fire symbolically, for even when the military victory was still fresh, the spiritual meaning was greater still and needed a fitting ceremony to mark it. For many centuries, especially since the destruction of the Temple and the dispersion of the Jews, nationalistic aspects of the holiday have lain dormant. It would have been foolish, to say the

131

least, for the Jews in medieval ghettos to celebrate a military victory, so while—in the words of a Yiddish song—the *"kleyne likhtelakh"* [little lights] remind us of tales of valor, bravery, and might in bygone days, the miracle of the oil has become a poetic substitution for the miracle of Jewish survival.

Any party or gathering will include the lamp-lighting ceremony; whichever way one chooses to interpret the flames, their light never fails to spread hope and joy. The candles are lit anytime after sunset, except on Friday night when they are lit immediately before the Sabbath candles. Whether you have one lamp for everyone to share or one for each participant, try to make certain that in the course of the holiday everyone—children, women, and men—will have an opportunity to kindle at least one light. The *shammash*, or servant light, is lit first. Before kindling the other lights, the following blessings are said:

ברוך אתה יי, ·אלהינו מלך העולם אשר קדשנו במצותיו
וצונו להדליק נר של חנכה.

Barukh atah adonai elohenu melekh ha-olam asher kiddshanu bemitzvatav vetzivanu lehadlik ner shel Hanukkah.
["Blessed are You, O Lord our God, King of the Universe, who sanctified us with His commandments and commanded us to kindle the Hanukkah lights."]

ברוך אתה יי אלהינו מלך העולם שעשה נסים לאבותינו,
בימים ההם בזמן הזה.

Barukh atah adonai elohenu melekh ha-olam she-asa nissim la-avotenu bayyamim hahem bazzman hazzeh.
["Blessed are You, O Lord our God, King of the Universe, who performed miracles for our ancestors in days gone by at this season of the year."]

On the first evening only we add the Sheheheyanu prayer, which is said at the beginning of every festival and on special occasions when something unique—such as a Bar Mitzvah—is happening or when one tastes a seasonal fruit for the first time that year.

ברוך אתה יי אלהינו מלך העולם שהחינו וקימנו והגיענו
לזמן הזה.

Barukh atah adonai elohenu melekh ha-olam sheheheyanu vekimanu vehigiyanu lazzman hazzeh.
["Blessed are You, O Lord our God, King of the Universe, who has kept us in life and enabled us to reach this day."]

After the candles or oil wicks have been lit and the *shammash* replaced, it is customary to chant the following:

הנרות הללו אנחנו מדליקין, על הנסים ועל הנפלאות
ועל התשועות ועל המלחמות, שעשית לאבותינו בימים
ההם בזמן הזה, על ידי כהניך הקדושים, וכל שמונת ימי
חנכה הנרות הללו קדש הם, ואין לנו רשות להשתמש
בהם אלא לראותם בלבד, כדי להודות ולהלל לשמך
הגדול, על נסיך ועל ישועתך ועל נפלאותיך:

["We kindle these lights on account of the miracles, the deliverances, and the wonders You performed for our fathers, by means of Your holy priests. During all the eight days of Hanukkah these lights are sacred, and it is not permitted for us to make any use of them, but only to look at them, in order that we may give thanks unto Your Name for Your miracles, Your deliverances, and Your wonders."]

Jewish bookstores, synagogue gift shops, and in some locations department stores have an increasing variety of Hanukkah lamps for sale, or you may be fortunate enough to have an antique candelabrum. Or you may want to consider making your own *hanukkiah*. In recent years I have been making a new one every year. This gives me the sense of rededication which is what Hanukkah is all about. All the lamps I've made are not necessarily of equal quality; I don't think they will *all* be heirlooms, though I hope some will. I enjoy using the new lamp along with those made or bought in previous years. Having many lamps allows everyone present to light a lamp, thereby participating more fully in the celebration.

Many people confuse the nine-light *hanukkiah* with the seven-branched *menorah*. There are two religiously significant lamps in Jewish life. The older of the two is the *menorah*, which symbolically combines the tree of life and the light of the seven planets of the ancient world. According to Exodus 37:17 ff., the first of these lamps was made in the desert from a single block of gold by the divinely inspired Bezalel. This lamp was eventually installed in Solomon's Temple. When the Maccabees relit the Temple candelabrum, it was probably a copy of this early *menorah* (the original having been melted down or lost in one of the periodic Temple sackings). The earliest lamps used for Hanukkah were most likely the single-wicked, pear-shaped ceramic oil lamps common throughout the Mediterranean world. These were lined up, adding an additional one each evening, on a pedestal in front of the house. In time

59 Ceramic lions and elephant, by Keren Rockland, hold the Hanukkah candles
(photo: Jim McDonald)

the single lamps were combined into a bench-form nine-light lamp. The *menorah* form was not used for Hanukkah lamps until the Middle Ages, because it was felt that to reproduce the Temple *menorah* would be profane. By the Middle Ages it was reasoned that, since the Hanukkah lamp needed nine branches and was of a different scale entirely, it was not a transgression to make *menorah*-form *hanukkiot*.

An easy way to approximate the feeling of the very early lamps is to simply accumulate nine small bottles or dishes and use them with candles or oil. The bottles India ink comes in, for example, are attractive and make nice little lamps. If you want to make an oil-burning lamp, fill the bottle with salad oil and use a pipe cleaner or the string from a mop as a wick. Bukharan Jews often use inverted handleless teacups as candleholders for Hanukkah. My daughter made the group of ceramic lions with a warrior elephant as a *shammash* shown in Fig. 59 when she was seven years old.

I brought back a 3"-thick slab of tree trunk from last summer's vacation in Maine. Back in the city a friend with a power drill then made nine depressions 1" in diameter to hold utility-size candles.

The stoneware lamp in Fig. 61 was made by cutting the back from a ½"-thick slab of clay and the base from a 1" slab. The triangular side supports and the *shammash*-holder were also cut from the ½"-thick slab. The entire surface of the lamp was textured with a sharp-pointed knife, which was also used to cut out the Hebrew phrase   נס גדול היה שם   [*Nes gadol hayah sham*—"A great

134

miracle happened there"]. The slab parts were assembled with the lamp lying down, using slip made by adding a bit of vinegar to the clay to liquefy it. The lamp was dried and fired horizontally in order to avoid warping or cracking. After the firing, a dimestore mirror was glued to the back with epoxy so that, when the candles are lit, they are reflected within the mirror-lined letters.

Since Hanukkah lasts for eight days, there are many opportunities for different types of get-togethers. You are assured of at least one weekend, if you want to have a large Sunday event or to make a Hanukkah Melaveh Malkah (departure of the Sabbath Queen; see pp. 249–253 for more about this). Among many Moroccan Jews it is customary to have a festive family gathering on the evening of the sixth candle, since that is Rosh Hodesh—the new moon—and marks the beginning of the new month of Tevet. *Couscous*—a dish of bulgur wheat, usually combined with ground lamb and raisins—is the favorite food for this reunion. In medieval Spain it was common for women friends to share a light supper of cheese pancakes sometime during the holiday; traditionally,

60 Hanukkah lamp made by Myron Tupa from a slice of birch-tree trunk (photo: Kenneth M. Bernstein)

61 Ceramic Hanukkah lamp (photo: Bill Aron)

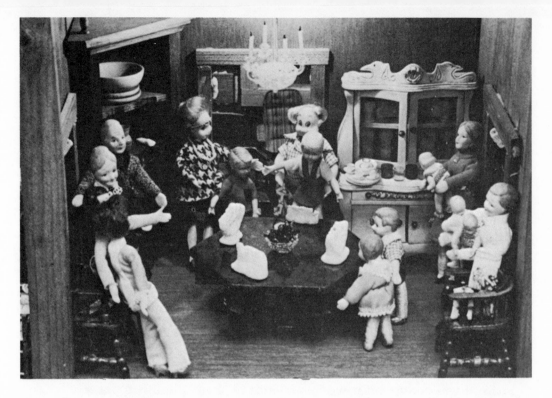

62 The dollhouse family celebrating Hanukkah with tiny porcelain Hanukkah lamps made to match our full-scale ones (photo: Bill Aron)

women are to cease from their labors while the Hanukkah lights are burning. This custom, as well as that of eating cheese foods during Hanukkah, is in tribute to the brave Judith, who, it is said, lulled General Holofernes to sleep with a meal of wine and cheese and then cut off his head. When the head was exhibited on the town wall, Holofernes' troops took fright and deserted; thus the Jews of Bethulia were saved. Today, though cheese pancakes are still popular, the humbler potato *latke* has superseded them on most Hanukkah menus, and wine-and-cheese-tasting parties have become a contemporary way of commemorating Judith's valor. For the past seven or eight years, I've made a big weekend *latke* party where guests did as much of the cooking as I did.

While candle-lighting and food are central to a Hanukkah party, before getting on to the recipes I'd like to make a few comments about decorations, invitations, games, and gift-giving. Try as I may to accommodate myself to the many requests I receive for ideas and workshops on Hanukkah decorations, I am very uneasy with the whole idea of "decorating for Hanukkah." I am aware that, with the world at large covered with visual manifestations of the Christmas season, there are many people who feel the need for a parallel Hanukkah display. My own feeling, both aesthetic and religious, is

136

to avoid as much as possible simplistic and tacky solutions. It has never been traditional to decorate for Hanukkah—Shavuot and Sukkot have been the customary times for that—but, knowing as we do that Hanukkah is in the process of growing into a more prominent holiday and will therefore take on certain of the practices common to holidays in the surrounding culture, it behooves us to make sure that whatever decorations are made have some authenticity about them rather than being simply Jewish versions of Christian ornaments.

Turning back to the First Book of Maccabees, we find that when Judah and his men reclaimed and rededicated the Temple, they cleansed and refurbished it and "they decked the front of the Temple with crowns of gold and small shields." Crowns in that period were wreaths, and the Maccabees were embellishing the Temple doors with victory wreaths. Another reason for the wreath was that in its early years Hanukkah was celebrated as a second Sukkot, and wearing leafy wreaths was part of the Sukkot celebration. Indeed, wreaths were so commonly used as part of Jewish observance that in the fourth century C.E. an early church father issued a warning to Christians to avoid the use of wreaths, a "custom of Greeks and Jews." Ironically, the Christians paid no attention to this and used the wreath with increasing frequency. Jews continued to use the crown as a symbol but, as fashion changed, the wreath form was abandoned and the more hatlike modern crown became a common Jewish motif. There are many symbols we share with other faiths, such as cherubim, bells, and angels, which we can use freely; it is a little late, however, to reclaim the wreath, which has been so totally associated with Christianity and Christmas in particular. Still, if one wants to decorate for Hanukkah, a nice surface to think of embellishing is the door.

Too often we think of a door as something to keep people out; how much nicer, especially at holiday time, to have the door itself extend a welcoming greeting. The last house I lived in had a glass panel in the front door. I made a batik cloth for it, incorporating a Hanukkah lamp and the phrase ברוך אתה בבאך ["Blessed shall you be when you enter"—Deuteronomy 28:6]. I chose this phrase because it was often used on Hanukkah lamps during the period when they were hung on the doorpost opposite the *mezuzah*. The design for this batik was very much like that of the paper-cut party invitation shown in Fig. 65. Fabric banners for the door, incorporating holiday motifs, can be made either by printing on the fabric or with embroidery and appliqué.

63 (photo: Bill Aron)

As for decorating the inside of the house—again my tendency is
to avoid excess: to clean it up as the Maccabees did, and to use
Hanukkah as a time for adding another Jewish artifact to my collection. For example, it's a good time to make a *mizrah* for an eastern
wall that may not have one. I like to set out all the Hanukkah lamps
I have and, after they are lit, to place them in the windows. Over
the years my children and I have also accumulated quite a few
dreidels. These are set out in a handsome bowl, along with another
bowl of candy and nuts, to encourage anyone who wants to play.
Other Hanukkah games, including a felt appliqué version of "pin
the candle on the *hanukkiah*" and a new board game called
"Aliyah," are also left around as invitations to play. For me the
holiday atmosphere and warmth of the home are decoration
enough.

STAMP-PAD PRINTING

This past year at Yadaim, the Brandeis Hillel Jewish Craft Design
Workshop, my students and I ran a Sunday-afternoon Hanukkah
craft workshop for the general community. The purpose of the
two-hour session was not to make instant ornaments but to explore

Hanukkah symbols, motifs, and thematic material and to learn a simple printmaking technique which could then be used to interpret some of these symbols and eventually to print them on fabric or paper. We spent about twenty minutes looking at slides of Hanukkah artifacts from different periods and talking about some of the Hanukkah lore discussed earlier. Then everyone picked a symbol to work with. Participants were given artgum erasers and fine-pointed hobby utility knives. They lightly drew their symbols on the erasers and cut away the backgrounds with the knives (single-edge razor blades can also be used, but it is harder to be precise with them). The carved designs were then printed, using a variety of different-colored India inks which were soaked into small sponges, making homemade stamp pads. Commercially available stamp pads can of course be used, but they don't come in as wide a range of colors as India ink does; also, for a large group the sponge pads are more economical. Since the workshop did not have as its intention the production of any "finished" work, participants felt free to experiment with forms, colors, and patterns. At the end of the afternoon, we discussed the possible projects toward which they could use their newly acquired skill. These included playing and greeting cards, tablecloths and napkins (both paper and fabric, using cold-water dye for printing), wrapping paper, streamers, and banners.

The stamp-pad printing technique is very useful for making per-

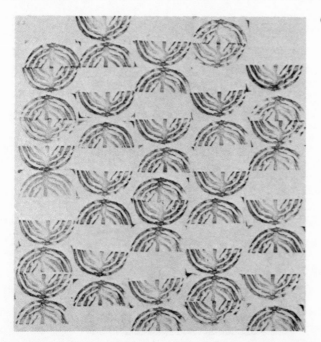

64 Stamp-pad printing

sonalized notepaper or cards which can be used for party invitations. It seems, however, that every time I set about designing a party invitation, I revert to my favorite technique: paper-cutting. Paper-cuts reproduce beautifully and, with so many instant copying services around, it is a simple matter to have attractive offset cards made from paper-cut designs. The Hanukkah invitation shown here was made for a party a few years ago. This year's invitation appears in the chapter on Housewarmings (Fig. 34), because we dedicated our new home as part of our annual Hanukkah party. The design was printed on the front of a folded card, and sent in 6"x9" manilla envelopes. It was printed without a message, because I wanted to use it as notepaper as well as for invitations.

Since the Middle Ages, playing games to while away the long winter Hanukkah nights has been a popular domestic tradition. Old engravings, woodcuts, and paintings often show serene family scenes with the Hanukkah lights aglow in the window and the household engaged in playing games of cards, chess, and dreidel. It is said that the custom of playing dreidel originated during the Maccabean struggle—that when groups of pious Jews would gather to study the Torah, which had been outlawed by Antiochus, they would keep a dreidel on the table along with the holy books. If they were discovered by soldiers, they could protest that they had only gathered to gamble. There were spinning tops in the Graeco-Roman period and the Jews may very well have been familiar with them, but we are more certain that the dreidel as we know it came

65 Paper-cut party invitation

66 Playing with the dreidel (photo: Bill Aron)

to be strongly associated with Hanukkah among Ashkenazic Jews during the Middle Ages, when playing put-and-take with a spinning top marked with letters was a popular Christmastime diversion adopted by Jews. The dreidel is marked with a letter on each of its four sides: נ *(nun)*, ג *(gimel)*, ה *(he)*, ש *(shin)*. They represent the Yiddish words meaning "nothing" *(nisht)*, "all" *(gants)*, "half" *(halb)*, and "put" *(shtel)*. These letters were then reinterpreted to stand for the phrase נס גדול היה שם [*Nes gadol hayah sham*—"A great miracle happened there"]. In Israel the dreidel is called a *sivivon* and the last letter is a פ *(pe)*, to stand for the word "here," so the phrase becomes "a great miracle happened *here*." Thus a simple game borrowed from the non-Jewish world serves to remind us not only of the miracle in ancient Judea but of that of modern reborn Israel.

Every player contributes an agreed-upon amount of candy, nuts, or matches to the kitty, spins the dreidel in turn, and pays the penalty indicated by the letter that is on top when the dreidel falls: *nun*, nothing happens; *gimel*, the player wins the pot (everyone must then contribute to the kitty again); *he*, the player gets half of what's in the kitty; and *shin*, the player must contribute whatever has been agreed upon to the kitty.

141

67 Elephant grab bag (photo: Jim McDonald)

Gift-giving at Hanukkah grew out of the older tradition of giving children Hanukkah *gelt* [money]. Just as I have always associated the Hanukkah lights with the spiritual victory in ancient Judea, I have linked the custom of giving children a few coins with the political aspect of the Maccabean triumph. When the Maccabees finally achieved independent status, one of the first things they did was to coin their own money—a governmental process we take for granted but which was a privilege won only after many battles. So even though I do give my children gifts at Hanukkah, I also give them coins. It is my custom to give them one penny on the first night, two the second, and so on, until by the end of the week they have accumulated the grand sum of thirty-six cents. This has a nice symbolic quality to it since the numerical values of the letters spelling ''life'' in Hebrew (חי) add up to eighteen, and thirty-six is twice eighteen.

Unless it gets out of hand, exchanging gifts at holiday time is a universally heartwarming custom. A grab bag is always fun and can be handled in a number of ways. Rather than the host's providing presents for everyone, the guests can be assigned other guests to bring gifts for, or everyone can simply bring some little thing to contribute to the grab bag and then randomly pull a package from the sack. The velvet ''warrior elephant'' in Fig. 67 was made as a

68 Elephant pattern with grid

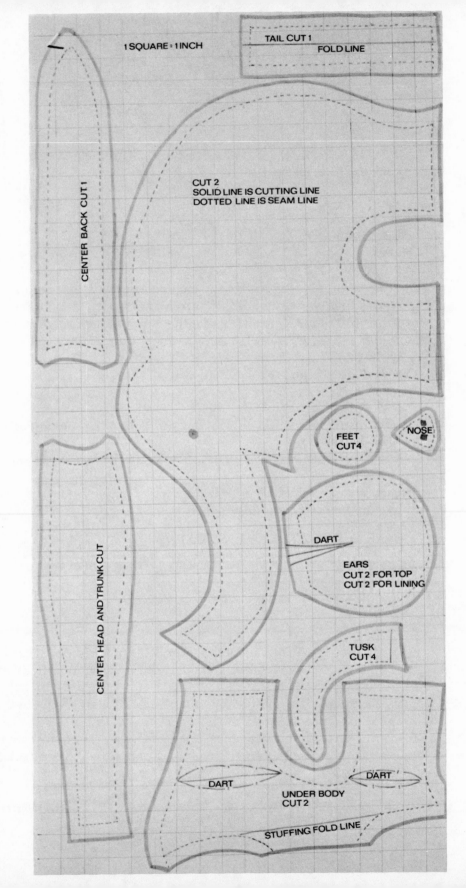

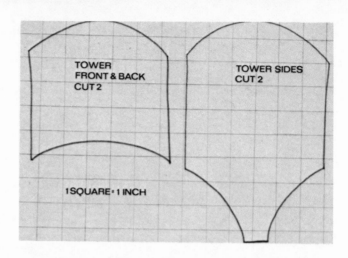

69 Tower pattern
   with grid

centerpiece for a children's party; each child brought a small gift, which was then tied with gold ribbon so another child could fish it out. During the Maccabean struggle, the Syrian-Greeks had quite a few Indian elephants, which carried a tower on their back. Five or six arrow-shooting soldiers rode in these towers.

To make the elephant as shown, you will need:

³/₄ yard of 54"-wide velvet (or ⁷/₈ yard of 44/45" velvet)
¹/₄ yard (or the equivalent in remnant squares) of felt for the tusks, snout, and feet
¹/₂ yard of 36" patterned fabric for the blanket, its lining, and the tower letters
¹/₂ yard of 36" solid-color fabric for the tower
7"x12" scrap of fabric to line the ears
2 plastic eyes
2 buttons to hold the tower to the blanket
18" of thin ribbon to tie the blanket under the elephant's belly
2 ¹/₂ pounds polyester stuffing
thin cardboard to stiffen the tower

1. Enlarge the patterns and cut them out.
2. Pin patterns to fabric and cut out the required number of each.
3. With right sides of fabric together, seam each underbody to each main body.
4. Seam back and trunk panel to both sides of main body. Seam bottom of the trunk and front legs.
5. Turn right side out (the only open seams are the belly seam, the snout, and the feet). Topstitch felt toes to bottom edge of feet.
6. Line the ears and sew them in place by hand.

70 Letters, full size

7. Attach the eyes according to the manufacturer's directions (some are glued, some sewn; others have back washers).

8. Turn inside out again, and seam felt circles to the bottom of the feet, and a felt triangle to the end of the trunk.

9. Turn right side out again. Stuff, using a wooden spoon handle or a dowel to pack the stuffing tightly into the legs and snout. Sew the belly seam.

10. Sew, turn, and stuff the felt tusks; sew in place by hand.

11. Make the tail by folding the fabric, turning in the seam allowance, and topstitching many lines, ridging the velvet to look like corduroy. Sew in place by hand.

12. No pattern is given for the blanket, which is a lined narrow rectangle, 7"x23". Make it to show your patterned fabric to the best advantage.

13. To make the tower, cut two of each form from cardboard. Place these alternately on folded fabric ½" apart. Draw around each panel with a pencil. Do not cut the panels apart, but cut ½" outside the pencil line along the top and bottom edges of the lined-up panels.

14. Appliqué the letters in place. The letters are the same as those on the dreidel.

15. With right sides together, seam the top and bottom curves of the four connected tower panels.

16. Turn right side out. Gently ease the cardboard patterns into their places. Topstitch between each panel.

17. Seam the two ends together, forming the tower.

18. Put the blanket and tower on the elephant and determine where to place the button and the ribbon which will hold the blanket and tower in place even when children are pulling their packages from the tower.

FLAMING TEA

It is just as gratifying to prepare a special treat for adults as it is for children. An old Russian Hanukkah custom was to provide each guest with a glass of hot tea and several lumps of brandy-soaked sugar in a teaspoon. While songs were sung, a candle was passed around to ignite the spoons of sugar. When all the cubes were aglow, the burning brandy was poured into the tea. Since it is difficult to duplicate old customs in large groups without being stagey and artificial, this might be nice to try at dessert, with just family or a few friends.

71 Pouring the flaming cognac
(photo: Jim McDonald)

POTATO LATKES

When I first began making *latkes,* it seemed such an involved and messy procedure that I'd make only enough for the immediate family. Now Hanukkah isn't complete for me unless I make a *latke* party for fifty to sixty people. Since the work increases with the number of potatoes, I usually have quite a few helpers for the preparations and the cooking. The pre-party party is as much fun as the party itself. The recipe below will feed about sixty people (depending on what else you serve).

30	pounds (about 100 medium) potatoes	32	tablespoons flour
		8	tablespoons salt
6	pounds (about 24) onions	4	tablespoons baking powder
28	eggs, slightly beaten	1¾	tablespoons pepper

Remove any blemishes from the potatoes and wash them thoroughly; it isn't necessary to peel them. Use the coarsest side of the grater to grate the potatoes into a large mixing bowl. Let them sit in the bowl for about 10 minutes, and then turn them into a colander. Squeeze out as much liquid as you can. Peel and chop the onions; fry them in small batches in just enough salad oil to cover the bottom of the skillet. (When I do a family-size quantity of this recipe, I fry the onions while the potatoes are draining. When I am making a huge batch, I usually fry the onions before I even begin doing the potatoes. Or, when enough people are helping, one or two do the onions.) Return the drained potatoes to the mixing bowl, add the fried onions, and stir in the eggs, moistening the potatoes thoroughly. Add the

147

72 (photo: Bill Aron)

flour, salt, baking powder, and pepper, and mix well. More liquid will continue to form, but once the other ingredients have been added to the potatoes, do not pour it off; stir the mixture from time to time as you remove spoonfuls for frying. Heat about ¼″ of salad oil in a large skillet and drop tablespoons of batter into it. Flatten with a slotted metal pancake-turner. When the edges are brown, turn and brown the other side. Drain on paper towels.

Unless you have restaurant-size mixing bowls, you will have to divide the mixture into smaller batches. As long as you keep track of the number of grated potatoes in each batch, and divide the fried onions and other ingredients proportionately, you will not have any problems. If you have many helpers, assign one person to oversee the mathematics of the recipe. If you are doing it alone, start the night before. Even with several people grating and frying, it takes longer than you would imagine. I usually start the preparations about four hours before guests are meant to arrive. That way, when people come, the frying is still going on; they help themselves to sangria, beer, or cider while nibbling on cheeses and giving a hand with the cooking. As the *latkes* are finished, they are kept warm in a large ceramic serving pan in the oven. When most of them are made and the guests have all arrived, we gather around the dining-room table to light the Hanukkah lamps. Once lit, these are placed on the windowsills and the *latkes* are served, along with a huge bowl of sour cream and one of homemade applesauce.

Parties, regardless of the age group, benefit by having a pivotal activity of some sort. In Israel, *sufganiyot*—doughnuts, plain or

148

filled—are a favorite Hanukkah food. If you have never made your own, you'll find it easy and fun to do. A doughnut-making (and -eating) party is a pleasant way to get together after school during Hanukkah week or for a Youth Group meeting. The directions and ingredients given below are simple and sufficiently unmessy that younger children could also make them, as long as they are of an age to be careful with the hot cooking oil. Making stained-glass cookies can also be the focal point of a party.

FILLED AND FROSTED DOUGHNUTS

	salad oil for frying		butterscotch morsels
4	packages refrigerated pan-ready		raisins
	biscuits (10 per package)	¼	cup granulated sugar
	semi-sweet chocolate or	½	teaspoon cinnamon

Using a ¾" round cutter (a bottle top will do if you do not have a cookie-cutter that size), cut out the center of each biscuit. Press 6 chocolate or butterscotch bits and 3 or 4 raisins into the top of each of 20 biscuits. Mix the sugar and cinnamon together in a small shallow bowl. Dip the tops of the rest of the biscuits into this mixture, then place them, sugar side down, on top of the candy-topped biscuits. Press the edges firmly together. It is a pity not to use the leftover biscuit "holes," since they taste just as good as the doughnuts. So tuck a chocolate bit or two into

73 (photo: Bill Aron)

them and cover them with their cinnamon-dipped counterparts also.

Put enough oil into a 10″ or 12″ frying pan to come halfway up the side. If you use an electric skillet, set the control for 380°; for an ordinary frying pan, use a medium flame. When the oil is heated, use a slotted spoon to gently place about 10 doughnuts into it. As the doughnuts brown on the bottom, they will float to the surface of the oil. When this happens, gently turn them, using your slotted spoon and a long-handled fork. Brown the other side. Remove the doughnuts with the slotted spoon and place them on paper towels to drain.

As soon as you have blotted off the excess oil but while they are still warm, dunk the doughnuts in any of the toppings given below. If you use the chocolate or sugar glaze, you can then dip them again into flaked coconut or ground nuts.

CINNAMON SUGAR: Mix 2 teaspoons cinnamon into ½ cup granulated sugar.

SUGAR GLAZE: Add 2–3 tablespoons of water to 2 cups of confectioners' sugar, stirring until well blended.

CHOCOLATE GLAZE: To the sugar glaze, add 2 tablespoons of cocoa and a little more water.

These glazes can be varied by using orange, lemon, or other juice or flavorings as all or part of the liquid.

Fry the doughnut "holes" too, and devour everything with apple cider or milk shakes (strawberry) to wash it down.

STAINED-GLASS COOKIES

Stained-glass cookies can be as simple or elaborate as you like, but they are always special. Consider making them with particular people in mind and giving them as Hanukkah presents. The dough can be formed into names, initials, story-telling pictures, or holiday symbols. Use them as place cards or stand them in a window for decoration. They are almost too pretty to eat, but since they keep so well you can enjoy them as sculpture for a while before nibbling. The process itself is fun for a group of children, teenagers, or adults. Just make certain you have enough table space for the number of people who are going to be baking. The cookies can be made with any hard sugar dough, even a mix, but I prefer using the Gingerbread and Lemon–Honey dough recipes used for the edible *sukkah* (pp. 120–121). You will also need lollipops or other colored hard candy to use as the "glass." Make certain that the candy you buy is the clear variety; the more milky candies don't produce as spectacular results. Separate the candies into different-colored batches and crush by placing in double-thick paper bags and beating with a hammer or mallet. It's not necessary to completely pulverize the lollipops; just try to have all the lumps less than ¼″ in size. Then place the different colors in paper cups.

74 Stained-glass cookies depicting Adam and Eve, a Hanukkah lamp in the window, children dancing the *hora*, Eliezer's attempt to kill a Syrian warrior elephant, pitchers of oil, and dreidels (photo: Jim McDonald)

Roll, pat, or cut the dough into ¼"-thick strips and shapes. Use the strips or ropes to make outlines of the designs you want. The photographs can give you some ideas, but go on to invent your own. As usual, children prove less inhibited than their elders in creating spontaneous masterpieces.

If you are using the Gingerbread and Lemon–Honey recipes from this book, make certain to keep the dough not immediately being formed wrapped in plastic to keep it from drying out. Use available tools, such as a garlic press, to make "hair" and to form and decorate the cookies, combining dark and light dough. Use a drop or two of water to attach pieces.

Construct the frame on ungreased pieces of aluminum foil. When the cookies are ready for the oven, place the foil on a baking sheet and bake in a preheated 350° oven for 8 minutes. Remove from the oven and very carefully fill in the spaces with the crushed candy. Return to the oven and bake for another 4 minutes. If the cookies are still not quite done, return them to the oven for another minute or two. Too much baking can scorch the candy. If there are spaces in the candy, push the hot sugar around with a toothpick. Cool completely on the aluminum foil on wire racks.

What makes it a *Hanukkah* party is the lighting of the candles. Plan your party to get all the cooking done. Then light the Hanukkah candles, sing a few songs, and eat.

בנו בתים וישבו ונטעו גנות ואכלו את־פריך

TU BI-SHEVAT

Tu Bi-Shevat, a minor holiday which is also called the New Year for Trees, means the fifteenth day of the Hebrew month of Shevat. Originally a nature festival, combining elements of tree worship and celebration of the midwinter full moon, by the first century before the Common Era it had no religious significance except (so it is said) that when on the fifteenth day of Shevat, with winter half over, the sap begins to rise in the trees, the age of fruit trees is reckoned for the purposes of tithes and similar laws. The Talmud makes no mention of any special liturgical observance on Shevat 15 except that fasting is forbidden and certain penitential prayers are not said. Mystics in the seventeenth century saw profound symbolic meaning in the verse "For is the tree of the field man?" (Deuteronomy 20:19) and began developing a special ceremonial for the New Year for Trees. Among Ashkenazim this only meant eating fruit identified with the Land of Israel, but among Sephardim a ritual developed in which fifteen different fruits accompanied four glasses of wine and appropriate readings from the Bible, the Zohar, and the Talmud. The Safed kabbalist Hayyim ben Joseph Vital (1542–1620) compiled a Seder* for Tu Bi-Shevat, including readings in Hebrew, Aramaic, and Ladino, called *Pri Etz Hadar* ["Fruit of the Goodly Tree"], which was eventually published in Laverno, Italy, in 1758.

Most contemporary Jews, if they think of Tu Bi-Shevat at all, know it as a kind of Israeli Arbor Day. In Israel it has become customary to plant saplings on the day. Americans participate in the reforestation program by giving money earmarked for trees to the

---

*Seder means simply the order of service; we think of it particularly as the domestic order of service on Passover Eve.

75 Paper-cut: "Build houses . . . and plant gardens, and eat the fruits of them"— Jeremiah 29:5

Jewish National Fund. Imagine my surprise when a few years ago I was invited to two different Tu Bi-Shevat Seders. When the first invitation came from a vegetarian friend, I thought it was a joke; the second invitation made me realize that my friends had a growing interest in continuing the kabbalistic tradition of ceremonial Seders for Tu Bi-Shevat begun in the seventeenth century.

I have since been to a number of these Seders and, while the manner of presentation varied quite a bit, depending both on the leader and on the participants, the basic elements were the same. Always present was the wonderful feeling of participating in the historic process of developing a holiday ritual. Whether your interest is ecological, vegetarian, mystical, or broadly cultural, making a Tu Bi-Shevat Seder provides a wonderful opportunity to explore less familiar facets of Jewish expression and to enjoy the headiness of eating a variety of fruits in the dead of winter.

While most commonly held on the eve of Tu Bi-Shevat, the Seder is not bound to any hour, so it can take place at the most convenient time of the day. Unlike the Passover Seder, where the symbolic foods are there for a didactic purpose and the *real* eating takes place at the meal served after the ritual foods have been sampled and explained, the foods at a Tu Bi-Shevat Seder are simultaneously symbolic and pleasant to eat.

The basic order of the service is:

An introduction. This of course depends on your group, but stories such as the talmudic one about the Sage Honi are helpful. It seems Honi was walking along the road when he came upon a man planting a carob tree. "How long will it take for this tree to bear fruit?" he asked the planter. "Seventy years," the man replied. "Why then are you planting if you will never eat the fruit of your labors?" asked Honi. To which the man responded, "I found a fruitful world because my forefathers planted for me; so will I do for my children."

The first cup of wine (see below if this is a children's Seder). The blessing for wine is said, then the wine drunk. The blessing is repeated before each cup of wine. The first cup is white, light and very dry, signifying winter when nature is asleep, dry, and cold.

A fruit not eaten before that season is introduced. It is nice to use the carob,* also known as St. John's bread and in Hebrew as *bokser*.

---

*If carob isn't locally available in health-food or religious stores, it can be ordered from Bloom Packaging Co., 4222 Tenth Ave., Brooklyn, N.Y.

The Sheheheyanu blessing is said, followed by the blessing for fruits of the tree, and the carob is sampled.

Then the fruits (some say fifteen; others thirty)—which have been divided into three categories representing ascending levels of spirituality—are blessed and partaken of alternately with three more glasses of wine. Interspersed with the eating and drinking are stories, poems, questions, and songs about fruit, trees, planting, and the Land of Israel.

Eat from the first category of fruit, the lowest, representing our simple physical being. These are fruits that have a protective inedible shell, as our bodies are a shell for the soul. Fruits in this category include pomegranates and almonds (which are especially nice to use because they are native to Israel), coconuts, grapefruit, and pineapple. Some people use bananas and watermelon in this category, but if one is strictly thinking in terms of celebrating trees one has to remember that bananas grow on *plants* and are considered herbs, and that watermelons grow on vines and in pickled form the skin is edible. Pomegranates are hard to find in midwinter, so I would suggest buying some around Sukkot when they are in season and keeping them in the refrigerator until Tu Bi-Shevat (they keep well). In the Salonic edition of the kabbalistic Tu Bi-Shevat Haggadah mentioned earlier, there is a Ladino poem by Judah Kalai'i which has the following verse to be chanted while contemplating and eating nuts in the first category:

> De mal la alma esta harta; Dio mira que razon es
> Mandes ya que se parta esta casca de la nuez.

> Sin, like a stubborn shell and hard,
>   is wrapped around our soul;
> Lord, break the husk and let the nut
>   come out whole!

Drink the second glass of wine. This is to be a darker, golden, but still basically white wine. Some people use the same white wine as the first cup, mixing in a bit of red in order to darken it. My preference is to keep the wines as distinct as the fruits, using a very dry hock for the first wine, for example, and a golden sherry or Concord wine for the second glass, which is meant to represent the thaw when the sap begins to run in the trees.

Fruits from the second category are eaten. These are fruits that are totally edible except for the pit. They represent a slightly higher level of spirituality, where (depending on the point of view) the heart is protected or inaccessible. Everyone present, even children, can be encouraged to come up with individual interpretations of how a person is like this or that type of fruit—and what it means if one is. Fruits in this category include plums, dates, apricots, olives, and peaches. Some add avocados. The carob can be eaten again here.

The third cup of wine is drunk. This is meant to be a pink or rosé wine, symbolizing the approaching spring when the fruit trees are in blossom.

Eat fruits from the third category, such as figs, grapes, pears, apples, cranberries, and oranges (candied rind). These totally edible fruits represent the level of spirituality closest to the highest form of creation, that of emanation—which is so pure that it is beyond representation by any fruit.

The fourth and last glass of wine is drunk. This is a red wine, symbolizing fertility and fruitfulness.

While there are many Haggadahs available for Passover, none is commercially available for Tu Bi-Shevat. Sy Hefner, at the Jewish Community Center in Wilkes-Barre, Pa. (60 S. River Street), and the American Zionist Youth Foundation (515 Park Avenue, New York, N.Y.) have prepared very complete and useful materials for planning and making a Tu Bi-Shevat Seder. These are available for a nominal fee, or you might want to make a Haggadah of your own. If you want maximum participation, it is helpful to have at least a one- or two-page order of service for everyone present. This can be decorated with appropriate pictures of your own creation or borrowed from seed catalogues, plant books, encyclopedias, and so on. A group in Connecticut based much of its Seder on questions and answers about trees from *The Book of Knowledge*. Other groups have structured their Seders around biblical readings dealing with fertility of the earth and trees, such as Genesis 1:11–13, where the creation of the plants and trees is described; Ezekiel 17, which tells the parable of the spreading vine, symbolic of the people of Israel; Leviticus 26:3–13 and Deuteronomy 8:1–10, which deal with the divine promise of agricultural abundance for those who keep the commandments; and psalms such as 65:10–14, which vividly describes the blossoming of spring, and 72:16, which makes a parallel between nature and governing. A visit to the library will turn up books on the folklore of plants and fruits, as well as scientific and ecological material. Indeed, it is possible to structure your Seder to suit many diverse groups. However, I would caution you not get too "heavy," lest the enjoyment of the day and its celebratory quality become buried in didacticism and pedantry. Intersperse the complex philosophical thought with lighter stories and songs.

The songs and other readings you use will depend very much on what the group is familiar with. If the group includes a skilled songleader, then new material can be taught. If not, emphasize songs or poems set to familiar melodies which will enable as many people as possible to sing along. Because many people have heard it set to music and called "Turn, Turn, Turn," Ecclessiastes 3:1–8 is very suitable as a responsive reading or a song.

If you are planning a Seder for a large number of people, ask everyone to bring something. Have them bring it cut into individual servings or bite-size pieces.

If the Seder is to be a sit-on-the-floor event, trays of mounds of cut-up fruit can be passed around, as well as trays of cups of wine. Since this is the height of the respiratory cold season, it is unlikely that everyone will enjoy drinking from the same shared goblet, though in an intimate group this can be very nice. Sitting at tables gives you the opportunity of using the table setting itself to enhance the celebration. At each place have four cups of wine and three small dishes, each containing segments of the five fruits in a category. You might want to use attractive paper dishes and cups. If you use a paper tablecloth, perhaps you'd like to write the order of service on it. This is especially helpful if you have no Haggadahs. Obviously make this as attractive as you can.

Just as the Passover Seder has a tray of symbolic foods, consider having such a tray for this Seder; it might consist of the seven species that are native to the Land of Israel: wheat, barley, grapes, figs, pomegranates, olives, and honey (Deuteronomy 8:8). Like the Passover foods, these should be explained.

In planning a Seder with children, replace the wine with four glasses of juice: apple, orange, cranberry, and grape (or white grape, then apple, cranberry, and purple grape). Remember, too, that while a congenial group of adults may very well be content to sit around for hours eating, drinking, and exploring the symbolism of the event together, a Seder with children should be paced according to their age and attention span, usually not lasting more than an hour.

The Passover Seder, which is designed for families, includes several devices to keep the attention of the children. Besides parables, stories, and songs, there are the famous four questions and the disappearing *afikomen*. Just as the four questions are designed to elicit the response which will convey the message of the holiday to the

76 (photo: Bill Aron)

next generation, so the questions for Tu Bi-Shevat can be formulated according to what you would like to stress about the holiday. Perhaps if enough people deal with this over the next several hundred years, we will have a universally accepted set of questions!

Give some thought to having something special at the end, perhaps a special story dessert such as carob ice cream. Another device might be to break up a story (even a joke or riddle) based on holiday-related material, telling a "chapter" with each cup of wine and the punch line at the very end. Take for example the statement by Yohanan ben Zakkai that if you are planting a sapling and are told that the Messiah has come, you should first finish planting the tree and only then go out to greet the Messiah. In typical fourth-grade fashion, you can ask near the beginning of the Seder: "If you are planting a sapling and someone rushes up to you and says, 'The Messiah has come,' what should you do?" Tell the children that they should think about this with a corner of their minds; the child who comes up with the answer at the end of the meal will receive a jar of maraschino cherries or a tree planted in Israel in his honor.

After the Seder, socializing can of course continue with or without more food. If you decide to serve more food, try to keep it in the spirit of the holiday. It's a good time to emphasize vegetarian dishes. You might serve fruitcakes and bread, or use the Cake of Milk and Honey on p. 229. Seeds from some of the fruits can be planted. Especially nice would be to get the carob seeds to grow. They don't need to be sprouted; they can simply be planted in a pot of earth. If you succeed and have the first carob tree in your neighborhood, you can use it as a centerpiece for next year's Tu Bi-Shevat Seder.

77 (photo: Mae Rockland)

PURIM

Purim is a minor but wonderfully joyous holiday which comes at the end of winter, about a month before the spring festival of Passover. It is unique both in its background and in the manner in which it is celebrated. We cannot really understand the nature of Purim without first exploring the Book of Esther, which describes the events upon which the holiday is based.

The story told in the Book of Esther, the Megillah, which is read in the synagogue on both the eve and the morning of Purim, is a marvelous one. A long time ago in Shushan, the capital of Persia, lived a rather foolish king named Ahasuerus. He tired of his wife, Vashti, and put her aside. The land was searched for a suitable new queen, and from all of those presented to him he chose the beautiful Jewish Esther. The introduction was arranged by the orphaned Esther's guardian and cousin, the good Mordecai. The king's advisor, the evil Haman, was rather an anti-Semite and had a personal grudge against Mordecai as well. He convinced the simple king to issue a decree that on a certain day to be determined by the casting of lots (purim), all the Jews of the kingdom were to be slaughtered. A one-day Final Solution.

Esther, who spent most of her time in the women's quarters of the palace, didn't know much of what was going on, but when Mordecai explained all to her she immediately came to the aid of her people. She fasted to prepare herself spiritually for the test to which she would put herself, then approached the king for an audience. Since it was her duty to wait to be called rather than to ask to see the king, this was an act of great bravery. He of course was enamoured of her and was ready to grant her request, which was that he come to a feast she would prepare for him. At the feast she requested him to come to yet another party and to bring Haman. There she finally told him what was on her mind. There was someone in the land who wanted to destroy her and all her people. "How can I endure to see the evil that shall come unto my people? or how can I endure to see the destruction of my kindred?" she asked. The

161

king, overcome by his love for her beauty and goodness, ordered the death of Haman and his family and gave the Jews permission to slaughter thousands of their enemies. Mordecai then decreed that the Jews would celebrate their deliverance from destruction with "days of feasting and gladness, and of sending portions one to another, and gifts to the poor."

It is extremely unlikely that the events in the Purim story happened as they are told in the Megillah. Historians point out that, among other things, Persian monarchs were obliged to select their brides from a limited number of royal families, and it is highly improbable that a king would allow the Jews to slaughter thousands of his subjects. It is suggested that the Scheherazade-like Book of Esther, like the books of Daniel and Judith, was a novel of the classical period, written as a sort of underground literature to keep the Jews' spirits up during the turbulent Second Temple period.

But many things that never happened are true nevertheless. While the Book of Esther may not be history, we can see it as an allegory which functions both to explain and to transform end-of-winter New Year customs much older than itself into a celebration of deliverance from physical annihilation, much in the same way that the miracle of the Hanukkah oil is but a poetic substitution for the miracle of deliverance from religious oppression. Throughout our long history there have been more than enough Hamans to justify a holiday when one is encouraged to become so drunk that one can no longer distinguish between the good Mordecai and the evil Haman.

When the Megillah is read, every time "Haman" is mentioned it is immediately drowned out with as much noise as possible. The uninitiated coming to hear the Megillah read for the first time may well be amazed to find the synagogue totally lacking in decorum. Some people may be in costume or masked; the children and many adults will have noisemakers of one sort or another. Typical is the *gragger*, very much like the noisemaker used on the secular New Year's Eve. Others will have cymbals and horns. The volume of noise can be truly deafening, but the crowd calms down in order to listen to more of the story and have the opportunity to blot out Haman's name again and again.

Even as we celebrate Purim as a festival of Jewish salvation, we can see in customs such as noisemaking—an age-old device for driving away evil spirits—the wearing of masks, and the choosing of a new queen links to ancient change-of-season celebrations. Exchanging gifts of food *(mishloah manot)* and giving charity to the poor, two other customs associated with Purim, are no less valid because they are not original. Until this century, Purim was for most of the world's Jews a much more important and joyous holiday than Hanukkah. Even though it was only a semi-holiday in the sense that candles weren't lit or the *kiddush* for wine said, and work continued more or less as usual, it was characterized by a great deal of revelry, paralleling that of the Christian carnival. Feasts and masquerades were popular; comic theatrical products were staged; children would go from house to house in costume, clowning and begging for coins and goodies (remember Halloween); cooks outdid themselves in their eagerness to make beautiful and delicious confections to share with their neighbors and friends.

Now, with the exception of those of us who have children in Hebrew schools, most American Jews don't remember when Purim is and have a difficult time understanding its derivation and relevance for us today. This is a pity, because—with its underlying values of faith, sharing, charity, and sheer joy in Judaism—it is a marvelous folk festival. I hope I am not alone in seeing a growing interest in this holiday. Since the 1960's, as Hanukkah has grown in observance, those Jews who are more comfortable with themselves as Jews in an American environment are stronger about expressing their Jewishness at other times. Purim is a perfect time for this. I'm always delighted to see Purim carnivals at Jewish centers and *hamantash–latke* debates, which have become popular on college campuses, usually under the sponsorship of the B'nai Brith Hillel Foundation. These "debates," which are in a sense descendants of the old Purim spiel, have the opposing sides argue the relative virtues of the Purim *hamantash* (a triangular pastry filled with fruit or poppy seeds, made in the shape of Haman's hat) and the traditional Hanukkah potato *latke*. The audience is overcome with hilarity as the debaters argue about the religious significance of the circle and the triangle, the political effect on the welfare of the world of using oil to fry in, the medicinal and other properties of the standard prune *hamantash* filling, and so on. After the debate, which seems usually to be held at a Sunday brunch, there is a substantial sampling of both *hamantashen* and *latkes*.

Like most Jewish centers and synagogues, the Princeton Jewish Center issues a monthly newsletter. In it the rabbi has a page or so to express his views on whatever topic he currently wishes to bring to the attention of the congregation. Last year about a month before Purim the rabbi's page was provocatively entitled "Your Rabbi's Fantasies." I read that before anything else. Along with his desire

The invitation reads (hand-lettered):

Purim Masquerade Party
at
The Bet Am Shushan Palace
on
Saturday Night March 12, 8:30
Featuring: Ethnic and Exotic Dancing,
Food, Drink and Atmosphere
Wear Costumes & Masks or Tie & Tails.
Free Admission
Bring Food and Drink to Share
Teenagers Welcome
Limited Capacity
Pick up your Tickets
at the J.C. Office
10-12 2-4
Drink Exotic/
Kosher Dainty

for how can I endure to see
the evil that shall come unto
my people? or how can I endure to see the destruction of
my kindred?'

Purim Masquerade!
Costumes
Food & Drink
Music

78 Invitation to the Masquerade

for greater attendance at services, more art work, and better lighting for the second floor, was a daydream which caught my attention
immediately: "I wish we could have an old-fashioned Purim masquerade just for fun, with no fund-raising connections." I picked
up the phone, dialed the Center number, and said: "Rabbi Glatt,
I'd like to fulfill your fantasy." He was a bit taken aback, but as I
explained that if the Center would turn over the Bet Am—the recently purchased eighteenth-century house adjacent to the Center
which was used for some Hebrew-school classes and social

events—to me for an evening, I would undertake to turn it into a "Persian Palace" and invite the membership for an evening of costumed fun. He was of course delighted, and we agreed to a meeting the following morning to discuss the details, because such an event would necessitate approval of the Board.

Since I had envisioned this party as simply an extension of something I would do at home, the thought of anything as official-sounding as the Jewish Center Board almost convinced me to forget the whole idea. But the next morning the rabbi's enthusiasm reignited my own. He translated my ideas into a project outline which could be presented to the Board at a meeting I would attend in order to answer any questions the members might have. I won't bore you with a detailed account of the meeting. Suffice it to say, all went well and although there was some dissension from those who wanted the party to be used to raise always much-needed money, it was finally concluded that occasionally having a really good time in and around the synagogue was as important as fund-raising. I'm including an abbreviated version of the outline we presented to the Board, so that if you should decide to have such a masquerade it will help you see some of the details that must be taken into consideration. You will notice that we called the party a *Post*-Purim Masquerade. This was because the first difficulty we encountered was that the Center was already booked for the Saturday night closest to Purim and so we had to delay our party for a week. The general feeling was that this not only didn't matter, it allowed us to enjoy the holiday for even longer.

POST-PURIM MASQUERADE

TIME: Saturday evening, March 12, 1977.

PLACE: Bet Am, which will be decorated as a Shushan Persian Palace.

DETAILS: Mae Rockland will coordinate the event. She will organize and direct all aspects of the evening, including:

Decorations: to be done on Thursday, March 10.

Designing and supervising the production of an invitation.

Running a Mask Workshop a week or so before the event at no cost to participants except for materials.

Arrangements for people to lead dancing and other entertainment. Such people would be volunteers and come as a favor with no charge to the Jewish Center.

CENTER'S ROLE:

1. Pay for printing and mailing of invitations; secretarial staff would address and mail them.

165

2. Provide paper and plastic eating utensils for the refreshments.
3. Allot up to $50 for decorations.
4. Provide cleanup volunteers.

VOLUNTEERS: Besides the core of helpers which Mae will secure on her own, 4 to 5 additional people will be needed to help with the decorating.

PARTICIPANTS:

1. Would come at no cost.
2. Must come in some type of costume; even a mask would suffice.
3. Would bring refreshments—food and drink—to share.
4. The Masquerade is for everyone over Bar/Bat Mitzvah age.

AREAS TO BE RESOLVED:

1. Ascertain the number of people legally permitted in the Bet Am at one time. Obtain this through the House Committee Chairperson.
2. It is suggested that no smoking be allowed in the Bet Am during the party. People who wish to smoke are to do so outside of the building. Signs to this effect will be posted in the various rooms of the Bet Am.
3. Invitations to have an RSVP. If necessary for fire laws, a cut-off number of participants to be established.

ADVANTAGES OF THIS AFFAIR: The way in which this Post-Purim Masquerade is envisioned, it will provide a fine social context for our members. There will be a good time for all, fun, participation. It will be in good taste, is linked to a traditional festival, and can be a stimulus for other such social affairs.

After the Board meeting I was fired with new enthusiasm when I met with the four friends without whose help I couldn't have managed and set about designing the invitation, planning the Mask Workshop, and organizing the food and decorations.

The four volunteers completely took over areas of the Masquerade planning and arranged for their own sets of helpers. One took over planning and organizing the food and decorations; another the music and dancing; a third the drinks and general house management and cleanup; and the fourth handled publicity.

Since Purim has always been of special importance to Sephardic Jews and the holiday traces its origins to Persia, we decided to try to create an Oriental atmosphere by having all the food, décor, and music as Sephardic and Middle Eastern as we could make it. When the invitations went out to the entire Center membership, people were requested to pick up tickets at the Center office and to sign up for the kind of food they would bring to share. Each person, couple, or family was asked to bring enough *interesting* kosher dairy or *parve* food to feed eight to twelve people. A chart at the Center allowed spaces for main dishes, salads, appetizers, and desserts. The person in charge of food made herself available with recipes and suggestions for foods such as stuffed grape leaves, baklava, and eggplant concoctions.

More often than is necessary, social events at religious institutions are arbitrarily divided up by age or sex. This or that is for the Youth Group, the women's division, the men's club, or the senior citizens. Sometimes this is both unavoidable and even desirable, but it seems that a greater attempt can be made to share more events. With this in mind, we decided to invite anyone over Bar/Bat Mitzvah age, reasoning that that gave us a Jewish way to establish the adult age for what was to be a Saturday-night adult party. We hoped to encourage teenage participation by having the Mask Workshop an event for all ages.

The invitation was drawn on typing paper, using motifs from an early sixteenth-century French Megillah and an eighteenth-century Dutch woodcut from a Sefer Minhag [Book of Customs]. The camera-ready artwork was printed by offset on gold cardstock. We felt that it was worth the additional few cents good-quality paper cost so that the Masquerade would get off to an elegant start, making everyone feel the special nature of the event. The bottom 2½" of the design was planned so it could be cut off and used for the tickets.

When they picked up their tickets, participants were also asked to bring wine, beer, or soft drinks for eight to twelve people. We envisioned a long party. Recognizing that some people might want expensive hard liquor—after all, on Purim we are encouraged to drink and be merry to such an extent that we no longer know the difference between evil Haman and good Mordecai—but might not want it to quickly disappear, leaving them with only a bottle of soda pop in exchange, a system was set up at the bar to identify numerically anyone's private stock. This worked out very well, with people bringing some drinks to share and a bit to indulge in with their cronies. Ice and glasses were provided by the Center.

The Center had given us a small allowance to use for decorations, and we used just about all of it to rent plants from a nearby greenhouse. Thus we had large potted trees in almost all the corners. Weeks in advance we all trimmed our forsythia bushes and brought as many branches as we could into the house to be forced. On party night the Bet Am was lush with vegetation. We asked everyone who came by for a ticket to lend large Indian-type tablecloths or bedspreads, which we hung and draped throughout the

79 (photo: Bill Aron)

"palace," as well as cushions and beanbag chairs which replaced the schoolroom chairs we moved to the basement. A non-Jewish neighbor lent us a thronelike chair she said had been used by President Woodrow Wilson. We wanted this so people could "play" king and queen.

One of the highlights of the evening was the dancing. Most of the participants could barely believe that this was their same old Jewish Center. Two professional belly dancers performed, and to everyone's delight they invited some of the less timid men present to join them. A folklorist and folk-dance instructor also taught some simple dances and soon had quite a large group of people dancing to Middle Eastern music.

The day after the party, as we were cleaning up, we were really a bit sad to see the decorations come down. It had been a lovely evening, a reminder that we Jews haven't survived this long without taking time out for a drink and a laugh now and then.

THE MASK WORKSHOP

Two kinds of masks were introduced to the group. The first, made from the bottoms of cut-off blue jeans, were very popular with the

168

80 Pant-leg mask (photo: Bill Aron)

teenagers. Since they are simple to make at home, we decided to use the workshop time to concentrate on the plaster masks.

PANT-LEG MASKS

For each mask you will need the discarded bottom of a pant-leg which is wide enough in circumference to fit over the wearer's head. Old bell-bottom pants are very useful; these should measure 3"–5" in length. If you want the mask to be a hat as well, cut the leg material longer to go over the head.

Place the band over the face and form a vertical pleat in the fabric above the nose; then gently mark the places where the eyes are to be cut. Remove the pant-leg and cut the fabric where the eyes have been marked with a horizontal and a vertical slash, forming a +.

81 Making the pant-leg mask

Fold the flaps back and stitch in place. Other decorations, such as feathers and embroidery, can be added, but for speed and simplicity this is hard to beat.

CAST PLASTER MASKS

To make the masks shown here, you will need surgical casting tape, Vaseline, scissors, water, old nylon stockings or shower caps to protect the model's hair, and plenty of paper towels for the general mess. Surgical casting tape, which is used to make casts for broken limbs, is gauze tape that has been impregnated with plaster. When dampened it is easily molded to conform to whatever you wish to cast; it dries hard in less than half an hour. If your local pharmacy does not stock it or will not order it for you, it is available from hospital-supply houses. Look in your phone book for one near you or ask your doctor where his office gets the tape. A high school in Trenton, New Jersey, used this tape to cast teenagers dressed in Revolutionary War costumes and constructed a beautiful and impressive all-white Bicentennial tableau. Clothes were protected with plastic wrap before applying the tape. I mention this here in case anyone becomes enamoured of this medium and would like to make costume parts or sculpture with it. The basic process is the same as that described below.

The tape comes in various widths; depending on what is available in your area, each roll of tape will make two or three masks. Cut

82 Cast plaster mask workshop (photos: Jim McDonald)

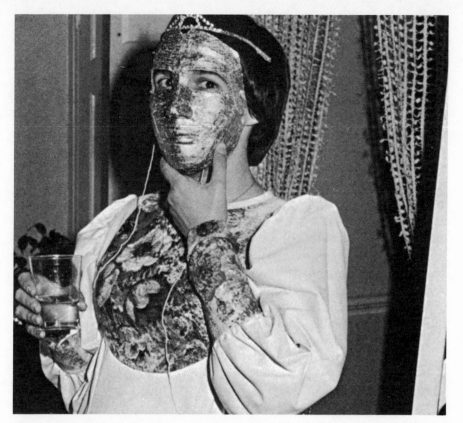

83 (photo: Bill Aron)

the tape into 1″ x 2″ strips. Cut some of these in half, some into quarters. Put these strips into a small shoebox-size carton to keep them dry. Place a small container or basin of water nearby. You can do your own mask using a mirror, but it is easier and more fun to work in pairs.

The hair of the person to be masked should be protected with a nylon stocking or a shower cap and the face generously greased with Vaseline. The Vaseline should go right up to the hairline and under the chin; if the person is bearded, make certain the facial hair is well coated. It's messy and feels awful, but you can begin to enjoy it. Dampen a plaster strip by dipping it quickly into the water and place it immediately on the face. The first strip usually goes on the forehead, the next two along the sides of the face, then down the nose; the jawline and entire outer shape are determined, then the mouth and nose area; the eyes are usually last.

The tape sets quickly, so there is little time to correct mistakes, and the second layer must be applied while the first is still wet. Too much tape is better than too little. Excess can be cut away later with scissors or a sharp knife. The model must keep the same expression throughout. Don't attempt to do a smiling mask as your first one:

171

you have to work pretty quickly for that and finish before the person being masked can no longer hold the smile.

After all the tape is on, the mask will begin to feel warm and a bit oppressive. The masked person should then go to a mirror and begin wiggling his eyebrows and smiling under the mask. When he feels that it has just about completely loosened from his face and is beginning to get cool, it is time to remove it gently. When it is totally dry, it can be trimmed if necessary and colored with acrylics or spray paint.

Rather than decorating the mask elaborately, my preference is to paint it a solid color, with either plain or metallic paint, or to simply leave it white. The startling effect of these masks is that they really do look like the person they are modeled on, so the fun is more in what can be done with them than in adding decorations. For instance, the same mask can be made for many people so everyone in the group is John for the night. Friends can wear each other's masks and clothes. Partial masks can be made so that natural facial hair combines with the mask. A smiling mask can be worn on the face and a frowning version on the back of the head.

Use a yarn needle to sew strings to the sides of the mask to hold it in place.

While Purim provides a wonderful opportunity for adult fun and games, it is of course an ideal time to have children's parties and activities of every description. My sister made an afternoon party for her three-year-old daughter which featured a simplified reading of the Purim story and was complete with noisemakers, fancy hats and masks, *hamantashen*, and musical chairs. She knows the party was a success because at the end of it Shoshanah asked: "When can we have Purim again?"

Most Jewish centers and Hebrew schools have Purim carnivals, yet I feel that it is also very important as well as fun to bring Purim back to the home environment, making it a family celebration and personalizing the festival.

A perfect way to do this is by giving *mishloah manot*, a gift of at least two types of food, to friends. In Eastern Europe, children or sometimes servants carried platters of delectable goodies from house to house. The Purim plates themselves were often very lovely and special for the holiday. The women outdid themselves in the elaborateness of their confections. There is a delightful story of two servants meeting in the street, each *en route* to the household of the other. As they exchanged gossip they began to nibble at the Purim

84 Jester cookies, stamped with the mold at right (photo: Bill Aron)

cakes. By the time they delivered the platters, very little was left on them, allowing each mistress to feel very smug in the fact that her pastries were much nicer than her neighbor's.

As part of its "*Mitzvah* Campaign," the Lubavitch Student Organization distributes Purim kits containing two different cookies, two pennies with instructions to give one coin to each of two poor people or to put them into a charity box, and holiday blessings and directions. Simple and attractive containers can be made for the food gifts you give your friends by cutting out patterned paper or tissue paper and pasting it onto existing small boxes or paper plates. Or the goodies can be wrapped in cloth napkins, bandannas, or specially embroidered, batiked, or otherwise ornamented cloths.

While *hamantashen* are the traditional Purim pastry, I've admired antique cookie molds for so long that I decided to make a ceramic Purim mold to shape my *mishloah manot* cookies. Figure 84 shows the triangular glazed mold with a figure of a jester carved into it alongside a plateful of cookies with the figure in relief. Molds can also be carved in wood if you have the skills, or, simplest of all (though not very satisfying from the point of view of making a lastingly lovely object), in plaster of Paris, which is inexpensive for classroom use. After the mold is carved, paint it with acrylic sealer or wax to prevent bits of plaster from sticking to the cookie dough.

Any dough that will hold an embossment can be used. I've made them with almond dough (p. 205), lemon—honey and gingerbread doughs (pp. 121, 120), as well as packaged peanut-butter-cookie mix.

173

HAMANTASHEN

Hamantashen can be made with almost any basic cookie or sweet yeast dough. It is said that to avoid eating unkosher food while she was in Ahasuerus' court, Queen Esther (like Daniel in Nebuchadnezzar's court) was a vegetarian, eating mainly fruits, beans, and nuts; poppy seeds were her favorite. Perhaps that accounts for the popularity of poppy-seed filling for *hamantashen*. Other favorites include prunes, particularly among Jews of Hungarian background, and plum jam combined with chopped nuts among Jews from Bohemia. For a very American version, consider filling the *hamantashen* with peanut butter and jelly (my boys loved them when they were little).

No matter what dough or filling you choose, the important thing about *hamantashen* is their triangular shape, meant to suggest the turbanlike hat worn by the villain Haman. Others say the shape represents the purse or pockets Haman planned to fill with Jewish loot. A recipe for *hamantash* cookie dough is given here; if you would like to make a yeast version, double the sweet dough recipe for the Cake of Milk and Honey (p. 229).

4	cups sifted flour	4	eggs, well beaten
4	teaspoons baking powder	⅓	cup vegetable oil
1	cup sugar		grated rind of 1 lemon or orange
¼	teaspoon salt		

Sift the flour, baking powder, sugar, and salt together into a large bowl. Add the eggs, oil, and grated rind. Mix very well. Turn onto a lightly floured surface and roll to a thickness of ⅛"–¼". Cut into 4" rounds. Place a heaping teaspoonful of your desired filling in the center of each round. Bring the edges of the cookie dough together to form a triangle. Pinch to seal, leaving a bit of filling visible in the center. Place on greased baking sheets and bake in a preheated 375° oven until lightly browned—about 30 minutes.

POPPY-SEED FILLING:

1	cup ground poppy seeds	¼	cup chopped dates
½	cup water or milk	¼	cup chopped raisins
⅓	cup honey or sugar		cinnamon and nutmeg to taste,
	pinch of salt		if desired

If the seeds are not purchased already ground, pour boiling water over them, drain, and put them through a fine-bladed grinder or mash them in a mortar. Combine them with the other ingredients in a saucepan and cook over low heat about 10 minutes, stirring frequently as it has a tendency to scorch. Cool before using. (The amount of honey or sugar can be reduced or increased to taste.)

PRUNE OR APRICOT FILLING: Cook 1 pound of pitted prunes or dried apricots in a little water until soft. Drain and chop fine. Add sugar, honey, cinnamon, nutmeg, and lemon or orange rind and juice to taste. Ground walnuts (½ cup) can also be added.

PLUM FILLING: Combine 2 cups of plum jam or preserves with ¾ cup of chopped nuts and ¾ cup of cake or bread crumbs.

85 (photo: Bill Aron)

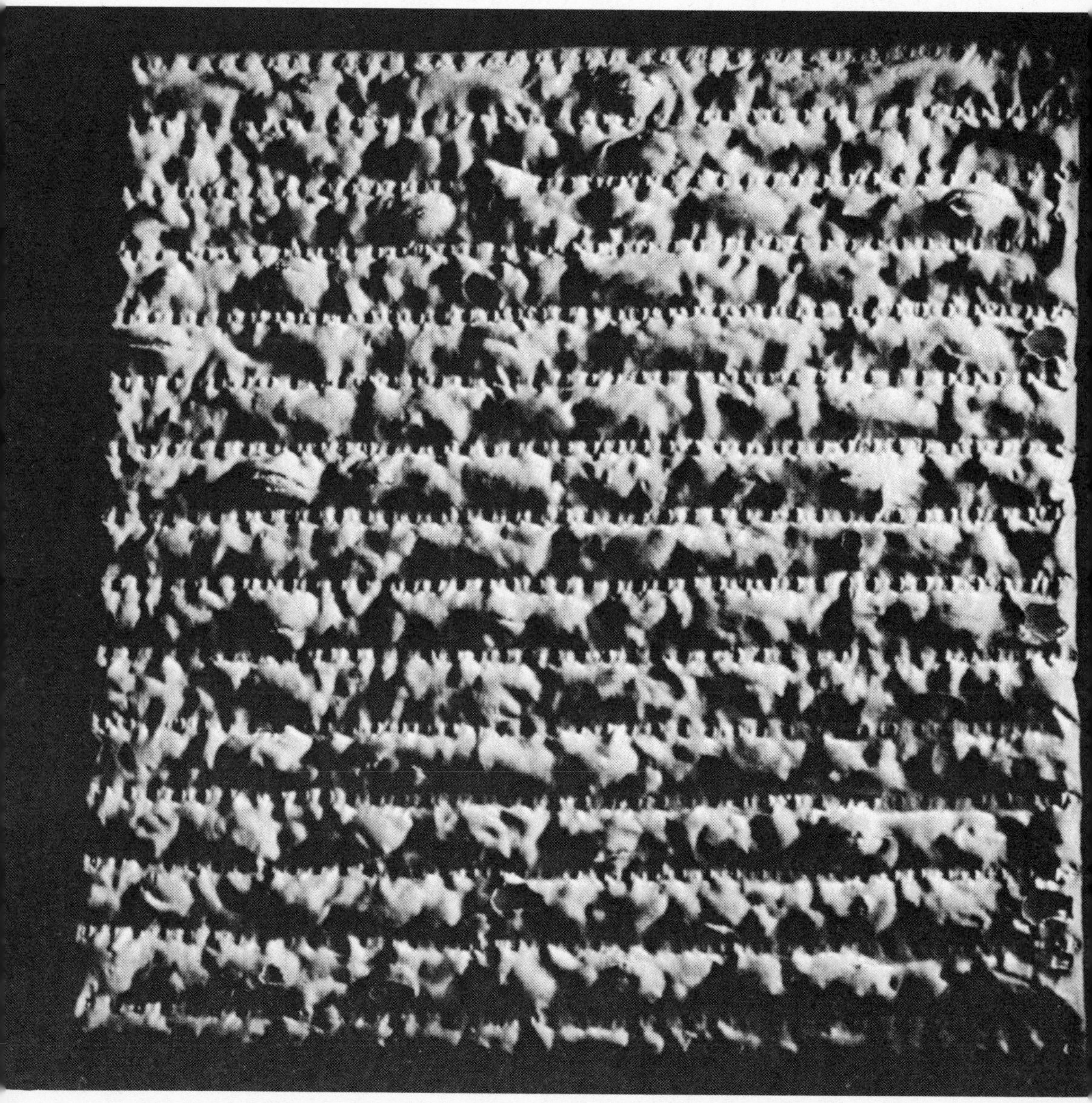

PASSOVER

Every year on the night of the full moon in the month of Nisan (March–April), Jews around the world enter into sacred time as we reenact the Exodus from Egypt in the oldest continually celebrated religious ceremony in the world. At the Seder table we suspend time in the conventional sense, and through ritual, theater, fantasy, food, and sense memory once again experience the liberation from Egyptian bondage, which becomes symbolic of all slaveries, for, as the Haggadah tells us, the festival is celebrated "because of that which the Lord did for *me* when *I* came forth out of Egypt." Passover is so old that its origins and even the meaning of the word Pesah are shrouded in history. Some historians believe that the roasting and eating of a ritually sacrificed lamb and the sprinkling of blood on the doorposts (tent flaps) were an ancient spring rite even before certain of the nomadic Hebrew tribes went down into Egypt and that it was to enable them to perform this ceremony that Moses petitioned the pharaoh for freedom. Later, when the Jews settled in the Promised Land, the agricultural New Year festival of the unleavened bread was coupled with the Passover celebration.

The customs and symbols of every holiday are always much older than their interpretations. As we sit at the Seder table and retell the ancient Passover stories and explain the symbolic food, all the epochs of Jewish history are there simultaneously. We feel ourselves to be a link in the unbroken chain of time, for not only once but, according to the Haggadah, in "every generation they rise against us to destroy us, but the Holy One delivers us from their hand." We know that it was not just our ancestors who were redeemed from bondage, but each of us has also been freed, and we cannot have real peace until everyone is free from oppression.

The ceremony we follow today has absorbed and reinterpreted the ancient derivations of the holiday and has gone almost unchanged since the Middle Ages. Among Ashkenazic Jews the Passover meal is called a Seder (meaning "order," since a set procedure is followed) and among the Sephardim it is called Haggadah ("narration" or "telling"). The book of ceremonial procedures, stories, and prayers used throughout the home service is also called a Haggadah. The table service and ceremonial meal become in a sense a theatrical event with parts for everyone. Although the thematic material is not simple, the children are at once the audience and the featured players. Invariably there are moist eyes as the youngest child who is able asks, "Why is this night different from all other nights?" The Seder is designed to respond to that question and to elaborate upon the themes of physical and spiritual oppression and liberation.

If you have never made your own Seder, all this lyricism about the beauty and meaning of it can be very intimidating. My intention is just the opposite. There is no such thing as the "perfect" Seder. Moses, Aaron, and Miriam wouldn't be any more at home with the Chief Rabbi of Israel than at your table if you are enthusiastically committed to the ideals expressed by the ritual. A good place to begin is by reading and studying the Haggadah.

But *which* Haggadah? It seems that every artist and every writer and every group for hundreds of years have wanted to make their own Haggadah—a striking testimony to the fact that this festival, its literature and folklore, are very deeply rooted in the Jewish heart. Since you will want to have a copy of the Haggadah for every guest (or every two guests) and it's much more pleasant and unconfusing if everyone has the same edition, buying Haggadahs can represent a considerable investment. Visit your local Hebrew bookstore or synagogue gift shop and browse shamelessly and intensely. Also ask your rabbi and friends to see copies of theirs. Years ago I directed a Sunday school for American children living in Madrid under the auspices of the United States Air Force on the base at Torrejon de Ardoz, Spain. The U.S.O. provided us with Haggadahs printed by the National Jewish Welfare Board. This was a simple, unfootnoted Haggadah in which the structure of the Seder could clearly be seen. Until recently I used it as my basic Haggadah. But every year I found more readings I wanted to include, and my collection of other Haggadahs with lovely illustrations or more poetic interpretations has grown so much, that I am now on the verge of buying a dozen matching books for next year's Seder. I have narrowed my choice down to the following four Haggadahs, and by next year I may be ready to make the commitment to one of them. They are:

A Passover Haggadah, with illustrations by Leonard Baskin (New York: Central Conference of American Rabbis), a careful combination of tradition and Reform Judaism; it includes stirring material

86 Frogs, one of the plagues with which God afflicted the Egyptians. Illustration from Mark Podwal, *Let My People Go: A Haggadah*

about the Holocaust as well as musical scores for Passover songs and hymns;

Let My People Go: A Haggadah, illustrated by Mark Podwal (New York: The Macmillan Company), which presents the traditional text with powerful drawings related to the plight of Soviet Jewry;

The Passover Haggadah, edited by Nahum N. Glatzer (New York: Schocken Books), the most scholarly of the four, with excellent English notes, explanations, and traditional quotations;

The Passover Haggadah, compiled and edited by Morris Silverman (Bridgeport, Conn.: The Prayer Book Press), which presents the traditional material clearly for the family Seder and includes readings pertaining to the Nazi annihilation of six million Jews, the creation of Israel, and the struggles of Soviet Jews.

As you can see, I favor the traditional Haggadah. Every year Haggadahs are written with attempts at "relevance" to this or that movement. While I like to collect examples of different Haggadahs and even to incorporate material from them into my Seder, I find that each year different issues demand our attention, and by Xeroxing or mimeographing additional readings we can add immediacy without sacrificing depth or historical continuity. This is not to say that the traditional Haggadah is static; it too changes, but slowly over time. Haggadahs for future generations will probably have memorial prayers for Holocaust victims and thanksgiving prayers for the reestablishment of the State of Israel as fixed parts of the order of the service. Now such prayers, if they are included, vary markedly from one Haggadah to another, and most of us use readings we have adapted or borrowed from various sources or written ourselves.

A custom which has grown up in recent years and is incorporated into many of the newer Haggadahs reflects our identification with the Jews of the Soviet Union, who are denied both the right to live full Jewish lives within their country and the right to emigrate to a country of their choice: this involves setting aside a *matzah* for the Soviet Jews (some people also have an empty chair and extra place setting). The leader lifts up the special *matzah*, shows it to the assembled company, and says:

> This is the *Matzah* of *Hope*.
>
> This *matzah*, which we set aside as a symbol of hope for the Jews of the Soviet Union, reminds us of the indestructible link that exists between us.
>
> As we observe this festival of freedom, we know that Soviet Jews are not free to learn of their past, or to learn the languages of their ancestors, or to pass on their religious traditions, or to train their children to be the teachers and rabbis of future generations. Nor are they free to leave without harassment.
>
> As they bravely struggle toward freedom, we add our voices to theirs, and we will be joined by other people of conscience who see the wrongs suffered by Soviet Jews. We pledge ourselves to continue to work for their freedom, for until all Jews are free, no Jew is free; until all people are free, no individual is free. Thus they will know that they have not been forgotten, and they that sit in darkness shall emerge into the light of freedom.*

I've included this reading here to show how Haggadahs do grow and change to interpret contemporary events in the light of our past. If your Haggadah does not have anything in it about the Soviet Jews, you might consider adding this, either when the *matzah* is first shown or, just before the meal takes place, when the *matzah* is distributed and tasted for the first time. Commemorative materials for Holocaust victims and the Warsaw Ghetto uprising (which began on Passover Eve) have not yet taken a definitive form, and I would suggest reading widely and coming up with your own pieces—maybe something from Anne Frank or Elie Weisel or a poem by Danny Siegel. Rabbi Herschel Matt suggests postponing opening the door for Elijah until the end of the Seder and including the Ritual of Remembrance there, climaxing with the singing of "*Eliyahu Hanavi*."

*The first two sentences of this reading have just about become standard; the rest is a composite with a few additions and variations of my own.

180

The Seder is a participatory event; as you do your preparatory reading of the Haggadah, think of the abilities and sensibilities of your guests and plan whom you will ask to read or chant the different parts. Ask them before the Seder begins—give them as much notice as possible so they can perhaps embellish the reading, if they want to, and children can practice and feel more confident. When you invite your guests, ask them if they would like to read in Hebrew or English. There is no point in embarrassing people at the Seder by asking them to read in Hebrew when they can't.

Decide how the four questions will be done. This year my niece will be old enough to recite the questions, yet my daughter is reluctant to relinquish her status as the "youngest child," so they will alternate, with Keren chanting in Hebrew and Shoshanah reciting the recently learned English questions. Like much of the Seder service, the four questions are traditionally chanted rather than simply read. And it is these familiar Passover melodies that reunite and stir us every year. As a child I chanted the questions in Yiddish to an East European melody; my children sing it in Hebrew, using the Israeli melody given here. (The remaining three questions will be found in any Haggadah.)

MA NISHTANAH

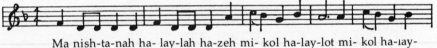

Ma nish-ta-nah ha- lay-lah ha-zeh mi- kol ha-lay-lot mi- kol ha-lay-

lot she-be- khol ha-lay-lot a-nu o-khlin ha- metz u-ma tzah ha- metz u-ma-

tzah ha- lay-la ha-zeh ha- lay-la ha-zeh ha- lay-la ha-zeh ha- lay-la ha-zeh ku-

lo ma- tzah she-be-

How is this night different from all other nights?

On all other nights we eat bread or *matzah*, on this night only *matzah*.

As you go over the Haggadah planning which readings to include, you might consider moving some of the songs usually sung

at the end further forward and interspersing them with the readings. This makes for a livelier Seder and keeps the children involved. Hebrew bookstores and synagogue gift shops have recordings with Passover melodies if you want to do some practicing beforehand. Also add your own stories and songs. Spirituals such as "Go Down, Moses," from the Black experience with slavery in this country, are popular at many Seders, as are some of the contemporary protest songs such as "We Shall Overcome" and "Blowing in the Wind."

Whatever Haggadah you pick, the basic order of the Seder is this:

1. *Kadesh**: The name of God is sanctified and the holiness of the festival proclaimed. *Kiddush* [blessing for the wine] is said and the cup of wine is drunk. The Sheheheyanu prayer is said, thanking God for having enabled us to reach this season.

2. *Urhatz:* The hands are washed but, since the meal is not begun at this point, the blessing is not said. A pitcher of water and a basin and towel are passed around, with the guests helping one another.

3. *Karpas:* Each participant dips a piece of green vegetable, symbolizing springtime and the renewal of nature, into salt water. Any green vegetable may be used—parsley, lettuce, and watercress are favorites. The salted water represents the tears of the Jewish mothers when their infant sons were killed by the Egyptians. Before eating the *karpas*, the following blessing is said:

ברוך אתה יי אלהינו מלך העולם בורא פרי האדמה:

Barukh atah adonai elohenu melekh ha-olam, bore peri ha-adamah. ["We praise You, O Lord our God, King of the Universe, who creates the fruit of the earth."]

4. *Yahatz:* There are three ceremonial pieces of *matzah* on the table. These are either covered by a layered cloth cover to separate the different *matzot* or are on a Seder tray. The three *matzot* signify the three ancient classes of Jews: Kohanim, Levites, and Israel (the priests, the temple attendants, and the people). In our own day we are still called up to the Torah in that order. The middle *matzah* is broken in two and the largest piece is wrapped in a napkin and put aside as the *afikomen*, to be eaten at the very end of the meal. The word *afikomen* derives from the Greek word for after-dinner entertainment and revelry; we call it the dessert, for after it is shared no more food is eaten. At some point during the Seder the wrapped

---

*Some people light the candles before the opening sanctification; others do it after. In any case, they are lit before the first cup of wine.

afikomen mysteriously disappears. In some families the leader of the ceremony hides it; in others, the children "steal" it. In any case, it must be ransomed from the children at the end of the meal so it can be eaten and the Seder ceremonies continued. This is a delightful and time-honored device to keep the children watching the Seder leader throughout the Haggadah reading.

5. *Maggid:* The story of the Exodus is narrated. This begins with one of the oldest parts of the Haggadah, the offering of hospitality to the poor, which is written not in Hebrew but in Aramaic. The leader of the Seder lifts the platter of *matzah* and says: "This is the bread of poverty which our forefathers ate in the land of Egypt. Let all who are hungry enter and eat; let all who are needy come to our Passover feast. This year we are here; next year may we be in the Land of Israel. This year we are slaves; next year may we be free." This is followed by the four questions, the parable of the four sons, the recital and description of the ten plagues with which God afflicted the Egyptians, the singing of *"Dayeynu"* (a stirring hymn of thanksgiving), and other powerful readings and prayers which together explain the meaning of the festival. The second cup of wine is drunk. Some people have the custom of dedicating each cup of wine to something special: the Jews of Syria, for example, or the memory of those slain in the latest terrorist attack, or the struggles of the women's movement or that of Black Americans.

6. *Rahatz:* Everyone washes his hands before finally beginning the meal. The following blessing is said:

ברוך אתה יי אלהינו מלך העולם אשר קדשנו במצותיו
וצונו על נטילת ידים.

["We praise You, O Lord our God, King of the Universe, who sanctifies us with Your commandments and enjoins upon us the *mitzvah* of washing the hands.]

7. *Motzi-matzah:* Pieces from the top and the broken middle *matzah* are distributed to all the participants. The usual *hamotzi* [blessing for bread] is recited, followed by the special blessing for the *matzah*. The *matzah* is eaten while reclining toward the left.

ברוך אתה יי אלהינו מלך העולם המוציא לחם מן הארץ.

Barukh atah adonai elohenu melekh ha-olam, hamotzi lehem min ha-aretz.
["We praise You, O Lord our God, King of the Universe, who brings forth sustenance from the earth."]

ברוך אתה יי אלהינו מלך העולם אשר קדשנו במצותיו
וצונו על אכילת מצה.

Barukh atah adonaı elohenu melekh ha-olam, asher kiddshanu be-mitzvatav vetzivanu al akhilat matzah.

["We praise You, O Lord our God, King of the Universe, who sanctifies us with Your commandments and enjoined upon us the *mitzvah* of eating unleavened bread."]

9. *Maror:* Bitter herbs—usually horseradish—are dipped in *haroset,* a mixture of ground fruit, nuts, spices, and wine, and eaten. The bitterness of the horseradish is reminiscent of the bitterness of slavery. The *haroset* is meant to look like the mortar with which we labored as slaves in Egypt.

10. *Korekh:* The bottom *matzah* is broken and every participant receives two small pieces; these are made into "Hillel sandwiches" with a little bit of the *maror.* This is a custom begun by the sage Hillel, who felt that the bread of poverty—which then became the bread of freedom—should be eaten with a reminder of the bitterness of slavery, so that in times of slavery we would keep alive the hope of freedom and in times of freedom we would not forget the bitterness of oppression.

11. *Shulhan orekh:* The festival meal is served. It is customary to begin the meal with a hard-boiled egg dipped in salt water. For many this is a sign of mourning for the destruction of the Temple; it is also a sign of new life and rebirth.

12. *Tzafun:* Now is the time to rescue the hidden *matzah* from the children so that it can be divided among the participants and eaten and then the Seder continued. The *afikomen* is said to be a substitute for the pascal lamb. In ancient days the roasted lamb was the last thing eaten at the Passover feast, as is the *afikomen* today. The third cup of wine is filled.

13. *Barekh:* The Grace after Meals is chanted. The third cup of wine is drunk while reclining. The wine cup is filled for the fourth time. The door is opened for Elijah, the beloved prophet of hope. In the Middle Ages the door was opened so that all passersby could see how baseless were the blood-libel accusations against Jews. Elijah's cup is also filled. *"Eliyahu Hanavi"* is sung. Hallel [psalms of praise] are sung and recited, and the fourth cup of wine is drunk.

14. *Nirtzah:* The Seder is officially concluded with the phrase ["Next year may we celebrate in Jerusalem."]

לשנה הבאה בירושלים

Songs were interspersed throughout the Seder, but now that it is "officially" concluded, the singing goes on until everyone is exhausted.

That is the basic outline of the Seder and is what you will find amplified in every Haggadah. I include it here both for those people who have Haggadahs in which it is difficult to see this structure and for those readers who have never been to a Seder or seen a Haggadah, in the hope that they will get some idea of what Passover Eve is all about. The midrashic parable of the four sons, related during the evening, recognizes that at the Seder there are many different kinds of people with different levels of understanding and involvement, and it is the leader's responsibility to clarify the story and meanings according to the capacity of each participant.

Some years ago at a community Seder in Spain, I heard a song that retold the story of the four sons, keeping the meaning clear and making it accessible to contemporary Americans (sometimes the traditional rabbinic ramblings in the Haggadah are a bit hard to follow). The song, called "The Ballad of the Four Sons," was sung to the melody of "Clementine." I have since heard it sung to "La Cucaracha" as well. I picked up a mimeographed song sheet with the words on it and have since used it at all of my Seders. Try as I might, I have not been able to locate the lyricist. If he or she reads these words, please step forward and allow me to congratulate you and to acknowledge you properly. Those who might object to including such non-Jewish melodies in the Seder service should be reminded that such time-honored favorites as *"Had Gadya"* and *"Ehad Mi Yodea"* had their origins in the non-Jewish world.

BALLAD OF THE FOUR SONS

Said the father to his children,
"At the Seder you will dine,
You will eat your fill of *matzah,*
You will drink four cups of wine."

Now this father had no daughters,
But his sons, they numbered four,
One was wise and one was wicked,
One was simple and a bore.

And the fourth was sweet and winsome,
He was young and he was small;
While his brothers asked the questions,
He could hardly ask at all.

185

Said the wise one to his father,
"Would you please explain the laws
Of the customs of the Seder,
Will you please explain the cause."

And the father proudly answered,
"As our fathers ate in speed,
Ate the pascal lamb ere midnight
And from slavery were freed,

"So we follow their example
And ere midnight must complete
All the Seder, and we should not
After twelve remain to eat."

Then did sneer the son so wicked,
"What does all this mean to you?"
And his father's voice was bitter
As his grief and anger grew.

"If yourself you don't consider
As a Son of Israel,
Then for you this has no meaning,
You could be a slave as well."

Then the simple son said simply,
"What is this?" And quietly
The good father told his offspring,
"We were freed from slavery."

But the youngest son was silent,
For he could not ask at all,
And his eyes were bright with wonder
As his father told him all.

My dear children, heed the lesson
And remember evermore
What the father told his children,
Told his sons that numbered four.

PREPARING FOR YOUR SEDER

In the traditional Jewish household, preparations for Passover
begin weeks before the holiday. If possible, new clothes are bought
for the children and the house is thoroughly scrubbed down. Just as

87 Searching for the *hametz* before Passover. Engraving from Bernard Picart, *Cérémonies et coutumes religieuses de tous les peuples du monde* (Amsterdam, 1723)

before Rosh Hashanah we do a spiritual housecleaning, before Passover we physically scour away the accumulated debris of the year. Before the days of packaged kosher-for-Passover foods, most of the special foods had to be prepared at home as well. All the cooking utensils and dishes are either made kosher for Passover by boiling or baking them for required amounts of time, or they are replaced for the eight days of Passover with special dishes reserved for the holiday and stored away the rest of the year. So intense are these spring housecleaning activities that Iraqi women have called Passover *"az frihli"*—"the festival of falling apart." During the eight days of Passover, no bread or any food with any trace of leavening or fermentation is eaten. So the cleaning is for the express purpose of ridding the household of all traces of leavened foodstuffs, *hametz*. While the roots of this passion for cleanliness can be traced to a superstitious desire to get rid of the last traces of the winter's "evil spirits" and to the agricultural preparations for a new season, our sages have symbolically compared *hametz*, the leaven in dough, to the corrupting influences in human life. By cleaning our homes of the last bits of *hametz*, we are trying to liberate ourselves from those habits and attitudes that mar our personal behavior and our relationships with others.

There is a nice custom that takes place on the evening before the night of the first Seder; some people may find it archaic, but it is both fun and, if seen in a deeper light, quite meaningful. The entire family searches the house for the last remaining bits of *hametz*. This "search" is carried out by candlelight, with the children holding the candles. (Flashlights could be used if the child is too young to hold a candle safely.) When they find the *hametz*, which has been purposely left behind after the meticulous housecleaning, a feather is used to brush it into a wooden spoon or bowl. I use a paper plate, because the next morning the accumulated *hametz* is burned along with the container it is in. Before starting the ancient ceremony of searching for and removing leaven (*bedikat hametz* and *biur hametz*), the following blessing is said:

"We praise You, O Lord our God, King of the Universe, who has sanctified us with Your commandments and enjoined upon us the *mitzvah* of removing *hametz* before Pesah."

After completing the search and wrapping all the *hametz* and container together, one says:

"May any *hametz* in my possession, which I have not seen or removed, be considered as nonexistent and regarded as mere dust of the earth."

On the following morning after breakfast, the package of leaven is burned and the following declaration is said:

"May all *hametz* in my possession, whether I have seen it or not, or whether I have removed it or not, be regarded as nonexistent and considered as mere dust of the earth."

As we have already seen, the Passover Seder is more than a meal or a family reunion; on that night the table becomes an altar and a stage as well as the setting for a special dinner. Set the table with the best you have. On it should be:

Candles to be lit at the beginning of the evening; these add an aura of spirituality to the event.

A ceremonial Seder plate placed in front of the leader. On it are: a roasted lamb shank bone (*zeroa*), representing the ancient sacrifice of the pascal lamb; a roasted egg (*betzah*), which symbolizes the required offerings brought to the Temple on all festivals and our mourning for the destruction of the Temple; bitter herbs (*maror*), usually horseradish (sliced, whole, or grated), to remind us of the bitterness of slavery; greens (*karpas*), such as parsley or lettuce, to represent spring and renewal; and a mixture of ground spiced fruits and nuts (*haroset*), resembling the mortar we used as slaves in Egypt.

Matzah. Three pieces (representing Kohanim, Levites, and Israel)

88 (photo: Bill Aron)

are covered with a layered *matzah* cloth separating them, or placed on a tiered Seder plate. There may also be another piece of *matzah* designated as the *Matzah* of Hope for the Soviet Jews, and either underneath the ceremonial *matzot* or on another plate on the table enough *matzah* for the group to eat with the meal (though this can of course be brought out when the meal is served). A napkin or little sack for the *afikomen* should also be provided.*

The cup of Elijah, filled with wine and displayed on the table throughout the Seder, in the hope that the prophet may appear to announce the coming of the Messianic Era.

Salt water in small dishes conveniently located around the table, in which to dip the greens and the egg that will begin the meal. It is also a good idea, if you are having many guests, to have several dishes of greens, *haroset*, and *maror* conveniently placed for every two or three guests or even divided individual dishes. My own preference, however, unless the assembled company is huge, is to have everyone share the ritual foods from the ceremonial plate. I enjoy the communal feeling of passing and helping one another.

*If you are going to provide a reward for the finder of the *afikomen*, I'd suggest that you have prizes ready for all the children and perhaps a ribbon or lollipop in addition for the winner.

189

A wine cup and a Haggadah at every setting. You also may want to provide *yarmulkas* for those guests who want them and do not have their own.

Either on the table or on a convenient sideboard, have a pitcher of water, a basin, and some decorative hand towels for the hand-washing. Ceremonial sets have been made in silver, brass, and ceramic, but if you don't have anything specifically designed for Passover, any lovely pitcher and bowl will do. One could certainly embellish the towels with embroidered decorative motifs.

The leader and preferably every guest should have pillows upon which to recline when reciting parts of the service. This custom goes back to Graeco-Roman times, when it was the practice at luxurious dinners for free men to lie on cushions; only slaves ate hurriedly. During the Middle Ages the rabbis tried to abolish this custom, reasoning that we were emulating the decadence of a style of life based on a slave economy; they weren't successful, and the pillows remain with us today as symbols of our freedom.

Beautiful ritual objects to grace the Seder table are increasingly available. As well as commercially manufactured items, there are handmade things by the growing number of people in the United States and in Israel who are committing themselves to the creation of attractive contemporary Judaica. You might want to try your hand at making some of the necessary items yourself. My book *The Work of Our Hands: Jewish Needlecraft for Today* has designs and patterns for *matzah* covers, pillows, towels, and an *afikomen* bag. If you admire hand embroidery but do not feel ready to take on an elaborate project, consider recycling some already existing embroideries and turning articles such as unused dresser scarves into Passover towels and *matzah* and cushion covers. For years at garage sales and flea markets I could not pass up odd pieces of old embroidery. I am very partial to the basket-of-flowers design so common in American folk needlework (it is also particularly suitable for the spring motif of Passover). In Fig. 88 you can see some of the old embroideries which were rescued and transformed into useful Passover articles.

The *matzah* cover was originally a long, narrow bureau scarf; thus, there was enough fabric for all four layers necessary to make a *matzah* cover with three pockets. The back also has a basket of flowers on it. Using embroidery thread in the same bright blue as other parts of the original embroidery, I added the words הא לחמא עניא ["Behold the bread of affliction"]. A small piece of the leftover fabric was made into a sack to contain the *afikomen;*

there was plenty of lace all around the scarf to use the parts that were not worn out for the edges of both articles. The cushion cover on the leader's chair was another bureau scarf which had a grid pattern embroidered on it, with flowers at each intersecting corner. The existing embroidered pattern conveniently provided fourteen squares in which I embroidered the order of the Seder service beginning with קדש [kadesh] and ending with נרצה [nirtzah]. For both objects I used a simple outline stitch. Another of the pillow covers (not seen here) for the youngest child has the opening phrase of the four questions on it, and yet another has the closing phrase of the Seder: "Next year in Jerusalem." Taken all together, it looks as if I had a very prolific grandmother; and since the work was probably done by *somebody's* grandmother, it adds to the traditional feeling of the evening. To set off the pastel embroideries and the old white cloths they were made on, I use a deep purple tablecloth and napkins. This may seem jarringly modern until we remember that when the tent of worship in the desert was made, one of its principal colors was purple.

If embroidery doesn't appeal to you, consider making some of the Passover articles using the batik processes described in the Rosh Hashanah chapter. Students at Yadaim, the Brandeis Hillel Jewish Craft Workshop, produced some lovely batik textiles for the holiday. Particularly charming were cushions in different forms—for example, one in the shape of a fish bearing the phrase כלנו מסבין "kulanu mesubin" ["We recline"] decoratively incorporated into its scales.

My sister and I collaborated on a pillow to give to our father this year as a Passover gift. I screen-printed the design on the fabric, using the same design we had used for our parents' anniversary party invitation (Fig. 30). She assembled it into a cushion, using brown velvet as the backing and the cording to complement the gold color of the front fabric. The Hebrew phrase, which is from the prayer book, says: "From generation to generation we will proclaim Your greatness."

The tiered Seder plate, with shelves for the three ceremonial *matzot* and purchased Bohemian glassware for the ritual foods (Fig. 89), was designed and made especially for this book by Myron Tupa. He has also provided the pattern for the shelves and the instructional diagram to help you make a similar one at home or using the facilities of a community center or school workshop.

191

89 Tiered walnut Seder plate, with glass dishes for the ceremonial foods (photo: Kenneth M. Bernstein)

The Seder plate was made of walnut. Select your wood by going to your local lumberyard and seeing what they have in the size you need. You want wood that will have a nice finished edge all around. If the wood isn't wide enough, it can be pieced. You can use a good grade of plywood (there are some on the market that do have an attractive edge when cut and finished) or a seasoned hardwood.

You will need four 11" x ½" squares and a length of ⅜" dowel to be cut into four 5¼" lengths. Buy a 6' length of 1" stock to be cut into 12" lengths and used to space the shelves when you assemble everything.

Enlarge the pattern in Fig. 90 and draw it onto heavy brown paper. Place the paper pattern on the wood and draw lightly around it with a pencil; mark the ⅜" holes for the dowels. Draw the shape on all four pieces of wood.

Cut out the gently curved square shapes using a hand (coping) or power saw. If you have a band saw, the wood can be stacked and all the shelves cut simultaneously.

Decide which shelf will be the top and, using a twist drill, bore ⅜" holes halfway through the wood of the four corners in the spots indicated on the pattern. Drill holes all the way through the four corners of the remaining three shelves. Finish the edges of the shelves with a file and sandpaper.

Sand the dowels lightly and stain them if desired. The shelves also should be sanded, steel-wooled, and finished before assembly. Apply stain according to the manufacturer's directions. Mineral oil was used for the final finish because it gives wood a pleasant luster, is not poisonous, and does not become rancid as would vegetable oil.

To assemble: Lay the top shelf upside down on your work surface. Place 1″ spacer bars on the shelf and place the second shelf on the spacer bars. Stack the remaining two shelves with 1″ spacer bars between them, as shown in the diagram. Make certain that all the holes align. Insert the dowels into the holes and tap them lightly with a wooden mallet or block of wood to drive them into the top shelf.

Carefully turn the assembled Seder plate right side up, keeping the spacer bars in place.

Use a brad about the size of a circular toothpick in the drill chuck (or a very fine drill bit) to drill holes through all four edges of each shelf three-quarters of the way into the dowel. Trim the points from twelve toothpicks, dip them into white glue, and insert them into the holes, driving them through the shelf edge into the dowel. The toothpicks act as miniature pegs, holding the shelves to the legs instead of nails. Trim the edge of the toothpick with a hobby knife and sand it with fine sandpaper. Finish with steel wool. A drop of glue can be placed in the holes in the top shelf to hold the dowels permanently.

The ceremonial foods can be placed directly on the top wooden surface, but I prefer using dishes, because some of the food is

90 Pattern for one-quarter of the shelf (drawing: Myron Tupa)

91 Assembling the Seder plate (drawing: Myron Tupa)

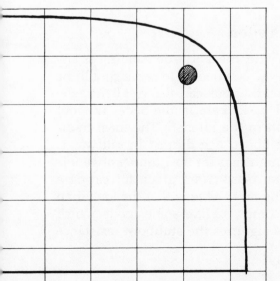

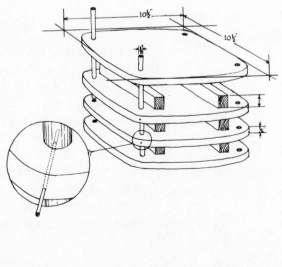

92 (photo: Kenneth M. Bernstein)

runny. If you are skilled at ceramics or metalwork, the dishes could be made of those materials. We were delighted to find the Bohemian glass dishes and wine goblet reasonably priced in a local store, because most of the designer's family comes from Czechoslovakia. An extra wooden plate to hold the *matzot* for the meal was made using the same pattern as that for the tiered plate. Directions and a pattern for the embroidered *matzah* cover shown with it in Fig. 92 can be found in *The Work of Our Hands*.

It can't be denied that it is nice to have lovely ceremonial objects, but don't let the lack of them prevent you from making a festive and meaningful Seder. You might find attractive dishes tucked in the back of your own china closet or at a shop, and by assembling them on a tray you can form your own Seder plate.

SEDER FOOD

Planning the food for the festive Seder meal is as demanding as any of the other preparations. Whatever you decide to serve should be cooked as early as possible, so that the cook can also rest before the guests arrive and can enjoy and participate in the Seder without worrying about what is going on in the kitchen. The meal traditionally begins by eating a hard-boiled egg dipped in salt water. Early in the day boil and peel enough eggs for the number of people who will be at the Seder. Several reasons are given for eating a hard-boiled egg at the onset of the meal. One is that the longer an egg is cooked the harder it becomes, unlike some foods which when cooked become softer; this signifies the stubborn resistance

194

of the Jews to those who tried to destroy us. The egg is also seen as a sign of mourning for the destruction of the Temple. Like most ancient customs it also has a universal seasonal meaning, that of new life and the emergence of spring.

Certain foods are so thoroughly associated with Passover that it is impossible to imagine a Seder without them. There is a Yiddish expression that describes a person who is not particularly interested in the narrative of the Exodus as someone who "comes to the Seder for the *knaydlakh* [*matzah* balls], not the Haggadah." Many of these traditional dishes, like the *knaydlakh*, are of East European origin, since that is where most of America's Jews come from. Recognizing our changing diets, and because the heavy East European food coupled with the wine tends to make everyone too sleepy to enjoy the continued readings and singing after the meal, I serve *small* portions of the traditional gefilte fish, followed by clear chicken soup with *knaydlakh*, but then have an Israeli-inspired Orange Baked Chicken as the main course, with usually the first asparagus of the season as an accompaniment. For dessert I like to emphasize spring again and have strawberries in raspberry sauce. I also like to serve roast lamb which has been marinated, Mediterranean style, in a mixture of lemon juice, garlic, thyme, and oregano, because it is reminiscent of the early Passover celebrations. For exactly the same reason many people object to serving any roasted food, and particularly lamb. I leave it to you to find the *minhag* [custom] that is most comfortable for you.

Adults usually come to the Seder table hungry, but it is a good idea to let children have both a nap and a snack in the late afternoon, so that they don't make themselves and everyone else miserable during the Seder.

Most people will offer to help with the Seder meal. Unless you have very good reasons for wanting to do it all yourself, it not only will make the task lighter and more enjoyable for you, but will give your guests a feeling of being participants rather than tourists. They might help not only by bringing something for the meal but also by preparing one of the ceremonial foods (roasting a shank bone can be quite an experience if you've never done it). Some people buy a horseradish root well in advance of Passover and sprout leaves from the top of it by setting the cut-off top in a dish of water, which is also a nice pre-holiday project. If anyone offers to bring wine, make sure he knows that everyone drinks at least four cups and how many people there will be.

The number of Jewish cookbooks seems to proliferate each time I go to the bookstore, and almost every one has a Passover section. The manufacturers of Passover foods also have recipe booklets, so with the wealth of available material I'm sure you will easily discover your own favorites. However, I can't resist sharing a few of mine with you.

HAROSET

Haroset is a mixture of fruits, wine, and spices chopped or ground together in such a way as to resemble the mortar which we used to build the pyramids when we were slaves. Unfortunately, some people make it taste as unappetizing as it looks. This is not necessary; only the bitter herbs are meant to be momentarily sharp. In this country we are most familiar with the East and Central European version of *haroset,* but Jews around the world use whatever fruits are local and available and have come up with some delicious concoctions. Why not prepare several batches, one for the traditionalists and another in order to share the taste of Passover as it is experienced in other communities?

EAST EUROPEAN HAROSET

1	cup chopped apple	2	teaspoons cinnamon
½	cup chopped walnuts or almonds		red wine (I use sweet wine)

Mix the apple, nuts, and cinnamon, using just enough wine to add color and bind it. Some people use dry wine. I usually add honey even when I use sweet wine.

ISRAELI HAROSET

1	apple, chopped	1	teaspoon cinnamon
3	bananas, mashed	½	cup red wine (dry or
	juice and grated rind of 1 orange		sweet to taste)
15	dates, chopped		sugar or honey, if desired
1	cup almonds or peanuts, chopped		matzah meal, if needed

Combine the fruit, nuts, cinnamon, and wine. If it is more liquid than you like, add matzah meal until it is the consistency you want it to be.

YEMENITE HAROSET

10	dates, chopped	1	teaspoon ginger powder
10	figs, chopped		red wine
1	tablespoon sesame seeds		matzah meal

Combine the fruit, seeds, and ginger. Add red wine and matzah meal to bring it to the consistency you want.

GREEK HAROSET

20	large dates, chopped	½	cup almonds, chopped
¾	cup walnuts, ground		trace of grated lemon peel
1	cup raisins, chopped		red wine

Combine the fruit and nuts. Add the wine to bring it to the desired consistency.

ORANGE BAKED CHICKEN (serves 6)

2	2½-pound frying chickens, cut up (or 8 chicken breasts or 8 chicken legs)	2	large onions, peeled and thinly sliced
2	teaspoons salt	1½	cups orange juice
¼	teaspoon black pepper	2	unpeeled juice oranges, sliced and seeded
⅓	cup cakemeal	2	cans mandarin orange segments or 4 navel oranges, peeled and sliced
½	cup salad oil		
2	teaspoons celery seeds		

Wash and dry the chicken parts. Combine the salt, pepper, and meal in a small paper bag. Shake the chicken in the bag, a few pieces at a time, to coat them evenly. Heat the salad oil in a large frying pan; add the chicken, skin side down; sprinkle with celery seeds. Keep the heat low and brown the chicken on both sides. When golden brown, place the chicken, skin sides up, in a 2-quart casserole. In the same skillet, sauté the onions until soft. Add the orange juice and heat it to the boiling point in order to loosen all of the crust particles from the pan. Pour this over the chicken, lifting it so the liquid and some of the onions get underneath the chicken parts. Place the orange slices on top of the chicken; cover and bake at 350° for 1 hour or until tender. To serve, remove the cooked oranges and replace them with the mandarin orange segments or freshly cut navel oranges.

PASSOVER POPOVERS

I really enjoy not eating bread for the week of Passover and feeling the distinction between the holiday and the rest of the year. But when the Sabbath which falls during that week arrives, *matzah* has already lost its novelty and doesn't seem special enough to have for the Friday-night meal. Other recipes I've tried for Passover rolls produce dense and heavy products. This one is so light and delicious that my family wants me to make them all year.

¾	cup water	½	teaspoon salt
¼	cup salad oil	1	cup matzah meal (regular or cake meal)
3	tablespoons sugar	3	eggs

Combine the water, salad oil, sugar, and salt in a large saucepan and bring to a boil. Remove from the heat and stir in the matzah meal. Beat the eggs, one at a time, and add each to the matzah-meal mixture, mixing well after each addition.

Wet your hands and form the very sticky dough into six large balls. Place them on a lightly greased baking sheet, leaving 2″ between each ball. Bake in a preheated 400° oven on the center rack. They puff up nicely. If desired, they can of course be made smaller. I've made them with honey instead of sugar, and they taste good but become heavier.

93 "Elijah the Prophet," illustration from Leonard Baskin, *A Passover Haggadah* (photo: courtesy Central Conference of American Rabbis)

94 A group of marchers, led by 102-year-old Yosef Doron, arriving in Jerusalem at the end of a three-day march (photo: courtesy Israeli Government Press Office)

ISRAELI INDEPENDENCE DAY

Sing with gladness . . . offer praises and say: "The Lord has saved His people, the remnant of Israel . . . gathered them from the ends of the earth. . . . The Lord has ransomed Jacob and redeemed him from the hand that is stronger than he. And they shall come and sing in the height of Zion . . . the young and the old together; for I will turn their mourning into joy, and will comfort them and make them rejoice from their sorrow."

—Jeremiah 31:7–8, 11–13

Israel's Independence Day, also called by its Hebrew name, Yom Ha-atzmaut, commemorates the establishment of the Jewish State on May 14, 1948. The holiday is celebrated by the Hebrew calendar on the fifth day of the month of Iyar. During centuries of exile the Jews have longed to return to the Holy Land, and the dream of return has been a recurrent theme in liturgy and poetry for all that time. In our own century we have been witness to an incredible ingathering as Jews from more than seventy countries "returned" home.

It takes generations of observance for a holiday to take on a distinctive character and manner of celebration; as we have seen with many of the other festivals discussed in this book, they wax and wane in popularity and profundity depending on many external circumstances and influences. The Reform Synagogue movement sees the establishment of the State of Israel in deeply religious terms and is working on developing suitable liturgy for the holiday; segments of the Orthodox community, on the other hand, are resistant to seeing the event as a partial fulfillment of the biblical prophecies foretelling the Return to Zion. The recitation of half-Hallel [psalms of praise] has been generally accepted, but exception is still taken to the recital of the accompanying blessing. I think it is terribly exciting to be around at the time when our own acts of participation and involvement may very well influence the course of a holiday our descendants will be celebrating as an ancient event.

In Israel Yom Ha-atzmaut is celebrated with official and unoffi-

95

cial parades and street parties. Platforms are set up in the city
squares for groups of entertainers; there are fireworks and much
singing and dancing. In Israeli embassies and consulates around
the world, receptions are held for the diplomatic community and
other well-wishers. On many college campuses in the United States
it is quite common for the Israeli students to sponsor an open
house, with Israeli food and music and sometimes professional entertainment. In recent years more American Jewish institutions
have been sponsoring Israeli-style activities of various sorts to
coincide with Israeli Independence Day. These include film festivals, local parades, and art shows, as well as dances and family
picnics.

You might want to plan a smaller gathering at home either before
or after such an event. Or, if there is no public celebration in your
area, consider organizing a cultural event yourself or together with
a few friends. If you decide to sell tickets, you can donate the
money to the Jewish National Fund, knowing that it will go to insure the possibility of many more years of Independence Day celebrations. Base the event on Israeli music, dance, and food. It is possible to rent Israeli films and hire Israeli performers. A call to your
nearest Israeli consulate will be very helpful in determining some of
the possibilities. There are also Israeli dance teachers who will
come and spend an informal evening with your group (for a fee),
teaching *you* how to dance. Your Jewish Center, synagogue, or
Hillel group might know of such a teacher.*

As party invitations or decorations, you might make paper-cut
dancing figures such as those shown at the beginning of this chapter. They are just a bit more complicated than the more common
paper dolls we made as children. These silhouettes were made by

*Also see my book *The Jewish Yellow Pages* for names and addresses of dance
teachers, performers, and film rentals.

folding a 12" x 18" sheet of construction paper in fourths. The figures were drawn with white pencil on one-fourth of the paper and then cut through all the folded layers simultaneously, using sharp scissors and a hobby utility knife. This gave me sixteen dancers to arrange as I liked. They can all be strung together to hang as a streamer, or they can be cut into smaller groups, with the date and time of the party written in white or a contrasting color, and used as the invitation.

If the weather in your area is dependable, you might want to plan your party as an outdoor *kumzits* ["come and sit"] in the evening around a campfire. In Israel many localities will have a public *kumzits* on the eve of Yom Ha-atzmaut and roast a whole sheep in the town square. The hindquarters of animals are not kosher (it is said because of the laming of Jacob when he struggled with the angel). In Israel there are specialists who can remove the necessary blood vessels and make the meat kosher. It is not easy to find someone in this country to do that and it can make the meat very expensive, but if possible it would be a lot of fun to roast a whole lamb. Or, if you are cooking over an open fire and you have a spit, try roasting a lamb shoulder over a bed of coals, or make shashlik according to the recipe given below.

A very simple way to mark the occasion is to think of it as a birthday party: have a birthday cake at the end of a family meal or invite over a few friends for birthday cake and coffee. This year, with Israel reaching the mature age of thirty, and because elaborately frosted birthday cakes seem to be losing their appeal for a diet-conscious generation, I made a tiered cookie-cake. Instead of birthday candles, I decorated the cake with thirty tiny Israeli flags which I bought from a Jewish bookstore. On the table I put a lit seven-branched *menorah*. Thus, the oldest of Jewish symbols is brought together with the newest.

ALMOND COOKIE-CAKE

This cake is made of rings of cookie dough, baked separately and stacked with a bit of frosting to hold them together. Cakes like this are often served at Norwegian weddings or anniversaries, with each ring representing a year of marriage. By adjusting the quantity of dough or the size of the rings, you can vary the size and shape of the finished cake. Instead of frosting, you can use a little jam to hold the rings together or even stack them with no "cement" and dust

the whole lightly with confectioners' sugar. Guests help themselves by breaking off serving-size pieces.

For a thirteen-ring cake as shown:

6¾	cups flour	3	cups shortening
2¼	cups sugar	4	medium eggs, beaten
¾	teaspoon baking powder	1	tablespoon almond extract
1½	teaspoons salt		

Sift the flour, sugar, baking powder, and salt together in a large bowl. Use a pastry blender or two knives to cut the shortening into the dry ingredients until the mixture is full of fine lumps. Add the eggs and almond extract, beating very well, until a soft dough is formed.

To make the rings, use a cookie press fitted with a ¾" metal tip, or roll out thirteen ¾" ropes in graduated lengths onto ungreased cookie sheets. The first strip for the smallest ring should be 4" long; each succeeding strip is 1½" longer, until the thirteenth strip measures 22". For the longest ropes, press several shorter pieces gently together. I really prefer a cookie press for this cake; if you don't have one, you might want to borrow one. It produces a handsomer finished product. The cake shown in the picture was done without a cookie press, because after I'd mixed the dough I discovered that mine was broken.

Shape each strip into a ring; gently press the ends together to join them. Bake each large ring separately on a cookie sheet; several small ones can be baked on the same sheet, allowing at least 3" between them. Bake in a moderate oven (350–375°) for 12–15 minutes, until lightly browned. Cool 10 minutes on the cookie sheet; gently loosen and slide onto a wire rack to complete cooling.

When all the cookies are baked and cooled, slide the largest onto a serving plate and decorate it with loops of any simple frosting or dabs of jam. Put the next largest ring in place before the frosting sets, and continue until all the rings are in place.

SHASHLIK

It is said that in biblical days meat from the sacrifices was prepared this way for the priests.

2	pounds tender lamb	2	cloves minced garlic
½	cup olive oil		salt and pepper to taste

96 (photo: Bill Aron)

Cut the meat into 1" cubes. Combine the oil, garlic, salt, and pepper, and marinate the meat for at least ½ hour, preferably longer. String the meat on skewers and broil. It is most traditional and delicious grilled over a bed of wood coals. Some people like to add a bit of oregano, wine, lemon juice, and/or thyme to the marinade. Experiment until you find your favorite combination. You can also vary the shashlik by alternating the meat cubes with tiny onions, tomatoes, or cubes of green pepper. The grilled meat cubes can be served over a bed of rice or informally piled into fresh pita pockets and augmented with a bit of salad.

PITA

Pita, which is also called Syrian or Armenian bread and is eaten throughout the Middle East, is a round flat bread with a natural "pocket" in the center. Because it is so adaptable as well as delicious, it has become quite popular in the United States. Cutting a round loaf in half provides two bread envelopes which can be filled with anything from Israeli *falafel* (see next recipe) to Mexican chili to hot dogs or tuna-fish salad. Pita is also good when cut into small pieces and used to scoop up dip or sauces (because of its softness, it is more flexible than the usual cracker and so is as good with runny sauces as with hard cheese). It is also good cut into strips, buttered, and baked in a slow oven until it is crisp and then served instead of crackers with soup or salad. Once baked and cooled, it should not be allowed to harden but should be stored in a plastic bag in either the refrigerator or freezer. Reheat it in a 300° oven for about 5 minutes.

3	packages dry yeast	1	teaspoon salt
1	teaspoon sugar	½	cup cornmeal
1¼	cups lukewarm water		
4	cups flour (all-purpose, or try half whole wheat and half white)		

Dissolve the sugar and yeast in the lukewarm water, stirring gently. Allow it to begin to ferment in a warm place for about 5 minutes. Sift the flour and salt into a large bowl. Make a well in the flour mixture and stir in the dissolved yeast mixture. Turn the dough out onto a floured work surface and knead well until it is smooth and elastic. Rinse out the bowl with warm water, dry it, and grease it lightly with salad oil. Place the kneaded dough in the bowl, turning it to grease all surfaces. Cover with a damp towel and let the dough rise in a warm, draft-free place for about 45 minutes to 1 hour, or until doubled in bulk.

Punch the dough down, turn it out onto a floured surface, and allow it to rest for 10 minutes. Divide it into six equal parts and shape these into balls. Don't let the balls stick together. Cover them with a towel and allow the dough to rest again for 30 minutes.

Preheat the oven to 500°. Flatten each ball with a floured rolling pin and roll each into a circle approximately 8" across and ⅛" thick. Sprinkle cornmeal on 3 large baking sheets and transfer the flat breads onto the sheets, placing two breads on each sheet. Bake one sheet at a time on the center rack of the oven, unless your oven is large enough to accommodate more than one or two sheets side by side. Bake for 5–8 minutes, until the breads have puffed up and are just very lightly browned. It helps if you have a window in your oven door, but in any case don't open the oven until the first 5 minutes are up. The pitas will puff up in the center; it is this puffing that produces the pocket. When the pita cools it will collapse again, but the pocket remains, waiting to be filled with your favorite goodies.

FALAFEL

Falafel, small deep-fried chick-pea balls, have become increasingly popular and international during these last few years. In Israel they are sold by street vendors and are often the staple of the ravenous sightseeing tourist. The most popular way to serve them is to heap several into a halved pita bread, along with some spicy salad and a healthy garnish of tahina sauce. They can also be speared with toothpicks and then dipped in sauce or yogurt.

The easiest way to make *falafel* is from a mix. An excellent Israeli product is on the market and available in most gourmet shops and many supermarkets. This enables you to save time while you support the Israeli economy, a very nice thing to do on Israeli Independence Day. If, however, you choose to make them from scratch, here is a basic recipe.

1	can (20 ounces) chick-peas, drained	¾	teaspoon salt
		½	teaspoon baking soda
¾	teaspoon garlic powder	¼	teaspoon chili powder
2	tablespoons flour	3	tablespoons minced parsley
1	medium egg, beaten	1	tablespoon salad oil
			vegetable oil for deep frying

Using a fork or potato masher, mash the chick-peas well. Add all the remaining ingredients and mix well. Let stand for 10–15 minutes. Heat about 2"–3" of vegetable oil in a deep skillet. Drop the chick-pea mixture by teaspoonfuls into the oil.

As they cook, the falafel balls will rise to the top. Fry them until golden brown, about 3 minutes. Remove with a slotted spoon and drain on paper towels. This makes about two dozen.

TAHINA SAUCE OR DIP

canned tahina	garlic powder
water	salt and pepper
lemon juice	parsley and paprika for garnish

Tahina is a paste made of ground sesame seeds. It is sold in cans and jars, much like peanut butter, and is increasingly available in the gourmet section of many supermarkets and in health-food stores, as well as shops that specialize in Middle Eastern ingredients. It is used in many popular Israeli dishes. The consistency varies somewhat from brand to brand. To make a sauce, use just about as much water as tahina paste; for a dip, use less liquid. The flavorings given above are the most popular; some people also like to add caraway seeds, ground cardamom, or coriander.

HUMUS

2	cans chick-peas (20 ounces each)	GARNISH:
¾	cup tahina	olive oil
½	cup lemon juice	paprika
½	cup water	parsley
1	teaspoon garlic powder	black olives (Greek, if you
¼	cup olive oil	can get them)
	salt and pepper to taste	pickles, sliced lengthwise

Drain and mash the chick-peas. Blend the other ingredients in another bowl until the mixture is smooth and creamy, and of the consistency of mayonnaise. You will need a bit more or less than ½ cup of water, depending on the brand of tahina you have bought. Combine the tahina mixture with the chick-peas and mix well. Garnish with a swirl of olive oil, some fresh snipped parsley, paprika, and a few olives and pickle slices.

97 Archery instruction at the Lag Ba-Omer picnic (photo: Bill Aron)

LAG BA-OMER

The seven weeks between Passover and Shavuot are known as the days of counting the *omer*. In Leviticus 23:15–17, it is commanded that from the day when the first sheaf (Hebrew: *omer*) of barley is offered in the Temple, forty-nine days are to be counted until the spring harvest is celebrated and two loaves of new bread offered to God. The ceremonial counting begins on the second night of Passover and continues until Shavuot (Pentecost). These seven weeks are considered a time of semi-mourning, the Jewish equivalent of Lent. During that time it is customary not to wear new clothes, have haircuts, listen to music, or get married. A number of reasons are

given for this period of mourning—principally that the students of Rabbi Akiba (ca. 40–ca. 135 C.E.) died of the plague in that period. It is more likely, however, that this period of austerity derives from the more primitive custom of associating seasonal happenings with human behavior. The days before the spring harvest of the first fruits and the inauguration of the agricultural year are in a sense similar to the period during Elul before the fall cycle of holidays that culminate with Sukkot and Simhat Torah—a time to limit frivolous activity and to wait until the fullness of the season is assured before normal life can go on.

Lag Ba-Omer, a minor holiday which really has no tradition other than that it is a holiday, marks the thirty-third day of the *omer* period. On this day, suddenly, the lenten restrictions are suspended—some authorities say for only twenty-four hours, others say until Shavuot. Just as it is difficult to explain the reason for the period of semi-mourning begun at Passover, the justifications for relaxing the prohibitions and having a festive holiday are equally obscure. The reason is often given that, since we sorrow for the students of Rabbi Akiba during the counting of the *omer* on Lag Ba-Omer, we commemorate the "fact" that on that day the murderous plague stopped. This seems to be yet another example of the way in which Jewish tradition takes universal seasonal holidays and invests them with greater meaning, while continuing ancient customs that are dear to humanity.

Lag Ba-Omer is very similar to the more familiar May Day. Both holidays probably originate with the desire to frighten away evil spirits on the eve of a new season. The obvious way to do this is by giving the demons a taste of their own medicine; bonfires and shooting bows and arrows are popular activities for both May Day and Lag Ba-Omer. Lag Ba-Omer is often called the Scholars' Holiday because, according to Jewish lore, during the Bar Kokhba rebellion against Rome (132–35 C.E.) the students of the aforementioned Rabbi Akiba would go to the forests with bows and arrows, ostensibly to have sporting contests but in reality to study the Torah and discuss ways of subverting the Romans. Another later tradition tells us that Rabbi Simeon bar Yohai died on the thirty-third day of counting the *omer* and the kabbalists who attribute the Zohar to him memorialize the anniversary of his death by a pilgrimage to the site of his grave. Since he died in joy rather than misery, the event is commemorated with all-night singing, dancing, and bonfires. We are, it seems, deeply rooted to this earth and to nature, whether we fight off gremlins or call ourselves mystics.

210

Religion can only add deeper meaning to holidays; it doesn't change their season or alter their spirit. So, for whatever reasons, Lag Ba-Omer is an ideal time for a students' picnic.

The one problem with planning a picnic for a classful of children is that it may very well rain. The Jewish holidays we celebrate are based on the climate of Israel, not the United States or wherever else we may find ourselves. So remember to make contingency plans, because once you have gotten permission from all the parents and the various teachers have planned the rest of their lessons around a "picnic," you really *must* deliver a picnic. When the Lag Ba-Omer picnic shown on these pages was planned for my daughter's Hebrew-school class, we were hoping to take the children to a nearby park where we could have field-day activities and do some outdoor cooking, but we nevertheless made certain to line up the use of the Jewish Center social hall in the event of rain. We also planned a craft–game project to replace the relay races if we had to be inside. We were hoping that all this anticipation, like carrying an umbrella, would keep the rain away; but of course it rained after all.

The party was broken into four different activities, each lasting roughly half an hour. The teacher, a very dedicated young Israeli woman, had done her homework with the children and laid the

98 Roman soldiers made from potato-chip canisters (photo: Bill Aron)

99 (photo: Bill Aron)

groundwork for the planned activities by telling the class about Rabbi Akiba, his students, the Roman occupation, and the Bar Kokhba rebellion. The parallels with modern Israel were not lost.

The first part of the afternoon involved the transformation by the children of cylindrical potato-chip containers into "Roman soldiers." Construction paper was taped in place to conceal the advertising; styrofoam cups and folded paper were made into hats; felt-tip markers were used for faces and details. These hastily but enjoyably assembled creatures were then used instead of pins in a bowling game. The idea, of course, was to vent a bit of anti-Roman aggression. It was still drizzling when we finished this game, but we were all eager to have a taste of what it was "really" like for Rabbi Akiba's students, so—a few at a time—children went outside for instruction and attempts at bow-and-arrow shooting. This was really the highlight of the day. The equipment was real (an 11-pound bow was used) and the instruction serious.

After all the children had had an opportunity to test their skill at stringing the bow and shooting at the target, we had a brief fireworks display. By then it was raining again, but the effect was dramatic nevertheless. To make the display, ¼"-thick aluminum wire was formed into the letters   לג בעומר   [Lag Ba-Omer]. These were attached to two horizontal pieces of wire. The lower wire had two legs, which were later pushed into the ground as supports. Each letter (but not the supporting structure) was then wrapped in strings of cotton rags. Charcoal igniter was carefully poured over the rags, soaking them completely. The display was put into the field at a distance from the children and set ablaze. We all looked on with the age-old fascination for fire while the holiday name appeared and disappeared in the flames.

While all this was going on, the other volunteer parent was in the kitchen assembling an Israeli-style supper: *falafel* balls and *humus* in pita bread, lettuce, cucumber, and tomato salad, *halvah* for dessert, and apple cider to wash it all down. Our little picnic was the envy of the school.

SHAVUOT

Shavuot [Pentecost] means "weeks," signifying the fact that this festival is celebrated seven weeks after Passover. It is an ancient holiday, and although it is not as old as Passover and doesn't take us all the way back to our days in the desert, its customs are as old as the settling of the Hebrews in Canaan and the beginnings of a settled communal pastoral and agricultural life. In the Bible the holiday has three names: the Feast of Weeks (Shavuot, Deuteronomy 16:10), the Feast of Harvest (Exodus 23:16), and the Day of the First Fruits (Numbers 28:26). All three reflect the dominant motif of agricultural celebration and thanksgiving. According to Exodus 23:17, there are three major pilgrim festivals—Passover, Shavuot, and Sukkot—for "Three times a year all your males shall appear before the Lord." It is interesting to note that, while today almost everyone has some idea of what the "minor" holiday of Hanukkah is about, very few people are at all familiar with Shavuot, which is a principal festival on the religious calendar.

In ancient times the outstanding ceremony of the festival was the bringing of the first fruits of the seven species for which Israel is known to the Temple in Jerusalem. These species are: barley, wheat, grapes, figs, pomegranates, olives, dates, and honey. Processions came from all the outlying cities; flutists headed the parade, and the people sang psalms as they marched along. An ox—its horn encrusted with gold and wearing a wreath of olive leaves on its head—went before them. When they got to Jerusalem, they were met by dignitaries and the artisans of the city. On entering the Temple, they were greeted by psalms sung by the Levites' choir. Both the produce and the baskets were given to the Temple; the poor had ordinary grass or wicker baskets to offer, while the wealthier farmers gave baskets ornamented with gold and silver. As each farmer made his offering he recited the verses from Deuteronomy 26:5 ff.: "A wandering Aramean was my father, and

100 Appliqué-and-embroidery Torah mantle (photo: Jane Kahn)

he went down into Egypt, and the Egyptians . . . afflicted us . . . and the Lord brought us out of Egypt with a mighty hand . . . and has given us . . . a land flowing with milk and honey."

In our so-called sophisticated and rational age, we tend to disparage early agricultural festivals. For me, however, they often embody the very basic concept of the relationship between humanity and God. Giving the first harvest fruits to God expresses the idea of the partnership between people and God, recognizing that it is not human labor alone which brings forth bread from the earth. Giving God the first portion of the crop is a way of appreciating and repaying divine efforts. People also have a natural awe and suspicion of anything new, so the agricultural first fruits as well as the firstborn of animals and humans were consigned by many primitive peoples to the gods or spirits. By offering the prime portion of everything to God—to whom nothing is new—the remainder is made familiar and safe.

Jews have never been satisfied with merely agricultural and seasonal meanings for our holidays; we have always added a historical interpretation as well. So, by the first centuries of the Common Era, it was an established tradition that on Shavuot—liturgically called the Time of the Giving of our Torah—the entire Jewish nation stood at the base of Mt. Sinai and received the Law. This is a natural outgrowth of the Passover story. Passover, an even more ancient seasonal holiday, commemorates the Exodus from Egypt. The seven weeks of counting the days of the barley-growing season, which begin on the second night of Passover, are now also seen as seven weeks of anticipation of the receiving of the Decalogue.

Just as with other holidays, the old seasonal folkloric customs are continued but reinterpreted to coincide with the historical meaning invested in the festival. For millennia it has been customary on Shavuot to decorate homes and places of worship and study with green branches and flowers and to eat dairy foods. It is said that the decorative use of foliage—even to crowning the Torah scrolls with garlands and strewing the synagogue floor with grass—is meant to represent the verdure on which Israel stood at the base of Mt. Sinai while receiving the Torah. We say that we favor dairy foods at Shavuot because the Torah "is like milk and honey." According to this tradition, when the people returned to their tents after receiving the Law, they were ravenous, and it would have taken too long to slaughter and make kosher an animal for a meat meal. Another version holds that eating meat would be reminiscent of the golden calf, and since we'd rather not be reminded of that episode we eat

216

dairy foods. These fanciful explanations only serve to make the ancient agricultural customs more endearing. Pastoral celebrations predate agricultural ones. Eating cheese probably harks back to the time when Shavuot was more concerned with shepherds than with agriculture, which is represented by the custom of decorating with greenery. At ancient spring pastoral ceremonies among the Canaanites, a kid was seethed in milk; stressing dairy foods both keeps the dietary laws and serves to differentiate Jewish celebrations from those of other peoples.

In 70 C.E. the Romans destroyed the Temple and drove the Jews from the land. During centuries of exile the agricultural beginnings of Shavuot were not forgotten, but the dominant motifs became those of revelation and Covenant. Readings for Shavuot include the Decalogue and the Book of Ruth, which is the compellingly beautiful story of a gentile woman's adoption of the Jewish faith set against the background of the barley harvest, thus linking the motifs of land and Torah. Psalms of David are also read, since King David was a descendant of the convert Ruth and it is said that he was born and died on Shavuot.

It was traditional among European Jews to start a child's study of the Torah on Shavuot, coating the first letters that the child was taught with honey and thereby emphasizing the sweetness and desirability of learning and of the Commandments. Today in most Reform and Conservative congregations religious-school confirmation ceremonies are held on Shavuot. In modern Israel the ancient custom of bringing first fruits is being reinstituted in many locales—even among secular kibbutzim—and baskets of fruit are donated by schoolchildren to worthy causes such as hospitals.

As with all Jewish festivals, feasting is part of Shavuot and, as has been mentioned, dairy foods are the favorites. But, except among the kabbalists, no special Shavuot social gatherings have evolved. The mystics instituted the custom of having a Tikkun Lel Shauvot—an all-night study session, which ends with the recitation of the morning prayers at dawn. One stays up all night with anticipation before receiving the Torah. Further, since Moses had to wake the Israelites who fell asleep the night before the Torah was given, we, in contrast, thus show our readiness to accept it. Friends who have had such study sessions suggest that it is a good idea to intersperse exercises, games, and food with the readings, which traditionally include the first and last verses from every book of the Bible as well as a passage or two from every section of the Talmud, in order to symbolically understand the full scope of what we are about to receive. It is a good opportunity to become familiar with the Book of Ruth, which can be read and discussed during the course of the evening.

If such a session seems beyond your endurance, it would certainly be in the spirit of the holiday to have a Tikkun dessert, perhaps serving cheese blintzes or one of the traditional cakes described at the end of the chapter. Twin *hallot* (consider forming them to represent the two tablets of the Law or two sheaves of grain) are also traditional for Shavuot.

Whether you celebrate Shavuot with an all-night Tikkun or a simple family meal, you might like to decorate your home for the holiday with foliage or with paper-cuts. Among the Jews of Eastern Europe, it was very popular to make paper cutouts for the windows at Shavuot. This was usually done by the *heder* boys and teachers before the holiday and was considered holy work. Many of them were round and called *roysalakh* [rosettes]. It is said that in the eighteenth century when Elijah the Gaon, of Vilna, took exception to the universal custom of decorating homes and synagogues with

101 Paper-cut *roysalah* with *magen Davids*

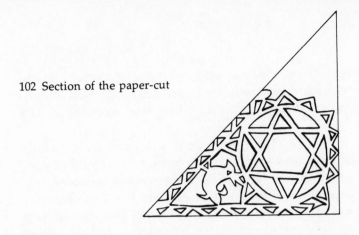

102 Section of the paper-cut

foliage—pointing out that it was a gentile one—the Jews began making paper-cuts. In reality the Jews had been making paper-cuts for at least several hundred years before that, as the lovely wedding contracts, Purim Megillot, and *mizrahim* from sixteenth-century Italy and other places show us. But it may have been at that time that the Jews of Eastern Europe took a particular liking toward using this folk craft at Shavuot.

My mother was born in Poland and lived there until she emigrated to the United States at sixteen. She taught me how to make paper-cuts when I was a child. She said that, while the men (whose efforts at this craft were taken more seriously) would tack the folded paper to a board and cut the design with a knife, women and girls would often cut paper designs with scissors. As you can see from the instructions and accompanying illustrations, I use both methods. She apologized for her lack of skill, saying that if her mother and her father's brother, both known for their artistry, could only be with us, I'd have the best of all teachers. I too wished that they could join us, little imagining the horror that they were experiencing as the Nazis obliterated their Polish *shtetl*. While some Jewish art and ceremonial objects survived the Holocaust, having been preserved for their intrinsic material value, most of the paper-cuts, being of humbler materials, perished along with the people who made them. Whenever I make a paper-cut, I feel as though I am making a memorial object. For that reason, and because paper-cutting is a simple and satisfying way to make decorative designs, I'd like to describe how they are made. In Israel today schoolchildren are once again making cut-paper designs for Shavuot, and I hope that you too will enjoy making them, not only for this holiday but for other projects as well.

For your first paper-cuts, confine yourself to symbols that can be easily shown in silhouette: a *magen David*, birds, a crown, the tablets, et cetera. When you are more expert you can go on to elaborately interlacing foliage, beasts, and thematic material. If you haven't done this before, you will be pleasantly surprised at how elaborate the simplest design becomes when it is reproduced as a multiple image.

Use thin, strong paper. Typing paper is excellent, as are some brands of shelf paper. Construction paper is a bit heavy and coarse, but if you are doing only a single-fold design or want the color, it is workable. Rice paper is nice for some effects but has a tendency to curl. There are several parchmentlike papers on the market that work very well; these are a bit expensive for practice, but when you have some experience and want to create longlasting, framable paper-cuts, you might want to try them.

Fold the paper in half or fourths, or, as in the case with the *roysalah* shown here, in eighths. This is done by folding a square sheet of paper three times: in half horizontally, then again in half, then in half diagonally to form a triangle.

Draw the design lightly on the reverse of the folded paper. Remember: you only need to draw one-half, one-fourth, or one-eighth of the design. To make the *roysalah* in Fig. 101, only the drawing shown in Fig. 102 was necessary.

Make sure as you draw that each shape is clearly delineated and that it touches a neighboring shape just enough (but no more) to keep it from falling apart when you begin to cut. Use sharp-pointed scissors or a hobby utility knife and cut away the background paper. I also use pinking shears for certain effects. If there is to be lettering included in the design, unfold the paper, lightly draw the letters on the front of the paper, and cut them out with a knife or scissors, whichever is more comfortable for you. Figure 103 shows an *alef-bet* design which is suitable for paper-cuts. Many of the letters present no problem. Some (such as the final *mem*) have hollow centers that fall out when the outline is totally cut away; these necessitate a unified *alef-bet* which keeps the letters intact.

When the cutting (which will take longer than you think) is completed, carefully unfold the paper and press it with a warm iron. If it is a Shavuot *roysalah*, you can attach it to your window with a bit of rubber cement or doublestick tape. When the painter Maurycy Gottlieb was twelve years old, one of his *roysalakh* in the window caught the attention of a non-Jewish passerby who then became his patron and helped him attend the Academy of Art in Cracow. Who knows who might see yours!

If you decide to mount your work rather than put it in the window, or if you are going on to make a *mizrah*, *shviti*, amulet, or

103 Stencil *alef-bet* for the paper-cut

a

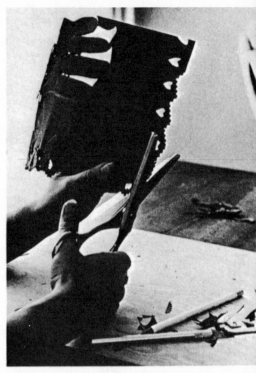

b

c

d

104 [a] The design is drawn on the folded paper. In this case, the paper was folded in half, and since it is black, a white pencil was used for the drawing

[b] The border is being cut with pinking shears. Some internal parts of the design have already been cut with ordinary scissors

[c] The paper-cut is held firmly against a cutting board and a hobby utility knife is used to cut details (a single-edge razor could also be used)

[d] The half-finished paper-cut is opened out. If letters are part of your design, they would be drawn now on the front of the paper (photos: Jane Kahn)

other wall ornament, the simplest way to preserve it is to use a tiny bit of white glue or rubber cement to attach it lightly to a contrasting background. Try the adhesive out first on the paper you are using to be sure it won't curl. If you have gone on to something very elaborate and are using good paper and want to preserve it indefinitely, however, it is better not to use any glue at all but to mat and frame the paper-cut as you would any fine artwork.

Once having mastered these basic instructions, you can go on to try your hand at many of the other paper-cut objects made by Jews over the centuries. Because I am so enamoured of this technique, I have used it extensively throughout this book, both for illustrations and as a means of designing other projects. Looking closely at these illustrations may be helpful to you with your own paper-cut designs.

105 Paper-cut *hamsa* that says MAZZAL TOV

106 In some villages in the Pale of Settlement, a popular Shavuot decoration consisted of making birds from hollow eggshells which were decorated with
feathers. These were then suspended on a string in the doorway, where they
would catch the breeze and look as if they were flying. In some places these
birds also made an appearance at Sukkot as part of the *sukkah* decorations.
This modern version is made with brightly colored tissue papers rather than
feathers, which can be hard to come by. Seven of the birds are suspended from
a round paper-covered embroidery hoop, which in turn is hung from the ceil-
ing by four strings tied into one. It would make a nice baby gift to hang over
the crib of an infant born near Shavuot (photo: Jim McDonald)

BLINTZES

I've already discussed the theories about the derivation of the custom of eating dairy foods on Shavuot. *Which* dairy foods, however,
were usually determined by the country where the particular Jews
found themselves. Greek Jews often enjoyed feta-cheese pie in
phyllo leaves, while the Jews of Italy favored manicotti filled with
ricotta cheese or pizza. The favorite Shavuot food among Russian
Jews was blintzes. These cheese-filled pancakes are an adaptation

of the Russian *blini*, which in turn are a Russian version of French crêpes, which probably came to Russia during the reign of Czar Peter the Great, who was so taken with French culture that he built his palace in imitation of Versailles and established the Royal School of Ballet.

For your blintzes, use the cheese filling in the *kolachi* recipe on p. 228 or one of these. The first one given is meant to save you a few calories; the second is more indulgent.

FILLING 1:

1½	pounds low-fat (1%) cottage cheese	⅛	teaspoon salt
		½	teaspoon cinnamon
1 or 2	egg yolks, beaten		sugar or dietetic sweetener
1	tablespoon melted butter, margarine, or diet spread		to taste

Combine all ingredients and refrigerate while preparing the pancakes.

FILLING 2:

		2	egg yolks
8	ounces cream cheese	5	tablespoons sugar
8	ounces farmer cheese	¼	teaspoon salt

Cream the two cheeses together until well blended. Add the remaining ingredients, mixing well. Put aside while making the pancakes.

PANCAKE BATTER:

1	cup sifted flour	1¼	cups milk
¾	teaspoon salt	4	tablespoons unsalted butter, melted
3	large eggs, well beaten		

Sift the flour and salt into a small mixing bowl. Add the eggs, beating until smooth (an electric mixer or wire wisk can be used). Add the milk gradually, beating until absolutely smooth. Strain the batter into another bowl if there are any lumps.

Let the batter rest for 20 minutes. Then add the melted butter, stirring thoroughly. This batter will make anywhere from 12 to 24 pancakes, depending on how thin you want them. I prefer them on the thin side.

Heat a 5½"–6" skillet or crêpe pan and add a dab of butter or margarine, moving it around to coat the pan. The pan should be quite hot before you pour in the batter. Spoon into the pan enough batter (about 1½ tablespoons) to form a very thin cake, tilting the pan from side to side to spread the batter evenly. Cook over low heat until the top is dry and blistered, about 1 minute. Some cooks turn the pancake to lightly cook the other side for half a minute; others remove the pancake when it is simply dry on top. Do whichever is easier for you. Stir the batter before you make each pancake. You probably only have to grease the pan for the first few pancakes.

As each pancake is finished, turn it out onto a clean tea towel. Then stack the finished pancakes on a plate which you've placed on top of a pan partially filled with hot water. Keep the water gently simmering; the steam will keep the pancakes pliable until you are ready to fill them.

When all the batter is used, fill the pancakes by putting 1½ tablespoons of filling on the edge of the less-cooked side of each pancake. Roll the edge toward the center, fold the sides in, and continue rolling toward the other end.

When all the blintzes are filled, sauté them, a few at a time, in a buttered frying pan until they are golden brown. Turn them to brown the other side equally. Instead of being fried, they can also be baked in a preheated 325° oven for 15 minutes. Serve the blintzes warm, with bowls of sour cream, applesauce, or your favorite preserves as a topping.

CHEESECAKE

There are almost as many cheesecake recipes as there are bakers; the two given here are my favorites. The first recipe is very easy to make, especially for children and novice cooks, and produces a dense, creamy, pielike cake. The second recipe is more demanding and time-consuming to prepare, but once you've tasted it you'll agree that it's worth the effort for special occasions. Both are best after they have been refrigerated for 24 hours. They can be served plain or topped with chopped toasted nuts; commercial sour cream; or fresh, canned, or preserved strawberries, blueberries, peaches, or cherries.

CHEESECAKE 1

CRUST:		FILLING:	
1⅓	cups graham-cracker crumbs (16 crackers)	12	ounces soft cream cheese
⅓	cup brown sugar (packed)	2	eggs
½	teaspoon cinnamon	½	cup granulated sugar
⅓	cup melted butter or margarine	½	teaspoon vanilla

Preheat oven to 350°. Mix all the crust ingredients and press the mixture to the bottom and sides of a lightly buttered 8"x8"x2" baking pan.

Use an electric mixer to beat the filling ingredients until the mixture is very light and creamy. Pour it into the crumb-lined pan. Bake 35–40 minutes, until the top is golden. It will puff up while it is baking, but then drop and become dense when removed from the oven. Cool on a wire rack, then refrigerate. Cut into sixteen 2" squares for serving.

CHEESECAKE 2

CRUST:

1	cup sifted flour	1¾	cups granulated sugar
1	teaspoon grated lemon rind	¼	teaspoon vanilla extract
¼	cup granulated sugar	½	teaspoon grated orange rind
½	teaspoon vanilla extract	3	tablespoons flour
½	cup soft butter or margarine	¼	teaspoon salt
1	egg yolk	½	teaspoon grated lemon rind
		5	medium eggs, plus 2 extra egg yolks
FILLING:			
5	8-ounce packages of soft cream cheese	¼	cup heavy cream

To make the crust, in a large bowl combine the flour, grated lemon rind, sugar, and vanilla extract. With a pastry blender or two knives, cut in the softened butter and egg yolk. Shape the dough into a ball; wrap it in plastic wrap and refrigerate it for at least 1 hour.

Roll one-third of the dough into a 9½" circle between two sheets of floured waxed paper. Place this big cookie on the lightly greased bottom of a 9" spring-form pan, trimming the edges to fit. Bake in a preheated 400° oven until golden, about 10 minutes. Cool in the pan on a wire rack.

Grease the sides of the spring-form pan and carefully fit it over the filled base. Roll the rest of the dough between floured sheets of waxed paper into a 15"x4" rectangle. Cut this in half lengthwise and use it to line the sides of the pan; patch if necessary.

For the filling, preheat the oven to 500°. With an electric mixer (or a wooden spoon and a very strong arm) beat the cream cheese until fluffy. Slowly add the sugar, vanilla, orange rind, flour, salt, and lemon rind. Beat continuously until smooth. Add the eggs and the extra 2 yolks; beat well after each addition. Stir in the heavy cream.

Turn the mixture into the lined pan. Bake at 500° for 12 minutes, until the cookie crust is golden. Reduce the oven temperature to 200° and bake 1 hour.

Cool on a rack, out of drafts. Remove the side of the pan and refrigerate the cake until cold. Garnish, if desired, as for Cheesecake 1. Serves 12 people generously.

KOLACHI

This pastry of Czechoslovakian origin has been a Shavuot favorite in Poland and France because its crownlike shape is reminiscent of the silver crowns adorning the Torah scrolls. For fruit fillings, which are as popular as cheese, try those in the *hamantash* recipe, pp. 174–175.

DOUGH:	7	cups flour
¾ cup lukewarm water		
1 ounce yeast	CHEESE FILLING:	
½ cup granulated sugar	2	cups cottage cheese
1 egg, lightly beaten	5	tablespoons sour cream
2 cups lukewarm milk	2	eggs, beaten
1 scant tablespoon salt	½	cup sugar
1 stick margarine, melted for the dough, plus another melted stick to brush pastries	½	cup raisins (white or dark)
	1	teaspoon vanilla
	¼	teaspoon cinnamon, if desired

In a large warm bowl combine the water, yeast, and sugar. Allow fermentation to begin. Add the egg, milk, salt, and 1 stick of melted margarine. Stir with a wooden spoon.

Stir the flour in gradually, using a large heavy mixing spoon. Continue stirring until the dough is well mixed and fairly firm and smooth. Cover with a damp cloth and set in a warm place to rise until doubled in bulk (about 1 hour).

Stir the dough down with the spoon and, if it is still sticky, add a bit more flour. Sprinkle lightly with flour and let rise again—about 45 minutes (or less may be needed this time), until again doubled in bulk.

Flour your hands and turn the dough out onto a well-floured surface. Form dough into small buns about the size of golf balls. Cover the buns and allow them to rest. By the time you have finished making the last of the buns, the first ones will be ready to be flattened and filled.

Flatten each dough ball into a circle with a floured rolling pin, or pat it gently into a circle with well-floured hands.

Mix the filling ingredients together. Put a heaping teaspoon of filling into the center of each circle. To close, bring the two opposite sides of the dough over the filling and pinch together. Bring up the other two sides, and also pinch those together. By stretching the dough a bit, you will have enough to close the pastries. Place the filled kolachi side by side in a well-greased baking pan. Brush them with the reserved stick of melted margarine and let them rise until light (about 30 minutes).

Bake in a preheated 375° oven until well browned (about 20 minutes).

Remove the kolachi from the oven and immediately brush them with more melted margarine. Sprinkle with granulated sugar and cool on a wire rack.

CAKE OF MILK AND HONEY

A slightly different version of this recipe includes raisins. It is then called a "Mount Sinai Cake."

DOUGH:
¼ cup milk
¼ cup sugar
¾ teaspoon salt
¼ stick margarine or butter
¼ cup warm water
1 packet (¼ ounce) active dry yeast
1 egg, beaten
2¼ cups flour, unsifted

GLAZE:
⅛ cup sugar

¼ cup honey
1 tablespoon margarine

FILLING:
1 package vanilla pudding (not instant)
1 cup milk
¼ cup heavy cream, whipped
⅛ teaspoon almond extract
⅓ cup slivered toasted almonds, plus 12–18 whole almonds for decoration

First prepare the dough. Scald the milk; remove it from the heat and stir in the sugar, salt, and margarine. Sprinkle the yeast into warm water in a large warm bowl. When the milk mixture has cooled to lukewarm, stir it into the yeast. Add the egg and half the flour. Beat well until smooth. Stir in the rest of the flour to make a stiff dough.

Turn the dough out onto a lightly floured surface; add a bit more flour if necessary. Knead until smooth and elastic (5–10 minutes). Rinse the bowl with warm water; dry and grease it. Place the dough in the greased bowl, turning to grease all surfaces. Cover with a damp cloth and let it rise in a warm place until doubled in bulk (about 1 hour).

Punch the dough down and turn it out onto a lightly floured surface. Form it into a smooth ball and place it in a greased 9" layer-cake pan. Spread evenly. Cover and let it rise again in a warm place until doubled in bulk (about 1 hour).

While the cake is rising for the second time, make and cool the filling. Combine pudding and milk in a saucepan (it's half the amount of milk called for on the package). Cook over medium heat, stirring constantly, until the pudding begins to bubble. Remove from heat; cool. Fold the whipped cream, almond extract, and almonds into the cooled pudding.

To make the glaze, combine the sugar, honey, and margarine in a saucepan. Bring to a boil and remove from the heat immediately. Spread some glaze over the top of the cake just before it goes in the oven. Bake in a preheated 350° oven for 30 minutes. Remove the cake from the pan to cool on a wire rack. While still warm, brush with the remaining honey glaze.

When the cake has cooled, split it and fill it with the almond/cream filling. Arrange whole blanched or toasted almonds on the top.

107 Poster design for
M.I.T. Hillel's
Rosh Hodesh
marathon in
honor of women,
nature, and
the moon

ROSH HODESH (THE FESTIVAL OF THE NEW MOON)

It is said that when God first created the sun and the moon, He made them both the same size. The moon wondered at this and asked, "Can two kings share a single crown?" To this God responded, "Go and make yourself smaller." The moon was upset and protested that the question had been a reasonable one. God realized this was true and, to compensate for making the moon smaller, promised that it would rule the heavens by night, that the months, days, and years would be determined by its waxing and waning, and that in the world to come the moon's light would be equal once again to that of the sun.

The Hebrew calendar is reckoned by the moon, and in earliest times Rosh Hodesh, the Festival of the New Moon, was a major holiday, more important even than the Sabbath. Marking the appearance of the new moon with prayers, song, and dance clearly goes back to a pre-partriarchal society, for the moon has been associated with women in almost all cultures since the most ancient times. The story of Lilith, Adam's first wife who demanded equality, parallels the folk tale of the moon. According to Jewish mysticism, the masculine and feminine aspects of God were equal at the beginning, and when the world is redeemed, the *Shekhinah* (the female dimension of God) will return from exile and women will be restored to a position of equality. For kabbalists, the *Shekhinah* is represented by the moon.

The appearance of the new moon marks the beginning of the Hebrew month. Originally the day was determined by observation, but now it is reckoned calendrically. When the preceding month has thirty days, the new moon is observed for two days—on the thirtieth day of the previous month and on the first day of the new month. During the period of the First Temple, Rosh Hodesh was observed as a semi-festival; everyone went to temple, no one worked, and family feasts were the custom. By the time of the Second Temple, the festiveness had disappeared and it had become a women's holiday, in that women could abstain from work in recognition of their refusal to turn over their jewelry to be melted down

231

to make the golden calf in the desert. But men did work, and only synagogue liturgy or the fact that in some communities schools were closed for half the day indicated that it was a holiday. Rosh Hodesh in its traditional form is one of those holidays that did not travel well, and most American Jews are totally oblivious to its existence. If one is in the synagogue on the day of the new moon, the recitation of half-Hallel and the Musaf [additional] service will remind him that it is a special day.

In the early 1970's, Jewish feminists found Rosh Hodesh an excellent vehicle for exploring and expressing feminine spiritual qualities within a traditional framework. The benediction for the new moon emphasizes the aspect of renewal in nature and interprets the renewal of the moon as symbolic of Israel's renewal and redemption. Feminists add another dimension to this interpretation of the lunar phases and indeed go back to the earliest meanings of the holiday by interpreting Rosh Hodesh to celebrate those characteristics that women share with the moon; the monthly cycle of renewal and rebirth of the moon is seen as corresponding to the feminine monthly cycle of renewal. In her article "This Month Is for You: Observing Rosh Hodesh as a Woman's Holiday,"* Arlene Agus says that "the celebration of Rosh Hodesh is the celebration of ourselves, of our uniqueness as women, and of our relationship to nature and to God." She has designed a ceremony that incorporates the traditional acts of giving charity, kindling lights, drinking wine, and feasting; she encourages people to expand upon these and personalize them with their own insights, readings, and creative interpretations. A particularly appealing suggestion is to use a floating single wick as the light to be kindled. With a tiny stretch of your imagination it is possible to see the resemblance between this single light, floating in a bowl of water, and the moon floating in the night sky. Most places that sell candles have the wicks and holders for burning oil. Use ordinary salad oil, pouring enough on top of the water to burn for twenty-four hours.

Moon, Moon, by Anne Kent Rush,** has a wealth of folkloric material about the moon and is based on the premise that "the position of the moon in a culture is the same as the position of women in that culture; our fates are inexorably shared." *Moon, Moon* presents a totally different design for a Rosh Hodesh service. It too is deeply

---

*This essay can be found in *The Jewish Woman: New Perspectives*, edited by Elizabeth Koltun (New York: Schocken Books, 1976), pp. 84–93.
**New York: Random House, 1976.

108 (photo: Jim McDonald)

rooted in tradition and combines the recitation of Hallel with dance choreographed by Fanchon Shur. Dance has been a part of the celebration of Rosh Hodesh from the very beginning, but as the holiday diminished in importance, physical movement shriveled to three tiny ritualistic bounces performed along with the verse "Just as I dance before you and cannot touch you."

For the last two years the Hillel at the Massachusetts Institute of Technology has sponsored a Rosh Hodesh marathon, using the holiday as an opportunity to socialize and explore some neglected areas of Jewish life. I designed the poster for the 1978 marathon to emphasize the evening's theme, honoring women, nature, and the moon (Fig. 107). Different speakers were invited to discuss such topics as "Literature of the Moon," "Rituals for Women," "Jewish Vegetarianism," and "Feminine Mysticism."

Rosh Hodesh is also called the Day of Good Beginnings. The new moon is seen as an auspicious day for new undertakings, and as such is an appropriate choice for joyous activities such as house-warmings, beginning a new course of study, wearing new clothes, or even eating a seasonal fruit for the first time that year. In line with feminist searchings for meaningful ritual which is neither re-bellious nor imitative, Rosh Hodesh presents many possibilities for innovative yet rooted ceremonies. One such is to celebrate a young woman's first menstruation on the first Rosh Hodesh following the event. The type of ceremony and festivity would depend on the sensibilities of the girl and her family. It seems very special to me to have luncheon or dinner in honor of the newly mature young wom-an, given by her mother and attended by grandmothers and aunts (if they live close enough) and any other women, such as teachers, who are especially meaningful in the girl's life; her friends of course could also be invited. I sounded this idea out on my young daugh-ter and a visiting classmate, and they were both very enthusiastic about it. They want the ceremony before the meal to include candle-lighting and think it would be really nice if we could bake

233

the *hallot* in crescent shapes. They'd rather have fruit juice or soft drinks than wine (why not?—it's their party) but would happily forgo childish balloons and have flowers on the table.

Whatever way you choose to mark the holiday, it is exciting and thought-provoking to be able to pour new wine in old bottles and to make an ancient festival meaningful for our own time. You have eleven chances a year (the new moon of Tishri is Rosh Hashanah) that you probably never thought of before as ready-made party dates. Whether you decide to have a dinner, a dance, or a women's study-group meeting, or just to share a new record with friends, allowing yourself to be aware of the new moon greatly enhances the day. As on Purim, Hanukkah, and the intermediary days of Passover and Sukkot, the general prohibition against gambling is lifted on Rosh Hodesh, so in planning a Rosh Hodesh gathering it would be entirely within tradition to include games of chance in the program. Dancing, as has been mentioned before, is traditional as well as fun and healthy. If your party is for women only, it might be an excellent chance to learn some of the women's folk dances from around the world. Instructors can often be found through your local Y or social center or folk-dance group. My book *The Jewish Yellow Pages* (pp. 147–50) also lists sources for dance teachers.

The one activity you must include in some form is feasting, since it is considered a *mitzvah* to feast on Rosh Hodesh. This tradition derives from the time when the new moon had to be sighted by two witnesses. To make certain that they would show up in order to wait in the Temple courtyard until the sliver of the new moon was sighted, a feast was prepared for them. We don't know with any certainty what the menu at these feasts was, but during medieval times, when Rosh Hodesh was considered a women's festival, the foods associated with it were symbolic of fertility: nuts, seeds, and fish. German Jews were partial to a midday meal including rice and *farfel* (baked crumbs of flour). In her article on the holiday, Arlene Agus suggests serving sprout salad or egg soup. Playing around with recipes—seeking to augment their symbolic value as well as their flavor—I came up with Rosh Hodesh Chicken (breasts and thighs in a sauce of pomegranates and almonds). This dish can be served with tongue in cheek.

For dessert, consider something flavored with the licorice-tasting aniseed or extract. Just as silver is the metal of the moon, anise is its herb. Anise-flavored liquor, such as Greek ouzo, Spanish anis, or French anisette, can be served over fresh seasonal fruit or ice cream.

Aniseed can be added to any plain cookie dough and cut with a glass into crescent shapes for moon cookies. (These, by the way, are a lot of fun for children to make.)

ROSH HODESH CHICKEN

3	whole chicken breasts, split	½	cup red wine
6	chicken legs	2	large pomegranates
3	tablespoons salad oil	½	cup toasted almonds
½	teaspoon garlic powder		

Cut the chicken breasts in two; separate the thighs from the drumsticks. Brown the chicken in the salad oil in a large skillet. When all of the skin has lost its yellow color and some of it is nicely browned, add the garlic powder and wine, and cover. Simmer gently over a low flame. Shell the pomegranates and add the seeds from one and a half of them to the chicken. Continue to cook for about ½ hour, until the chicken is tender and the pomegranate seeds have lost their color. Add the remaining pomegranate seeds and the toasted almonds. Serve on a bed of rice.

109 Lighting the Sabbath lamp in a seventeenth century Dutch household. The woodcut is from a Sefer Minhag [Book of Customs], *Philologus Hebreaeo-mixtus*, printed in Utrecht in 1663

THE SABBATH

Late one Friday afternoon a Jewish traveler found himself in a village too far from home to be able to return before sundown. The tiny village had only one Jewish family living there, so the traveler asked the master of the house if he could spend the Sabbath with them. "Yes," replied the man, "but it will cost you ten rubles." The traveler was visibly upset and said that that was a lot of money. But the host was adamant and would accept "not a ruble less." Since the disgruntled visitor had no other options, he agreed to pay the price. He stayed there the whole Sabbath and ate and drank his fill of the lavish and delicious meals which were served to him. When he was ready to leave on Saturday evening, he took out his billfold. The host indignantly refused the money, saying, "What kind of person would take money from a fellow Jew who did me the honor of spending the Sabbath at my table?" The guest was puzzled. "Then why did you make me agree to pay you, and so much, in the first place?" "Well," replied the host, "I wanted you to feel like a wealthy man who can drink and eat anything he wants because he has paid well for the privilege."

Whether I have a table full of guests or just my immediate family for the Sabbath, I always like them to feel like the traveler in the story: that there is plenty of delicious food and that they can eat and drink as much as they want.

From the very beginning, the Sabbath was observed with joy and celebration as well as with rest. During the Babylonian Exile and then after the destruction of the Second Temple in 70 C.E., the Sabbath—which, because it is so essentially personal and domestic, was more easily carried intact into exile than the three pilgrimage festivals of Sukkot, Passover, and Shavuot—grew in intensity and became the mainstay of Jewish life. The Second Temple period had produced sects such as the Essenes, Samaritans, and Sadducees which emphasized the strictness of Sabbath rest. However, the Pharisees—meaning most of the people—continued to stress the joyousness of the Sabbath rather than strict interpretations of

237

110 *Shabbat shalom,* New York City *ca.* 1945 (photo: Kronenberg. Courtesy of
   G. Fetterman)

the thirty-nine categories and subcategories of prohibited work
and worldly activity.

Before the Emancipation (which coincided roughly with the
onset of the industrial age), when Jews lived in ghettos or in the
East European Pale of Settlement, Sabbath observance was a magic
island of spiritual retreat in a sea of hostility or at best indifference.
In our madly rushing world, we too can greatly benefit from such a
refuge.

Like generations of Jewish homemakers, I like to be well prepared for any invited or casual guests, and, also like them, I want to
have all the shopping and cooking for all the Sabbath meals
finished by early Friday afternoon. Though there are still tragic
pockets of poverty among American Jews, most of us are indeed
fortunate that we do not have to stint on food all week in order to
have enough for these meals, as did our forebears in so many instances. But if you are anything like me and the many other women

today who have joined the work force, you are probably rationing your time even more than your money. Most of the week my family is lucky to have a simple and quickly prepared one-dish supper. Nutritious, of course—how could I admit otherwise?—and right out of some women's magazine, but I am in and out of the kitchen as quickly as I can be. On Friday, however, I love to cook. It becomes almost a pre-Sabbath meditation. I like to try new recipes, because the company we often invite will give me an audience for my successes or consolation for my defeats. Desserts, which, for reasons of diet and economy as well as time, are dispensed with during the week, are given a spot on the Sabbath menu.

When I was growing up, we almost invariably had roast chicken for Sabbath dinner. And just as invariably, the accompanying side dish was either noodle or bread pudding. It is said that the Jews eat so many noodle dishes because noodles are symbolic of the unity of the Jewish people; they are so entangled that they can never be separated. When I went off to college and was living in a women's cooperative, we began to get tired of one another's unpracticed cooking and planned a smorgasbord dinner party of recipes we wrote home for. While going through all my old looseleaf notebooks looking for recipes, I found the one my mother had sent me. It's as good now as it was then.

111 This *hallah* in the shape of a rooster was brought back from Poland by a friend. Consider making one of your own, using the recipes on pp. 92–100 (photo: Kenneth M. Bernstein)

MY MOTHER'S LOKSHN KUGL (Noodle Pudding)

½	pound thin egg noodles	1	rounded teaspoon bread crumbs
1	egg, beaten	1	scant tablespoon salad oil
¼	cup dark raisins	¼	teaspoon cinnamon
1	small apple, pared, cored, and very thinly sliced	1	teaspoon sugar

Preheat the oven to 350°. Boil the noodles in salted water according to package directions. Drain. In a large bowl combine the drained hot noodles with the other ingredients. Grease a 9″ or 10″ pie pan or skillet and heat it over a low flame. If you use a ceramic or glass pie pan, heat it in the oven.

Pour the noodle mixture into the hot pan and bake in a 350° oven for about 45 minutes, or until golden brown on top. The purpose of heating the pan before pouring in the noodles is to insure a nicely browned bottom crust.

To make bread pudding, use ½ pound of stale bread instead of the noodles. Soak and drain the bread and proceed as for lokshn kugl.

Since earliest times, fish has been a favorite Sabbath food; even the Talmud makes note that one shows delight in the Sabbath "with a dish of . . . large fish and cloves of garlic," and there are innumerable folk tales about the lengths to which people have gone to secure their fish. It is, after all, a foretaste of the leviathan upon which the righteous will feast when the Messiah comes. Fish has always been universally regarded not only as a symbol of redemption and fertility but as a positive aid to conception. In Europe during the Middle Ages, restrictive laws often kept Jews from buying fish because of the gentile fear that it would increase Jewish fertility. But the popularity of fish for the Sabbath survived those days too.

In Eastern Europe, fish was not as easily available as in the Mediterranean countries, and so low-esteemed fish such as carp (which many people today consider almost trash fish, because they live on the bottom of ponds and therefore have rather a muddy taste) became the basis of well-seasoned specialties. Gefilte fish, that Jewish basic, is a mixture of ground fillets of whatever freshwater fish are available, usually one part carp to two of whitefish or pike. My mother used to make it every Friday morning, and I can still almost hear the sound of her chopper against the wooden bowl. But then, as fish became more expensive and gefilte fish in jars appeared on every grocery shelf, even my stalwart mother stopped making her own. To my chagrin, despite the number of recipes available in almost every Jewish cookbook, I have never made my own gefilte fish. But, with an increasing number of vegetarian friends, I have developed several fish dishes which I feel are special enough for the Sabbath. Both of the following are beautiful to look at and, when they follow a soup course, feel as traditional as the meat dishes I grew up with.

HADDOCK STUFFED WITH GEFILTE FISH AND HERBS

1	haddock (3–5 pounds), washed, cleaned, and scaled	¾	teaspoon salt grated rind or juice of 1 lemon
1	medium onion, chopped		
½	cup chopped celery	2	gefilte-fish patties, cut up
6	tablespoons margarine	½	cup hot water
3–4	cups packaged stuffing or dried bread cubes	1	egg, beaten buttered bread crumbs margarine or butter for basting
1½	teaspoons sage		
½	teaspoon thyme		
½	teaspoon pepper		

Soften the onion and celery in the 6 tablespoons of margarine. Add the bread cubes, seasonings, lemon rind, cut-up gefilte fish, and hot water, mixing well to make a mixture that holds together. If necessary, add a bit more water. Sprinkle the inside of the haddock with a bit of lemon juice and stuff it with the mixture. Place it in a large greased baking dish. Brush with a beaten egg and coat lightly with buttered bread crumbs.

Use a fork to pattern the crumbs to resemble fish scales. Bake at 350° for 30–40 minutes, basting occasionally with melted butter or margarine. Makes 4 very generous servings.

SOUTH AMERICAN SALMON PIE

CRUST:		1	teaspoon baking soda
½	cup instant potato flakes	⅓	cup margarine
2	tablespoons melted margarine	½	cup milk (or non-dairy substitute)
2	cups flour		
½	tablespoon sugar	¼	cup mayonnaise
1	teaspoon cream of tartar		

Combine ¼ cup of the potato flakes with the melted margarine and set aside.

Combine the remaining flakes, flour, sugar, cream of tartar, and baking soda in a large mixing bowl. With two knives or a pastry blender, cut in ⅓ cup of margarine until the mixture resembles coarse crumbs. Add the milk and mayonnaise. Blend well into a soft dough.

Divide the dough into two balls. Roll out one ball between two sheets of floured waxed paper into a 10″ circle and place it on a greased baking sheet or pizza pan (the waxed paper makes it easy to invert the rolled-out pastry). Spread the filling to within ½″ of the edge. Roll out the other ball of dough and place it on top of the filling. Seal the edges by fluting them or folding and pressing with a fork (whichever produces the most decorative edging for you). Brush with milk and sprinkle with the reserved potato flakes. Bake at 375° for 20–25 minutes, until golden brown.

SALMON FILLING:

2	15½-ounce cans salmon, drained	3	tablespoons dehydrated minced onion
¾	cup mashed potatoes		
1	small green pepper, chopped	2	tablespoons lemon juice
10	stuffed green olives (with pimento), sliced in thirds	¼	teaspoon pepper
		½	teaspoon salt
2	stalks celery, chopped	½	cup parmesan cheese

Combine all ingredients and proceed with the pie recipe.

Even with the table beautifully set and delicious food prepared, it takes a bit more to turn a Friday evening into more than just another dinner party. A Florida friend, Rabbi Efraim Warshaw, has given this a lot of thought and come up with a "Seder" for Friday evening.* Many people are a bit intimidated at the thought of spontaneously blessing the candles, the wine, and the bread and find themselves forgetting in embarrassment the prayers they learned as children in Sunday school. Having a booklet or even a sheet of paper can be very helpful. Rabbi Warshaw encourages everyone to expand upon the model he has come up with, adding songs, stories, meditations, and prayers to suit the individual.

The Friday-night Seder designed by Rabbi Warshaw basically follows the order customary among traditional Jews for beginning the Sabbath. Even though his Seder is designed principally with the nuclear family in mind, it is still very useful for people living alone

*Write to him at Hebrew Day School of Fort Lauderdale, 5975 West Sunrise Boulevard, Fort Lauderdale, Fla. 33313, for more information.

or in modified families. Lighting the candles or making the *kiddush* over the wine is no less meaningful or beautiful if not done by Mother or Father. The domestic Sabbath service is begun by lighting the candles. There should be at least two. Some people use one candle for every person present; some use a seven-branched *menorah*. Most typical, however, is a simple pair of the loveliest candlesticks you have. The following blessing is said:

ברוך אתה יי אלהינו מלך העולם אשר קדשנו במצותיו וצונו להדליק נר של שבת.

Barukh atah adonai elohenu melekh ha-olam, asher kiddshanu be-mitzvatav vetzivanu lehadlik ner shel Shabbat.
["We praise You, O Lord our God, King of the Universe, who, having taught us the way of holiness through the *mitzvot*, has enjoined upon us the kindling of the Sabbath light."]

In traditional households, the husband at this point usually recites a selection from the Book of Proverbs (31:10–31) known as "A Woman of Valor," which is a lyrical appreciation of a wife. There is no reason why a wife couldn't choose an appropriate quotation to show her affection and appreciation for her husband at this point as well. The children are blessed, either by words or with a kiss.

The two angels who accompany the Sabbath Queen are welcomed with the song "*Sholem Aleykhem*" and the *kiddush* is chanted. The full *kiddush* can be found in the prayer book. If you can't read Hebrew, read it in translation.

ברוך אתה יי אלהינו מלך העולם בורא פרי הגפן.

Barukh atah adonai elohenu melekh ha-olam, bore peri hagafen.
["We praise You, O Lord our God, King of the Universe, who gives us the fruit of the vine."]

There are usually two *hallot* on the Sabbath table, symbolic of the double portion of manna which was gathered in the desert on Friday by the Israelites (Exodus 16:22). These are covered with a special *hallah* cover, which is said to be a reminder of the dew which covered the manna. The cover is lifted and a prayer is said over the bread. Some people like to hold the two *hallot* together, with as many people as possible holding them; others leave them on the *hallah* plate during the blessing. Some slice them and others insist on tearing the bread. After the blessing, it is customary to salt the bread before eating it, since salt is the mineral "food of the earth." This is the blessing for bread, which in fact begins any meal:

ברוך אתה יי אלהינו מלך העולם המוציא לחם מן
האָרץ.

Barukh atah adonai elohenu melekh ha-olam hamotzi lehem min ha-aretz.

["We praise You, O Lord our God, King of the Universe, who brings forth food from the earth."]

Now the Sabbath meal is served, and songs or stories are sung and told between courses. If observing the Sabbath is new for you, you might find it helpful to write out a "Seder" of your own and to make copies for everyone at the table. Even if you have a set way of welcoming and sanctifying the Sabbath, having copies of the blessings in English and transliterated Hebrew available for guests who are not familiar with them will enhance the evening for everyone. Even those of us who are totally steeped in the tradition can enrich our Sabbath experience by preparing for it rather than letting habit dull our senses.

One can prepare for the Sabbath in any one of a number of ways, finding new stories or songs to bring to everyone else's attention, baking *hallah*, cooking special foods, and making beautiful artifacts to grace the table. Previous generations invested a great deal of time in hand-embroidered tablecloths and *hallah* covers, and metalsmiths were often commissioned to make special plates and cups for the *hallah* and wine. While it is ritually proper to use any cup for the wine, any plate for the *hallah*, and any napkin to cover

112 Contemporary Sabbath platter and *kiddush* cup (photo: Jim McDonald)

113 Most of the work is already done on this recycled armchair doily en route to becoming a *hallah* cover (photo: Jim McDonald)

it, making one's own or in some way acquiring objects that are just for the Sabbath makes the meal more distinct from weekday ones.

Figure 112 shows a stoneware *hallah* platter made to resemble an altar. The Hebrew letters שבת are carved on the other side of the pedestal. A *kiddush* cup is formed like a huge split grape supported by a "vine." These were made without any special tools on my kitchen table and then fired in a friend's kiln.

Some years ago I began a collection of Sabbath plates made by other people. A pewter one I found, made in Germany or Holland in the latter part of the eighteenth century, has a design lifted almost line by line from the woodcut done a century earlier for a book of customs (Fig. 109). *The Work of Our Hands* has directions for retranslating this design once again into an embroidered *hallah* cover. After the book came out, I was gratified to get a letter from a woman who said that she had been searching for a design for a *hallah* cover for years and finally found this one. She took the idea one step further, however, and had her son photograph her in her own kitchen; she then transferred the picture of herself in her American kitchen to her *hallah* cloth. I invite you to come up with whatever variations you enjoy. For those of you who would like a beautifully embroidered *hallah* cloth but don't have time to make one, you might recycle an unused but still lovely doily or dresser scarf. Figure 113 shows just such a project in progress. (Recycled embroideries are also discussed on pp. 190–191.)

Children too can have a wonderful time preparing for the Sabbath. Camp Grossman, Boston's enormous Jewish summer daycamp, has the children making *hallah* and candles several times during the summer. The supplies are very inexpensive and easily

114 Children making candles at Camp Grossman, Massachusetts (photo: John Waite)

available, but, especially with young children, it is imperative to have adequate adult supervision and to make certain that the melted wax is never put over a direct flame but into a double boiler (even a makeshift one, using coffee cans for the wax, will do). Figure 114 shows the children circling the worktable, dipping their wick first into melted colored wax, then into water to solidify it. As they circle, the wax firms enough to allow them to dip into another color, and they continue until the multicolored candle is complete. They may not look exactly like their store-bought cousins, but the pleasure of making one's own Sabbath candles means more than a symmetrical product; besides, these unique candles are really pretty as well as special.

The second big meal of the Sabbath is the Saturday midday meal. It too is begun by blessings recited over wine and bread. Since all the preparation for this substantial meal should have been completed before the onset of the Sabbath on Friday night, generations of ingenious cooks have produced innumerable dishes that benefit from very long, slow cooking at low temperatures. These are variously called *cholent, hamim,* or *adafina,* depending on the country of origin. *Cholent* was the mainstay of the East European Saturday

246

meal. (For Jews in warmer climates, having hot food in the middle of the day was less necessary.) The dish consisted mainly of potatoes, buckwheat groats, and beans, with a meat bone or fat to give it flavor, as well as a dumpling and perhaps some onions. If one was prosperous, more meat could be added. In the Polish towns each family would mark its pot with chalk and set it in the baker's oven Friday afternoon, calling for it after synagogue on Saturday. This dish, which warmed the bodies and souls of so many of our forebears, tends to be a bit too heavy for a midday meal for contemporary Western Jews. It has undoubtedly also lost some of its flavor, since we no longer have bakers' ovens with wood coals to cook on, but must instead rely on a gas or electric oven set to 250°.

The Jews of Spain had their own versions of a slow-cooked meal. As with *cholent*, the number of recipes is equal to the number of cooks. The Spanish *adafina* can be baked in a slow oven or cooked on top of the stove over a low flame with a lot of water added to it. Pour off and serve the soup as the first course; then serve the meat and vegetables. After the expulsion from Spain in 1492, it is said the converts, to prove their loyalty to Catholicism, replaced the traditional eggs of the *adafina* with pork sausage. I plan to try adding chunks of kosher bologna or salami to a pot of *adafina*; it seems to me that would be quite good. The recipe given below is a basic one. In the south of Spain, sweet potatoes are often used instead of white; the unshelled eggs—which come out a dark brown on the outside and soft on the inside—can be omitted; more or less chicken or giblets can be used; cabbage is sometimes used; and, as with the *cholent*, a large *knaydl* [dumpling], called in Spanish a *pelota*, can be added. The basic ingredients remain the chick-peas, potatoes, and whatever meat you can afford.

ADAFINA

2	pounds boned chuck or breast of veal, cut in chunks	4–6	eggs, left in their shells
¼	cup olive oil	1	pound dried chick-peas
4	large onions, chopped or sliced	8	potatoes, halved
2	cloves garlic, minced	1	beef soup bone
2	tomatoes, chopped	4	carrots, sliced
½	cup fresh parsley, minced	1	tablespoon salt, or to taste
1	pound chicken wings, or half a chicken cut in parts		water to cover

In a large Dutch oven or heavy casserole, brown the meat in the olive oil. Reduce the heat and add the remaining ingredients, taking care not to break the eggs. Cover with water—at least 3 quarts. Cover and bring to a boil. Reduce the heat and continue simmering over a very low flame overnight. Or, once it comes to a boil, place it in an oven preheated to 250° and bake overnight. Obviously, it can also be cooked more quickly at a slightly higher heat (4–5 hours at 350° or a decent simmer) and eaten immediately or reheated before serving.

In talmudic times it was the custom to only eat two meals a day. In order to make the Sabbath special and to honor the day, the rabbis decreed that three meals would be eaten: one on Friday evening, one at midday on Saturday, and the third, *seudah shelishit*, in the late afternoon as the Sabbath began to come to a close. No *kiddush* is said at this third meal, but a special sanctity has become associated with it as the Sabbath Queen makes ready her departure. Among the Polish Hasidim, the *seudah shelishit* became an important part of their religious and social life, as they would gather at the rabbi's table, listening to the tzaddiks discourse and singing hymns and *nigunim* [wordless melodies] until late in the evening, thus prolonging the Sabbath as long as possible. Sometimes, on short winter days, this third meal could in reality be little more than a dessert following the big midday meal, but it was nevertheless called a *seudah shelishit*. If there was more time between the termination of the midday meal and the *seudah shelishit*, a light supper of cold food would be served. (My own favorite menu for this last lazy meal of the Sabbath is a variety of smoked fish or bagel, cream cheese, and lox sandwiches.) In the 1920's the poet Hayyim Nahman Bialik restyled the *seudah shelishit* as a cultural event rather than a strictly religious occasion. His students and friends would gather about two hours before sunset on Saturday afternoons for poetry readings, study, and discussion groups, thus keeping the spirit of the Sabbath without rigidly following its traditional forms. He called these reunions Oneg Shabbat, from the phrase "And you shall call the Sabbath a delight" (Isaiah 58:13). The name Oneg Shabbat has become synonymous with any cultural and social gathering on the Sabbath, whether held Friday evening or at any time on Saturday.

Havdalah and Melaveh Malkah

Just as the Sabbath begins with the *kiddush*, a blessing to sanctify it, so as the Sabbath ends there is a ceremony of separation and departure to mark the difference between it and the rest of the week. The Havdalah service consists of four blessings: for lights, wine, spices, and the "separation" itself. The blessings are preceded by several introductory passages from the Bible, and vary among the Sephardic and Ashkenazic rituals. The complete service can be found in your prayer book. After sunset, when three stars can be seen in the night sky, we reluctantly admit that the Sabbath is over. Before the ceremony begins, the Havdalah candle is lit. This candle must have at least two separate wicks; most Hebrew bookstores or synagogue gift shops have four-wick blue-and-white ones. Usually there is only one Havdalah candle, and a child holds it. There is a certain poetry in being in a darkened room with only the light of one mul-

115 Havdalah (photo: Bill Aron)

116 Multicolored Havdalah candle made by a
retired rabbi, who learned how to make
these unusual beeswax candles from his
father in Europe (photo: Jim McDonald)

tiwicked candle held by a child. Occasionally, however, it seems
better to have a candle for everyone who wants one. By the light of
the candle the same blessing over the wine as was recited Friday
night is chanted. The wine is not drunk at this point.

The spices—usually bay leaves, stick cinnamon, and cloves—are
then blessed and passed around to be smelled by everyone. Over
the centuries Havdalah spice boxes have taken the most fanciful
forms. They have been made to resemble towers, animals, and
plants. There are several interpretations for the use of spices at the
Havdalah ceremony. In the Middle East it was customary to burn
incense at the end of a meal, and since one couldn't burn anything
on the Sabbath, sweet-smelling spices were substituted. Legend
tells us that on the Sabbath we have an extra soul, and it is to revive
us as the extra soul leaves and to comfort us as the Sabbath also
departs that we use the spices. I've always associated the spices
with the symbolism of the Sabbath Queen–Bride. The spices are
like the lasting fragrance of the Sabbath which we hope will linger
during the coming week.

The blessing over the lights of fire follows the smelling of the
spices. At this point we usually cup our hands in such a way that
our fingernails are in the light and our fingers cast a shadow on our
palms. This symbolizes the distinction between darkness and light.

250

The last paragraph of the Havdalah service is then recited, and the person leading the ceremony drinks the wine or passes it around to be shared. (Folklore tells us that if a woman drinks from the Havdalah cup she will grow a beard.) Enough wine is left to pour into a dish, and the candle flame is extinguished in it. At this point everyone wishes one another a good week. Singing the songs *"Shavuah Tov"* ["Good Week"] and *"Eliyahu Hanavi"* (the same song of longing for the prophet Elijah, who will come to announce the Messiah, that we sing at Passover) as well as other melodies is the common way to keep the flavor of the Sabbath lingering a bit longer.

Havdalah at the 1977 Conference on Alternatives in Jewish Education was impressively beautiful. There were hundreds of people, and all through the week of the conference many of them had been making Havdalah candles and spice boxes, like those shown in Figs. 115 and 118, under the direction of Martin and Joan Benjamin

117 Antique-style Havdalah spice boxes (photo: Kenneth M. Bernstein)

118 Spice boxes made from ground-cinnamon containers (photo: Jim McDonald)

Farren. The candles are made by heating fireplace tapers in a folded heating pad. When the tapers are warm enough to be pliable, they are braided, using as many strands as the maker is capable of. The spice boxes are made from one-ounce metal and plastic spice boxes, with a flat cabinet knob for the pedestal and a rounded knob for the dome. Sheet-metal screws hold the knobs in place; predrill the holes for the screws. Also drill small holes in the top of the round knob for the flag, which is made from a piece of a metal coat hanger with a plastic flag cut from the side of an empty milk container. The boxes can be spray-painted with metallic paint, as one of those in the photograph was, or ornamented with découpage or colored paints; personally, I like them with no decoration, as an artifact of American popular culture.

After Havdalah, with the Sabbath over, there is an old custom of having yet another festive meal. This is called a Melaveh Malkah [Escorting of the Queen]. The root of the word Melaveh is *leb* [heart] and thereby signifies love for the Sabbath Queen. It is said that this custom of a festive meal in her honor originated with King David. It was prophesied that he would die on the Sabbath. Therefore, at the end of every Sabbath, since he was assured of another week of life, he gave a feast.

There is an element of sadness in the departure of the Sabbath. But since we are told that the Messiah will not come on the Sabbath, the new week begins with an air of anticipation. A Melaveh Malkah can begin the week for you on Saturday night with a meal or party which can take any form you want it to. I've been to some which were just simple family suppers and others where the dancing and singing went on until the middle of the night. The best Saturday-night party is the one that will help you hold on to the peace and joy of the Sabbath into the new week.

> Go your way, eat your bread with joy,
> And drink your wine with a merry heart;
> For God has already accepted your works.
>
> —Ecclesiastes 9:7

119 Contemporary ceramic Havdalah set, by Joan Meznick (photo: Kenneth M. Bernstein)

APPENDIX

The Hebrew Holiday Calendar 5739-5761 (1978-2000)

The Hebrew calendar is a combination of lunar and solar reckonings. Since biblical times the months have been determined by the moon, but the lunar months must conform to the seasonal changes which are determined by the sun. The twelve Hebrew months are: Tishri, Heshvan, Kislev, Tebet, Shevat, Adar, Nisan, Iyar, Sivan, Tammuz, Ab, and Elul. The solar year has approximately 365 days, which makes it about eleven days longer than the twelve lunar months; therefore a complicated system of adjustments was worked out to ensure that Passover always falls in the spring and Sukkot in the fall (in the northern hemisphere). We are familiar with the manner in which the inaccuracies of the civil calendar, which is solar, are adjusted by adding a day to February every four years and calling that a leap year. The system of adjusting the Hebrew calendar is based on the same idea, but since it is necessary to balance the lunar and solar years, it is more complicated. There are seven leap years in every nineteen-year period. During a leap year there are thirteen lunar months. The extra month is a second Adar, which roughly corresponds to February–March. In every nineteen-year cycle, the third, sixth, eighth, eleventh, fifteenth, seventeenth, and nineteenth years are leap years. This causes great swings in the civil dates of Jewish holidays. Even the Christian holiday calendar is affected by this, since Easter follows the Hebrew calendar and usually falls the Sunday after Passover. During a leap year, however, Protestants and Roman Catholics will celebrate Easter a month "early," the Sunday after Purim, while the Eastern Orthodox Church will celebrate Easter following Passover even when Passover is "late."

The day begins after dusk when the first three stars can be seen, so all Jewish Sabbaths and holidays begin the evening before the corresponding civil date. This means that events that take place between sunset and midnight belong to the following Hebrew calendar day, but to the preceding day on the civil calendar. Keep this in mind when determining Hebrew birthdays and anniversaries. The months have twenty-nine or thirty days; the first day of every month (and the thirtieth) is Rosh Hodesh (the new moon). Originally the first day of the month was determined by observation, and messengers were sent to outlying areas to announce the new moon and the holidays. Because of the delays, it became customary in the Diaspora to celebrate the major holidays for two days to ensure that Jews everywhere would observe the holiday on the same day. Today, with holidays determined by calculation rather than observation, this custom is still observed by Orthodox and Conservative Jews outside of Israel. Reform Jews disregard the second day of festivals. The following chart gives the civil and Hebrew dates of the holidays discussed in this book. To determine dates for Bar/Bat Mitzvahs, anniversary celebrations, and so on, you will have to consult a more complete calendar.

THE FIRST DAYS OF JEWISH HOLIDAYS   1978-2000 (5739-5761)

YEAR	Rosh Hashanah Tishri 1	Yom Kippur Tishri 10	Sukkot Tishri 15	Simhat Torah Tishri 23	Hanukkah Kislev 25
1978/79	October 2	October 11	October 16	October 24	December 25
1979/80	September 22	October 1	October 6	October 14	December 15
1980/81	September 11	September 20	September 25	October 3	December 3
1981/82	September 29	October 8	October 13	October 21	December 21
1982/83	September 18	September 27	October 2	October 10	December 11
1983/84	September 8	September 17	September 22	September 30	December 1
1984/85	September 27	October 6	October 11	October 19	December 19
1985/86	September 16	September 25	September 30	October 8	December 8
1986/87	October 4	October 13	October 18	October 26	December 27
1987/88	September 24	October 3	October 8	October 16	December 16
1988/89	September 12	September 21	September 26	October 4	December 4
1989/90	September 30	October 9	October 14	October 22	December 23
1990/91	September 20	September 29	October 4	October 12	December 12
1991/92	September 9	September 18	September 23	October 1	December 2
1992/93	September 28	October 7	October 12	October 20	December 20
1993/94	September 16	September 25	September 30	October 8	December 9
1994/95	September 6	September 15	September 20	September 28	November 28
1995/96	September 25	October 4	October 9	October 17	December 18
1996/97	September 14	September 23	September 28	October 6	December 6
1997/98	October 2	October 11	October 16	October 24	December 24
1998/99	September 21	September 30	October 5	October 13	December 14
1999/2000	September 11	September 20	September 25	October 3	December 4
2000/01	September 30	October 9	October 14	October 22	December 22

Tu Bi-Shevat	Purim	Passover	Israeli Independence Day	Lag Ba-Omer	Shavuot
Shevat 15	Adar 14	Nisan 15	Iyar 5	Iyar 18	Sivan 6
February 12	March 13	April 12	May 2	May 15	June 1
February 2	March 2	April 1	April 21	May 4	May 21
January 20	February 18	April 19	May 9	May 22	June 8
February 8	March 9	April 8	April 28	May 11	May 28
January 29	February 27	March 29	April 18	May 1	May 18
January 19	February 17	April 17	May 7	May 20	June 6
February 6	March 7	April 6	April 26	May 9	May 26
January 25	February 23	April 24	May 14	May 27	June 13
February 14	March 15	April 14	May 4	May 17	June 3
February 3	March 3	April 2	April 22	May 5	May 22
January 21	February 19	April 20	May 10	May 23	June 9
February 10	March 11	April 10	April 30	May 13	May 30
January 30	February 28	March 30	April 19	May 2	May 19
January 20	February 18	April 18	May 8	May 21	June 7
February 6	March 7	April 6	April 26	May 9	May 26
January 27	February 25	March 27	April 16	April 29	May 16
January 16	February 14	April 15	May 5	May 18	June 4
February 5	March 5	April 4	April 24	May 7	May 24
January 23	February 21	April 22	May 12	May 25	June 11
February 11	March 12	April 11	May 1	May 14	May 31
February 1	March 2	April 1	April 21	May 4	May 21
January 22	February 20	April 20	May 10	May 23	June 9
February 8	March 9	April 8	April 28	May 11	May 28

INDEX